Mark Greene and Ian Shaw write of se that "a core component of their ministry involves helping God's people live out their calling as royal priests in their Monday to Saturday lives." Exactly right – and yet so easily missed. It is the whole of God's people who constitute God's "royal priesthood," and those whose callings are to lead and serve in teaching and preaching are fundamentally pointing all God's people to this, their "priestly" calling – to separate out light from darkness, or the holy from the unholy (Lev 10:10), for the sake of the life of the (whole) world. This book comes at this core idea from multiple angles – scripturally, historically, culturally, practically – with something to challenge everyone. It could spark fruitful and down-to-earth discussions for faculties and educators of all kinds. May its readers be many, and may their own vision run to the ends of the earth, including their local Monday-morning workplaces.

Richard Briggs, PhD
Director of Biblical Studies and Lecturer in Old Testament
Cranmer Hall, St John's College, Durham, UK

Traditionally, evangelicals have been very good at reading the Bible, but really poor at "reading" society. It is as if all our energy has gone into understanding the sacred text, but we have failed to appreciate that all around us there have been seismic cultural and social shifts. *Whole-Life Mission for the Whole Church* sets out to address this problem with reference to the sacred-secular divide. It offers an important contribution, especially with regard to theological education. The church needs to engage with society afresh and it needs theologically educated disciples to do so; followers of Jesus Christ who see their mission as both ecclesial and societal in a globalized world. This book pushes the conversation forward and invites all of us to appreciate the impact that the sacred-secular divide has on our lives. I commend this book most warmly to church leaders, theological educators and students.

Mark J. Cartledge, PhD
Principal and Professor of Practical Theology,
London School of Theology, UK

This book gives a timely reality check on the sacred-secular divide in the Christian church as well as theological institutions which prepare Christians for the Great Commission in the world. Reality bites. Such a divide has been eroding the Christian mission in both Western and non-Western worlds. The remedy offered in this book thus hits the nail on the head by addressing the divide from biblical, theological and practical viewpoints of theological educators from various parts of the world. They point us to viable solutions for overcoming the divide through revising the programs and pedagogy of theological education to ensure an integrated life for both the church and institution.

Clement Mook-Soo Chia, PhD
Principal, Singapore Bible College

The belief that the mission of the church is of the essence, and that it is worked out in the whole of life through the vocations and discipleship of all Christians, is assented to in theory by some church leaders but put into practice in only a minority of churches. This essential book demonstrates that most church leaders have never been formed or trained to make whole-life disciples, and it addresses the problem at the source – the current practice and understanding of much theological education for ministry – and gives practical steps seminaries can take to reorientate themselves for this most vital task.

Bishop Graham Cray
Former Principal, Ridley Hall, Cambridge, UK

A problem with many theological seminaries is that in theory they teach the priesthood of all believers, but in their practices and unstated attitudes they teach the priesthood of official ministry workers. This problem is an example of the "hidden curriculum," which is the curriculum as actually experienced by learners, even when it runs contrary to the publicly stated curriculum. As this book shows, overcoming the sacred–secular divide in theological colleges involves a close look at the culture of the seminary – including a recognition that in many ways "the faculty is the curriculum." This book stresses the importance of whole of life discipleship, and how this discipling should extend to all believers as they are salt and light wherever they live and work.

James Dalziel, PhD
Dean and CEO,
Australian College of Theology, Sydney, Australia

The breaking down of walls marks watershed moments, whether these be the walls of Jericho or Berlin. Here is a book that seeks to dismantle an invisible, insidious wall, one that has restricted Christians from joyously whooping into the wide open spaces of life and service in the kingdom. The global aspects of this wall as presented here will both caution readers against indifference and motivate them into action.

Havilah Dharamraj, PhD
Head, Department of Biblical Studies,
South Asia Institute of Advanced Christian Studies, Bangalore, India

This is an impressive and important work. It address the issue of the "sacred-secular divide" (SSD) in theological seminaries from a global perspective and so appreciates the nuances of this challenge in different cultural contexts. At the heart of the SSD lie questions about the nature of Christian discipleship and mission – this means that no Christian theological educator should ignore the divide. This book is theologically informed and practically applicable. Indeed, it is this latter aspect that will make it particularly valuable for theological educators, as it provides specific advice on evaluating and designing effective curriculums, programmes, modules, lectures, and assessments. Like the church, theological education in service of the church needs to be "always reforming." *Whole-Life Mission for the Whole Church* is truly a fine resource in this ongoing task.

Simo Frestadius, PhD
Dean of Research, Regents Theological College, West Malvern, UK
Chair, European Pentecostal Theological Association

This global and multidisciplinary collection highlights and addresses one of the most pressing issues facing the church today – the sacred-secular divide. One African seminary leader is reported in this volume as lamenting, "We are sleepwalking on this issue." But it is not just African seminaries asleep at the wheel when it comes to addressing the sacred-secular divide. In dissecting the problem, the various authors helpfully identify a pathway towards addressing it through a reimagining of theological education of pastors and teachers. I recommend this book to all who are engaged in the crucial task of educating future leaders for the church.

Ian Hussey, PhD
Director of Post Graduate Studies,
Malyon Theological College, Brisbane, Australia

This book links two crucial aspects in the life of the church – the effective training of ministers and the need to encourage all God's people to live out their faith in everyday life. It asks important questions about how most effectively to do the first, in order to enable the second. Add in an international dimension which brings the conversation into a worldwide arena, and what emerges is a brilliant, engaging and practical book that will inspire and challenge theological educators – and the whole church – in the task of equipping the people of God.

Rt Revd Emma Ineson, PhD
Bishop of Penrith
Former Principal, Trinity College, Bristol, UK

These are challenging days for the church and therefore challenging for those training ministers to lead the church. But while some of these challenges come from outside – social change, cultural hostility – the biggest one is an own goal – the splitting of faith from life. There are lots of terms for split, but the editors of this essential book have chosen SSD (sacred-secular divide). It is a divide that theological educators (like me) need to take far more seriously than we seem to be doing. I am from a tradition that started in weaver's workshops, bakeries, and around commercial printing presses; it was a movement earthed in the everyday lives of its members, debating Scripture, social life and the politics of the day almost in the same breath, certainly in the same Bible study. One could say the arrival of theological education and professional ministers put paid to that; something vital was lost and we urgently need to recover it. This book, written by practitioners from across the globe, could be the key to that recovery. There are lessons aplenty for curriculum designers, teachers and learners that could just be the spark that enables us to recover the whole gospel for the whole world.

Simon Jones
Vice Principal and Director of Ministerial Formation and Training,
Spurgeon's College, London, England

The individual Christian is enthusiastic to express their faith in their workplace, their neighbourhood, their family, in all their life. However, that enthusiasm is stymied by churches led by pastors who have been taught to focus on biblical content and programs. The training that pastors receive is from institutions run by academics much more interested in the mind than the whole of life, and blissfully protected from engaging with everyday culture. This book identifies and addresses the urgent need for fundamental change in theological colleges and seminaries, to empower and enable the church to fulfil its call to the mission of God: participating in the reconciliation of *everything* on earth and heaven through Jesus. This book lays a firm foundation biblically and historically, and includes practical ideas representing a global conversation. There is silence from my part of the world – Oceania – but I recognize the need for change, and can testify to the momentum for change that is taking place in Australia.

Kara Martin
Lecturer, Alphacrucis College, Sydney, Australia
Speaker, and Author of *Workship 1 & 2*

Theological colleges can be bastions of Scripture-informed thinking and deep spiritual formation, developing leaders who in turn grow whole-life disciples. However, like any institution, they can be slow to keep up and change, disconnected from the real-life context of a barista, bus driver, child-care worker, manager, mother, entrepreneur, construction worker, or health-care worker – to name but a few examples of those who day-by-day engage in the joy and challenge of what it means to follow Christ on their particular frontlines. This compelling book reaches across this chasm and provides a wealth of ideas and convictions that theological colleges must address if they are to remain relevant. Our dynamically changing world desperately needs fruitful disciples in every sphere. This book is a must-read if you want to see change, and especially if you are in theological education and you want to play your part.

Dr. Lindsay McMillan
Managing Director, Reventure Limited

This book asks some searching questions of theological educators around the world. What is the purpose of theological education? If the answer is that it exists, not for itself but for the sake of the church, then how well are seminaries and colleges helping to equip students to be whole-life disciple-makers? To what degree is theological education captive to a sacred-secular divide? What needs to change and how can this be done? Asking good questions is one thing, but the strength of this book is that it also offers clear, compelling answers, based on solid theological foundations and drawn from a diverse range of global practitioners. The result is a practical manifesto for re-envisioning theological education to serve God's mission in the world. Highly recommended but with a warning – readers need to be open to the hard work of embracing change.

Patrick Mitchel, PhD
Director of Learning,
Irish Bible Institute, Dublin, Republic of Ireland

How does a church leader encourage their people to understand that the Christian life does not end when you walk out of the church door but begins there? How do those leaders inspire in their people the zeal and the compassion required to live out the gospel in daily life? If we can answer questions such as these, we'll be setting free countless witnesses to the gospel in every sphere of human life. This book is packed with fresh ideas, trenchant challenges and global insights which can help raise up Christian leaders able to form missionary disciples.

The Rt Revd Philip North
Bishop of Burnley, UK

This book presents a much-needed call to theological educators to recognize the deep impact of the sacred-secular divide in every aspect of church life and how doctrine is lived out, and of the key role of theological education in nurturing churches where people are discipled for their everyday lives and contexts. It is also a call to overcome this divide in theological education by bringing change in two dimensions: the values and goal of school and the educational process at macro and micro curricular levels. Examples from Asia,

Africa and Latin America of how this can be accomplished are inspiring and realistic. This is a must-read book for those committed to theological education that prepares for a whole-life perspective on God's mission in God's world.

Elizabeth Sendek
President,
Fundación Universitaria Seminario Bíblico de Colombia, Medellín, Colombia

The sacred-secular divide that has so bedevilled the church, and the theological institutions that seek to serve it, gets the treatment it deserves in this timely book. The divide is exposed for the dangerous lie that it is. It is exposed as a lie that has misshaped our theological colleges and the graduates we produce. But in *Whole-Life Mission for the Whole Church*, the lie is not just exposed, it is also countered with deep truth and practical wisdom. Of course, as those with an interest in whole life discipleship know, this is not the only book that shines light into the dark places where the SSD dwells amongst us. But it does what few do: it turns that light on our theological colleges. And it doesn't just expose the SSD, but gives biblical, theological, and practical resources to help us deal with it, including lived examples from colleges around the world. This is both valuable and greatly needed. For as readers of the gospels know, it's not enough to sweep our educational houses clean. They need to be re-inhabited by the light and truth of the gospel, in which not only is there no division between Jew nor Greek, but no sacred-secular divide.

Andrew Sloane, ThD
Associate Professor of Old Testament and Christian Thought,
Director of Research, Morling Theological College, Sydney, Australia

ICETE Series

Whole-Life Mission for the Whole Church

ICETE International Council for Evangelical Theological Education
strengthening evangelical theological education through international cooperation

Langham
GLOBAL LIBRARY

Whole-Life Mission for the Whole Church

Overcoming the Sacred-Secular Divide through Theological Education

Edited by

Mark Greene and Ian J. Shaw

Series Editors
Riad Kassis and Michael A. Ortiz

ICETE International Council for Evangelical Theological Education
strengthening evangelical theological education through international cooperation

Langham
GLOBAL LIBRARY

© 2021 Mark Greene and Ian J. Shaw

Published 2021 by Langham Global Library
An imprint of Langham Publishing
www.langhampublishing.org

Langham Publishing and its imprints are a ministry of Langham Partnership

Langham Partnership
PO Box 296, Carlisle, Cumbria, CA3 9WZ, UK
www.langham.org

ISBNs:
978-1-83973-072-6 Print
978-1-83973-110-5 ePub
978-1-83973-111-2 Mobi
978-1-83973-112-9 PDF

British Library Cataloguing-in-Publication Data
A catalogue record for this book is available from the British Library.

ISBN: 978-1-83973-072-6

Cover & Book Design: projectluz.com

Contents

Section 2: Addressing the Issue through Theological Education

Section 3: Effecting Change

The Many Hands to Thank

Many hands make light work. Or so the saying goes. This work has not always felt light but that's not been for lack of hands to help. And hands to thank.

It was John Stott who founded both the Langham Partnership and the London Institute for Contemporary Christianity. Those who were there will never forget his memorial service, held at St Paul's Cathedral in London in January 2012 to honour one of the most influential world Christian leaders of the twentieth century. When John Stott died, it was his wish that any money given to a memorial fund raised as a result of that service should be spent on a joint project. So this Langham/LICC project on tackling the sacred-secular divide through theological education would not have been possible without the many people who gave so generously in gratitude to God for a man who yearned and worked and prayed for the release of all God's people into whole-life mission. Thank you all.

We're grateful too to the scholars who took so much time away from their seminaries, churches and families to participate in the consultations that led to this book, to humbly share failures as well as successes and, subsequently, to contribute comments and insights to this volume and champion the cause in their own contexts. Their names are listed in the appendix.

Also we're grateful for the opportunities we've had to engage with North American theological educators through the Karam Forum so ably led by Greg Forster, and with scholars from around the world through the triennial ICETE conference in Panama in 2018. There, through the visionary leadership of Dr Riad Kassis, the issue of the impact of the sacred-secular divide on theological education was the core conference theme, enabling some of these ideas to be tested and refined.

Of course, no multi-national, multi-venue research project can even get off the ground without the make-it-happen team to make it happen. So enormous thanks to Elizabeth Hitchcock at Langham Partnership for her incredible effort involved in arranging travel and accommodation and to Anna Watkin and Pippa James at LICC for their help with developing slides, materials and presentations and for Pippa's meticulous editing work. We are also very grateful to Dr John Jeacocke for his help in compiling the index and with proofreading the text.

"I thank my God every time I remember you. In all my prayers for all of you, I always pray with joy because of your partnership in the gospel from the first day until now" (Phil 1:3–5).

Mark Greene and Ian Shaw
February 2021

Life's a peach, not an orange. (Mark Greene)

The Son is the image of the invisible God, the firstborn over *all* creation.
For in him *all* things were created: things in heaven and on earth, visible
and invisible, whether thrones or powers or rulers or authorities;
all things have been created through him and for him.
He is before *all* things, and in him *all* things hold together.
And he is the head of the body, the church; he is the
beginning and the firstborn from among the dead, so
that in *everything* he might have the supremacy.
For God was pleased to have *all* his fullness dwell in him, and through
him to reconcile to himself *all* things, whether things on earth or things
in heaven, by making peace through his blood, shed on the cross.
Colossians 1:15–20

The sacred-secular divide in the church is like a red handkerchief
in a washing machine full of whites –
everything comes out pink.
You may realise your mistake,
and never do it again,
but *everything*, apart from the handkerchief,
needs re-washing.
(Mark Greene)

Foreword

Remember those WWJD bracelets? "What Would Jesus Do?" was the message, optimistically nudging the wearers to consider their actions and choices as an answer to that question. For a while in my own leadership of Langham Partnership, I wore an invisible bracelet spelling "WWUJD." "What Would Uncle John Do?," or say, or think, about whatever issue was before us? John Stott was our founder, and his vision and wisdom shaped our ethos and objectives.

Well, while he was alive, we could always just ask him. However, in view of his request that any memorial fund on his death (in 2011) should be divided equally between Langham Partnership and the London Institute (which he also founded), I have no doubt whatsoever that this book is very much among the things that John Stott would have wanted to be done.

It is sometimes said that Langham and LICC represent both sides of John Stott's brain – which means of course that they were thoroughly integrated and coherent in his thinking.

On the one hand, Stott had the highest view of the pastoral ministry. Which is not to say that he endorsed clericalism. On the contrary, he despised and denounced the rigmaroles of clerical posturing. No, he believed in the biblical calling and gifting of "pastors and teachers" among the gifts of the ascended Christ to his church. And he believed, and practiced accordingly, that the primary responsibility of such shepherds is to feed the flock of God with the word of God through faithful, clear and applied biblical preaching and teaching alongside pastoral care. But in his travels, he saw that so many pastors in the Majority World lacked any adequate training or resources to equip them for that task. And as a result, churches languish in false teaching or grow in numbers but without depth of discipling and obedience. So he established the ministries now combined in the Langham Partnership to address that need.

On the other hand, Stott had an equally high view of the laity. Not that he liked that word either. He was passionate that ministry was not confined to "ministers" (ordained clergy), and that mission was not solely the task of church-supported "missionaries." Rather *all* God's people, in *every* dimension of their lives in God's world, including their various vocations, jobs, skills, interests, relationships and responsibilities, are "in ministry and on mission" – that is, are serving the Lord in daily life as salt and light. And for that role, they need to be equipped and resourced just as much as ordained pastors do. Indeed, it is precisely the role of pastor-teachers to "equip the saints for works of service" out there in the world where they live and work. And so, to foster such equipping, he established the London Institute for Contemporary Christianity, dedicated to enabling lay Christians to understand their faith and their culture, to listen to the word and to the world, and to work out what whole-life discipleship means in every dimension of life, culture, professions, economics, politics, medicine, education, the arts, sport and whatever else. And at the same time, LICC is also dedicated to helping pastors create church communities that empower all God's people for their ministry out in God's Monday to Saturday world. There is no part of life that is excluded or excused from the lordship of Christ. There is, in other words, no legitimacy to the sacred-secular divide that has so plagued the church. Stott was very clear on this.

And how do these two sides of his brain come together? Well, simply that those whom God calls to be pastor-teachers (the first side) need to be trained in a way that shapes and motivates them to facilitate the second side. They need to receive a theological education that does not simply reinforce that sacred-secular divide and embed it even further in their churches. They need to remember that ordinary believers do not come to church every Sunday to support the pastor in his or her ministry. It is precisely the other way round: the pastor comes to church to support and equip the people in *their* ministry – which is where it counts, out there in the public arena, as believers in a world of unbelief, as agents of God's kingdom in the kingdom of this world.

So that is what this book, the fruit of a joint project that would have delighted John Stott (and both sides of his brain!) is about. How can theological education be re-imagined and reconstructed to send out a fresh generation of pastor-teachers and leaders of God's church who are themselves free from the virus of the sacred-secular dichotomy and can rid their people of its toxic and disabling dualisms? That is a big challenge, and this is just a beginning. But it is a good beginning.

Chris Wright
International Ministries Director,
Langham Partnership

Introduction

The Journey Ahead

Theological Education and Mission
for All God's People

I deas have legs – they take you somewhere.

Good ones take you to good places, bad ones to bad places. Beliefs shape behaviour. Ethos shapes praxis. Every educator knows this.

This book is about trying to liberate the global church from the power of an idea that has been diminishing our understanding of God, our discipleship, our disciple-making, our missiology, our witness to the world, our grasp of the very scope of the gospel for hundreds of years. And that idea is the sacred-secular divide (SSD) – the false belief that there are some areas of life that are not important to God, some callings that are viewed as second-class, some spheres of society that aren't really worth engaging in.

Now the power of SSD as an idea is not the extent to which people consciously agree with it. Few do. You will not find many theological educators who would agree that godly pastors are more important to God than godly cleaners. And you won't find many pastors who think that godly Sunday school teachers are more important than godly school teachers. No, the power of the sacred-secular divide is not that people think it's true but that it shapes their lives anyway. In fact, it has successfully shaped the culture of the global church. It's so deeply embedded in the way we do things

> The power of the sacred-secular divide is not that people think it's true but that it shapes their lives anyway.

1

that often we don't notice it. SSD is not like a golf ball in a fruit salad: easy to spot, easy to fish out. No, SSD is like vinegar in the juice. It affects everything. And everything needs attention.

This project began in 2012 with a question: If the church inadvertently reflects the sacred-secular divide in its practice, do the theological colleges that train the church leaders also inadvertently manifest the sacred-secular divide?

We asked that question not only because we're committed to theological education but because we know how important theological education is. Ten faculty might engage with one hundred students in a year. Those one hundred students, if they become church leaders, will probably go on to impact the lives of at least 100,000 people in their churches over a lifetime of ministry. And that 100,000 will in turn probably engage meaningfully with at least two hundred people each in the course of their lives – family, friends, fellow-students, colleagues, clients, customers, health professionals, shop assistants. . . . That's twenty million connections.

> If the church inadvertently reflects the sacred-secular divide in its practice, do the theological colleges that train the church leaders also inadvertently manifest the sacred-secular divide?

Theological educators shape the leaders who shape the church that shapes our nation. John Stott once warned, "Pastors are either made or marred in the seminary."

We began by exploring the impact of SSD with a group of senior Majority World theological educators at a conference in Oxford, and then with a group of Majority World PhD students studying in a range of the leading Western theological institutions at a conference in Cambridge. Both groups were clear: the SSD is alive and well in most of their institutions across the world in ways the conferences had made them more sharply aware of.

The question was how might this debilitating scourge be addressed?

Given the global scope of the problem, we decided to set up four four-day collaborative workshops with theological educators from a range of institutions. The first, held in London, comprised key leaders from a range of global theological institutions. They helped us set the agenda for a series of three regional consultations held in Colombia (for Latin America), Kenya (for Africa) and Singapore (for Asia) to reflect on the issue in differing contexts.

In all, over thirty leaders participated, allowing us to draw on a wide range of experiences, contexts and insights.

The aims were three-fold:

1. Learn how the sacred-secular divide manifests itself in different cultural contexts.
2. Identify best practice – what works, why and what's transferable.
3. Test and develop tools that generate awareness of the issues, and tools that combat the issues and create a new whole-life culture.

We learned much along the way. Some were shocked by the impact of the sacred-secular divide. One warned, "We are sleepwalking on this issue." Another commented, "It is not enough to know and talk about it. It is indispensable to take some actions." And we were encouraged by examples of liberating practice in institutional culture, in curriculum design, and in courses and assessments. Indeed, there were more than enough examples of different interventions to convince us that anyone at any level in theological education can begin to make a difference in their own context – even if it takes longer to change an overall curriculum or the institution as a whole. This change does not need money or specialist training. Prayer and imagination and initiative are a heady and fruitful combination.

The sections that follow reflect that learning.

We begin by seeking to describe how the SSD expresses itself in church culture and affects the everyday lives of God's people in diminishing ways. And we offer a snapshot of the alternative vision: what does it look like when God's people are filled with vision, enabled, commissioned and supported for their ministry in daily life? The kid at school, the grandmother going to the shops, the corporate executive in their office and the cleaner who cleans it? Without such a vision, theological education will perish, and shrink back into a narrow focus on gathered church, pastoral care and neighbourhood concerns.

> What does it look like when God's people are filled with vision, enabled, commissioned and supported for their ministry in daily life?

The book goes on to look at the SSD in the light of Scripture, pointing to a "whole-Bible, whole-life" solution, exploring how the integrated life, and integrated view of cosmic reality, is at the heart of the biblical revelation. In chapter 2, Antony Billington reminds us of the deeper and wider nature of the gospel. The God who created all things is the God who will restore all things, and who calls us to flourish in his liberating lordship in every aspect of life. Then, in chapter 3, Edwin Tay surveys key sources in a series of historic reflections on the issues, reminding us that in past times preachers and theologians have promoted the integrated life. The Puritan William Perkins argued, "Theology is the science of living blessedly forever,"[1] and William Ames asserted, "Theology is the doctrine of living for God."[2] The way toward a solution, Edwin Tay argues, must be Christological. Antony Billington then takes the discussion on the SSD further, in chapter 4, by exploring how, from the eighteenth century to the present, many Christians have operated with a comprehensive, whole-life perspective on God, humanity, sin, salvation and the mission to which God calls his people. Chapters 3 and 4 show how the overall stance the contributors to this volume are taking and encouraging others to adopt in the task of theological education is not new to the pages of Christian history but stands in healthy continuity with those who have gone before us.

We then present six snapshots from around the world as key leaders seek to "name the issue" in their contexts. They show that all societies tend to exist with a basic dualism, and although the form of the "divide" differs with context, it casts a shadow over the life of the church in every nation. In chapter 6 the focus narrows, as our global seminary leaders explore how the SSD manifests itself in seminary life, and the key challenges they face.

> Although the form of the "divide" differs with context, it casts a shadow over the life of the church in every nation.

Reflection on practice should provoke transformative change, and in section 2, we move on from "naming" the issue to "addressing the issue." Three case studies of institutions in Brazil, Sri Lanka and Kenya explore different approaches that have been taken to overcoming the SSD.

---

1. W. Perkins, *A Golden Chain*, in *Works of William Perkins*, vol. 1 (London: Reformation Heritage Books, 1608), 13.

2. W. Ames, *The Marrow of Theology*, ed. John Dykstra Eusden (Grand Rapids, MI: Baker, 1968), 77.

In the light of the challenge and the missional opportunity of the SSD, we then explore the educational principles that can fuel concrete changes to curriculum, programmes, courses, individual lectures and assessments. We share examples both of how this can be done, but also of how it is being done in seminaries around the world. Progress must be founded on creating koinonia with academic colleagues and, importantly, students.

The purpose of this overall project, and this book that has arisen from it, is to promote transformation. So, section 3 explores the process of change and barriers to it that might need to be overcome. Even if major change is not possible all at once, the importance of small, incremental change – "one-degree shifts" – is outlined. Participants from the consultations then offer their own reflections on how they have begun to make progress towards change in institutional culture, and their own practice. All long to make their institutions places where whole-life missionary disciples and whole-life missionary disciple-makers are equipped. A final section of chapter 15 looks at how such a non-sacred-secular divided student might look, as the product of an infectious and dynamic whole-life disciple-making culture that our students can carry into their ministries in church and society.

Section 1

Naming the Issue

1

Naming the Issue in Our Churches and Institutions

Mark Greene

Victoria is an apprentice hairdresser.

She's nineteen and she's been in the job just over a month. It's a busy salon so there's always something to do, and it's almost always got to be done quickly. She's enjoying it, but she's been feeling the pressure. Three weeks into the job, her vicar commissions her into her role. She's been more at peace since then.

I ask her, "So, what difference does being a Christian make to the way you wash someone's hair?"

"I pray for them as I massage in the conditioner."

Victoria's praying is an invisible gift to her clients – soothing conditioner for the soul, not just the hair. But behind her prayers lie a whole set of beliefs.

Victoria believes that her daily context in a hairdressing salon is important to God.

She believes that the actual work she does is important to God. And that it can be done in a distinctive way.

She believes that God is alive and can move in a hairdressing salon.

She believes that God wants to bless her clients, and that she can be part of that.

She believes in the power of prayer and in God's freedom to respond in his own way and in his own time. She doesn't need to see the results of those prayers. Indeed, this side of heaven, for the most part she probably won't. But it's still worth praying – God will be listening to her.

She's confident in the God who sends her.

What kind of church community makes disciples like Victoria?

What kind of church leader produces disciples like Victoria?

What kind of seminary produces church leaders who produce disciples like Victoria?

The reality is that Victoria is rare. The vast majority of Christians, whether kid, teen, adult or retired, do not have a vision for daily engagement and service in the places they go on a daily basis – the fields, the factories, the school gates, the shops, the clubs, the offices. And the reason they don't have such a vision is because this is not the vision that grips the global evangelical church.

> The vast majority of Christians do not have a vision for daily engagement and service in the places they go on a daily basis.

In 2010 at the Lausanne Congress for World Evangelisation in Cape Town, we asked evangelical delegates from some 198 countries if this was the mission strategy in the church in their nation: "To recruit the people of God to give up some of their leisure time to support the mission initiatives of church-paid workers."

Virtually everyone there agreed that it was.

Now of course this strategy has borne much fruit, in all kinds of neighbourhood and community initiatives and increasing commitment to mission initiatives beyond our native countries' borders.

This is not a bad strategy; it's just an incomplete one. It ignores the daily contexts God's people naturally find themselves in, where they naturally meet people who don't know Jesus. And what that means is that 98 percent of God's people – all those not ordained to full-time paid church ministry – are not being equipped or filled with vision for discipleship and mission in the 95 percent of their time that isn't reserved for church-based activities.

Imagine a factory where 98 percent of the people were not consciously engaged in the main work of the factory. You'd think they were nuts.

We are nuts!

But imagine if we weren't nuts.

Imagine if the church globally had spent the last fifty years helping people to see how they could be salt and light and yeast and mustard seeds at school, at university, at work. . . .

Imagine if we hadn't convinced our young people that farming and business and defence and banking and media and law and politics and plumbing and building and cleaning were second-class callings. . . .

Imagine if the thousands of God's people in those arenas had been equipped and supported and prayed for and filled with vision. . . .

After all, apart from anything else, those are the places where major decisions about our societies are made, where our nations' cultures and priorities are shaped. Can we really fulfil the Lord's command to disciple nations without equipping our people for the contexts they find themselves in?

But inadvertently that's overall what we have done. Here's the first half of a quote from a full-time schoolteacher: "I spend an hour a week teaching Sunday school and they haul me up to the front of the church to pray for me." What's the second half of the quote? "The rest of the week I'm a full-time teacher and the church has never prayed for me." No one in that teacher's church is saying to that teacher that the forty-five hours they spend at school are less important than the one hour in the Sunday school class, but that is what is being communicated.

The reality is that SSD makes lay Christians think they are second-class Christians. It diminishes the value of their daily work, it blinds them to the fruit that God may be producing right where they are, it shrinks their ecclesiology to the gathered context, it prevents them recognising how the Bible addresses all of life, and it blunts their alertness to God's action in their ordinary daily lives, cutting them off from accessing prayer, wisdom and the support of the body. In sum, the SSD shrinks the very scope of the gospel itself. It is an affront to the all-encompassing, all-sufficient redemptive and renewing work of Christ. And it is alive and well in evangelical churches across the globe.

However, this is much more than a plea for a course on integral mission or workplace ministry or for a faith and work centre. In fact, such initiatives can serve to reinforce the problem by unintentionally suggesting that the SSD is a topic to be addressed in one corner of the curriculum, rather than a pervasive worldview to be rooted out.

SSD has affected every aspect of church life and the operational understanding of almost every doctrine. SSD shrinks our ecclesiology by putting more focus and value on the gathered church than the sent church. It shrinks our pneumatology by inadvertently limiting our expectation of the action of the Spirit to particular places and particular kinds of tasks. It shrinks our soteriology by focusing on individual conversion rather than on whole-life disciple-making and the *missio Dei* . . . and so on.

> SSD has affected every aspect of church life and the operational understanding of almost every doctrine.

We in the West have passed on this heretical virus to the global church. Yes, in the Langham/LICC project, we have learned that the SSD manifests itself in different ways in Guatemala than in Gujarat, in Singapore than in Sarajevo, but we have also learned that it remains a virulent and destructive force.

One of the implications of this for theological educators is the reality that most of us will be in SSD churches. And therefore may not have ever seen what a non-SSD church might look like. We may not have a picture in our minds of the kind of communities we are seeking to train our students to lead, just as we may actually not have a picture of what fruitful whole-life discipleship can look like for a hairdresser, a fieldworker, a university student, a housewife or a corporate executive. This presents a particular challenge to us. After all, as theological educators, we rightly need to be in dialogue with the academy in our discipline, and we rightly need to be in dialogue with the denominations and churches we serve. But we cannot rely on those conversations to inform our understanding of the dynamics of the places God's people find themselves in on a daily basis and the opportunities and challenges before them. We, too, need to understand not just the macro forces at work in our national cultures but also the places where God's people are called to be salt and light and to seek and pray for shalom in those contexts.

> We need to understand not just the macro forces at work in our national cultures but also the places where God's people are called to be salt and light and to seek and pray for shalom in those contexts.

The pervasiveness of SSD makes our understanding of our cultural contexts even more important precisely because most of our students come to our seminaries from SSD churches, and on the whole they go back into SSD churches. So the challenge to our institutions is to ask ourselves:

- Is my institution's culture affected by SSD?
- Is my teaching affected by SSD?
- Am I affected by SSD?

But also to ask:

- Do we have a vision for what Monday to Saturday discipleship could look like for the people in our own churches?
- Do we know what a whole-life disciple-making church might look like?

And the reason that is an important question to ask is because in reality such churches are extremely rare. On the whole, denominations have historically not asked seminaries to train whole-life disciple-making pastors. However, as Bishop Graham Cray, author of *Mission-Shaped Church* and former principal of Ridley College, put it, "Churches have to realise that the core of their calling is to be disciple-making communities, whatever else they do."[1]

Local church culture is deeply affected by SSD. It affects the songs we sing (which are rarely about Monday to Saturday life); it affects who and what's on the prayer list (rarely the Monday to Saturday mission fields of the congregation); it affects what's on the agenda of our meetings (rarely the discipling of all God's people). It affects the stories we tell in church, who we praise in public and how pastors spend their time, what they see in the Bible, what they choose to preach about and what illustrations they give.

A while back, when I was teaching at the London School of Theology, I conducted some research on evangelical preaching.[2] We discovered that over 50 percent of evangelicals had never heard a sermon on work and that, more significantly, a higher percentage didn't feel that they had a biblical understanding of work and its role in their lives.

How could that be?

---

1. From a lecture given by Graham Cray at LICC, summer 2010.
2. Mark Greene, "Is Anybody Listening?" *Anvil* 14, no. 4 (1997): 283–294.

After all, the Bible brims with material about work and applicable to work. From Genesis to Revelation, it's a recurrent theme, in creation and fall, in the construction of the ark and of the tower, in Jacob's dealings with Laban, in Joseph's growth, in Moses's practice, in Levitical and Deuteronomic instruction and command, in the exercise of authority by Deborah and the other judges, in Kings, in Boaz's counter-cultural workplace praxis, in David's frequent pleas in the Psalms for help in his often hostile work environment, and so on through Proverbs and Ecclesiastes and the Prophets and Esther and Nehemiah and the Gospels and Colossians and Philippians and Thessalonians and Revelation.

The theme of work is all over the Bible. It is not only absolutely obvious that work is in the text, it's absolutely obvious that it's an issue for anyone in a church over the age of four. So why haven't evangelical preachers preached it? That is the sacred-secular divide in action. Either we don't see it or we choose not to preach it when we do.

This is a hermeneutical issue, yes, and it's a homiletical issue and a doctrinal issue. But it's also a pastoral issue, a missional issue, a discipling issue. Somehow it is possible for graduates to leave our seminaries and not know that a core component of their ministry involves helping God's people live out their calling as royal priests in their Monday to Saturday lives. What vision, we might ask, of the role of the Christian in the world are we passing on?

Now this doesn't just have an impact on individuals; it has an impact on nations.

In the 1950s in Germany the church asked itself how the church and the nation succumbed, for the most part, so easily to Nazism? Now, of course, there were a host of factors but one of their main conclusions was this: the church did not have a robust enough doctrine of election.

Frankly, when I was told that by the person who'd done the research, I didn't understand it, and I didn't understand it because of what I thought the doctrine of election was. When I was taught the doctrine of election at college we focused on predestination and double-predestination, on the debate between Calvin and Arminius and those who followed them – who's in, who's out, and how many. It's an important question, and it's a very good issue to help students develop theological method – to combine exegetical, analytical, historical, philosophical and writing skills.

But that, my researcher friend pointed out, and as you doubtless know, is not the heart of the doctrine of election. The heart of the doctrine is that we have been chosen as a kingdom of priests in the world with a particular role to play. Now, if we don't understand our calling in the world, we are unlikely to work to fulfil it. And that is what happened to the church in Germany. And what has certainly occurred in my own nation.

Now this also matters in the local church hugely: who do God's people think they are called to be? What do they think their role in the world is?

If biblical preaching and doctrinal teaching are big issues that relate to one of the core drivers of church life – Sunday gathered teaching and preaching – let me give you an example of how SSD penetrates something as small as a slide with the words of a hymn on it.

Take a hymn like "Be Thou My Vision" which begins: "Be thou my vision, O Lord of my heart / Naught be all else to me save that thou art." Now often in Western churches the words of hymns and songs are projected on the background of a sunset over the ocean or a beautiful countryside scene. There's nothing wrong with those pictures. The heavens do declare the glory of God and many of us do feel closer to God out in his creation. However, such visuals, and it is almost always such visuals, imply that God is to be found in nature, in escape from our usual contexts, not *in* our everyday contexts.

What you would rarely see is the words of a hymn over a slum area in the local town, or over a factory, or over a picture of unwashed dishes in a sink, or over a nightclub. But the pastor who puts pictures like those behind hymns has a much richer view of the scope of God's concern, of where God may be found, and of what the role of God's people in the world might be than the pastor who uses a picture of a golden sunset.

And that pastor may have a completely different understanding of their own role as pastor in relation to God's people.

What are we training pastors to do? Are we training them to create communities that are intentionally seeking to help one another grow in fruitfulness for Christ in all of life? On the whole, we are not. In fact, it is quite hard to find modules or courses in seminaries that are about helping other people grow as disciples in Christ. Indeed, whilst pastors expect to care for people with pastoral needs, they don't expect to help them work out how to make an impact for Christ in the factory they work in, never mind equip and train them to do so. That's SSD.

A while back, my colleague, Neil Hudson, a pioneer in creating whole-life disciple-making churches, met a young man called Ed at a conference. Ed was working in a factory and was overqualified for his job and bored by it. He'd prayed for a new job. Nothing happened. He'd asked his home group to pray that he'd get a new job. Nothing happened. He'd asked the church to pray that he'd get a new job. Nothing happened.

I wonder what you might say to Ed?

Well, in many parts of the world, you might simply point out that he is deeply blessed to be employed at all and to be able to provide for himself and others through the work the Lord has given him.

You might respond pastorally:

"Ed, the Lord is teaching you patience and perseverance. The Lord is sovereign and he will provide in his time."

You might respond practically.

"Ed, maybe if you took the rings out of your nose, and got a haircut, you'd have more chance. . . ."

Neil said, "Well, if you and your home group and your pastor and your whole church have prayed and God hasn't given you a new job, then the question is: what does God want you to do there?" And he quoted Jeremiah 29:7: "Also, seek the peace and prosperity of the city to which I have carried you into exile. Pray to the LORD for it, because if it prospers, you too will prosper."

And Ed responded, "You mean I am meant to be a blessing there."

So from then on, Ed got in ten minutes early for his shift and connected to the people going off shift and to the ones coming on shift. He began to pray for people without them knowing it, and then began to pray for people *with* them knowing it. Was his job still boring? Yes. Was his day boring? No. He was working with God.

Now this looks like a little thing, but it's a big thing both for Ed and for what it says about the scope of the pastor-people relationship. Church members expect to be cared for in crisis; they don't expect to be equipped for mission in their daily activities. Pastors expect to try to respond pastorally to people in their churches who come in need, but on the whole they do not expect to respond missionally, and they don't expect to be disciple-makers. Preachers, yes; teachers, yes; counsellors, intercessors, leaders . . . yes. But disciple-maker? It's rarely part of an ordained person's self-understanding.

And this represents a significant but necessary shift: from pastoral care to whole-life disciple-making, from running the activities of the local church to inspiring and enabling people to make an impact for Christ in their daily lives wherever they are.

What Neil did was to help Ed see how he could participate in the mission of God right where he was. And that is one of the things that church leaders are meant to do: give people a whole-life missional vision and disciple them to live it out.

And we see this in Jesus's praxis. Yes, in his public ministry he spent a great deal of time teaching large groups of people, and indeed dealing with physical and spiritual disease, but he seems to have spent most of his time with a small group in an interactive, dialogical context – making disciples.

But it was not only in his praxis that he focused on disciple-making. In Matthew's account his famous last words were: "Go therefore and make disciples of all nations, baptising them in the name of the Father, and of the Son, and of the Holy Spirit, and teaching them to obey everything I have commanded you" (Matt 28:19–20).

First, he did not say, "Go and make converts."

He said, "Go and make disciples." And there is world of difference between a convert and a disciple. A convert has reached their destination. A disciple is on a journey of learning to live the way of Jesus in every area of life. Indeed, when Jesus spoke those words, I suspect that those early disciples who had spent the last three years with him would have understood him to say, "Go and have the kind of relationships with others that I've had with you."

And what kind of relationship was that? Interactive, ongoing, personal. Eating, drinking, travelling, responding to questions, addressing issues of character (who is the greatest?), reflecting proactively with them on their experience (we could not drive it out), and so on.

How many of us have ever had a relationship with an older Christian that's been like that?

How many of us have relationships with people in our congregations that look like that?

How many seminaries have trained their students to have disciple-making relationships with anyone? Globally, we found very few.

What the sacred-secular divide has done is not just shrink our understanding of the scope of disciple-making but it has blinded us to its necessity.

Theological education exists to serve the church but not necessarily to provide what the church tells us it needs. Instead, it must provide what the church needs to serve the *missio Dei* in our context at this time in history.

The challenge of creating Monday to Saturday disciple-making missional communities will not be met merely by new resources or new programmes or new training modules but by a concerted effort to change the core culture of the local church into a whole-life missionary culture. The role of seminaries is to ensure that students have the theological grounding, the exegetical skills, the leadership will and the practical skills to do it.

> Theological education exists to serve the church but not necessarily to provide what the church tells us it needs.

First, then, we turn to consider how the Bible grants us resources with which to tackle the SSD.

2

Naming the Issue from Scripture

Antony Billington

It is a wonderful privilege to be a missionary or a pastor, if God calls us to it. But it is equally wonderful to be a Christian lawyer, industrialist, politician, manager, social worker, television script-writer, journalist or home-maker, if God calls us to it. . . . There is still, of course, an urgent need for missionaries. . . . Pastors also are greatly needed to teach the Word of God. At the same time, there is a crying need for Christians who see their daily work as their primary Christian ministry.[1]

So wrote John Stott in *The Contemporary Christian*, first published in 1992. The issue to which he refers – the value or otherwise of different callings – is but one instance of what has become known as "the sacred-secular divide." This can be thought of as the view, or the underlying assumption, that there are some areas of life that are more important to God, such as church attendance, prayer, reading the Bible, evangelism and social action, and some areas of life that are less important to God, such as music, art, science, business, food, leisure, work and rest.

---

1. Quoted in John Stott, with Tim Chester, *The Disciple: A Calling to be Christlike* (London: IVP, 2019), 52.

That perspective works itself out in various ways in church life and mission, as well as in theological education. "The Cape Town Commitment" (reflecting the proceedings of the Third Lausanne Congress on World Evangelization, held in October 2010), issued a strong warning against it: "We name this secular-sacred divide as a major obstacle to the mobilization of all God's people in the mission of God, and we call upon Christians worldwide to reject its unbiblical assumptions and resist its damaging effects."[2]

What is meant by "secular" here is not secularization, the theory which holds that as societies modernize they become less "religious" – which has proven not to be the case after all. Nor is it secularism, where religion is excluded as a matter of principle from the public square and limited to personal belief. Rather, "secular" refers simply to the "temporal," the "earthly" or "mundane" realm of reality, the things of "this age." Strictly speaking, the *saeculum* (the Latin word from which "secular" is derived) is less the space we occupy and more the age in which we live. As James K. A. Smith puts it: "It is this time – between cross and kingdom come, between ascension and *parousia*, between the universal scope of [Christ's] lordship and its universal recognition – it is this time or season that is 'the secular,' the *saeculum*, the age in which we find ourselves."[3] Hence, we are not shuttling between the jurisdiction of two kingdoms so much as living in a period of contested rule in which we bear witness to Christ's lordship over all things.[4]

In this time between the times, it is all too easy to be held captive by faulty forms of dualism: between the "spiritual" and the "material," viewed as a hierarchy or two storeys, where one realm is higher than the other; or of grace versus nature, where the upper storey of grace supplements the lower storey of nature.[5] Or, as Graham Buxton

> In this time between the times, it is all too easy to be held captive by faulty forms of dualism.

---

2. Third Lausanne Congress, *Cape Town Commitment*, sec. 2A.3.

3. Smith, *Awaiting the King*, 159.

4. See Smith, 160.

5. For discussion of various "dualisms," see Boot, *Gospel Culture*, 53–60; Buxton, *Celebrating Life*, 1–23; Miller, *LifeWork*, 15–33; Snyder, *Salvation Means Creation Healed*, 11–61.

puts it: "The syndrome we are describing here is the 'sacred-secular divide,' and it has plagued the church throughout its life. Simply put, life is divided into two compartments, the holy and the unholy, or the sacred and the profane."[6]

Nancy Pearcey speaks for many when she argues that such a bifurcated approach does not hold with the clear testimony across the whole of Scripture to the comprehensive sovereignty of God, the rule of Christ and the renewing power of the Holy Spirit:

> The biblical message is not just about some isolated part of life labeled "religion" or "church life." Creation, Fall, and Redemption are cosmic in scope, describing the great events that shape the nature of all created reality. We don't need to accept an inner fragmentation between our faith and the rest of life. . . . The promise of Christianity is the joy and power of an integrated life, transformed on every level by the Holy Spirit, so that our whole being participates in the great drama of God's plan of redemption.[7]

So, then, what is the witness of the Bible on this issue?

Two Biblical Portraits

We begin with two compelling portraits from Scripture, one from the Old Testament and one from the New Testament, each of which demonstrates the significance of a "whole-life" perspective. Our biblical portraits start with someone who is versatile and resourceful, hard-working and skillful, with a remarkable range of manual, commercial, administrative, and interpersonal skills – the wise woman of Proverbs 31.

The Wise Woman (Proverbs 31:10–31)

Significantly, we reach the end of the book of Proverbs and discover that the model for lived-out wisdom to emulate is not a religious "professional," such as a priest or a prophet or a scribe, but a woman whose faith is shown in her daily life. In the words of Ellen Davis, this remarkable portrayal is "the Bible's

---

6. Buxton, *Celebrating Life*, 4.
7. Pearcey, *Total Truth*, 95.

> The model for lived-out wisdom to emulate is not a religious "professional," such as a priest or a prophet or a scribe, but a woman whose faith is shown in her daily life.

most extended description of the regular activity of an ordinary person," made all the more significant because "a book that purports to be 'the proverbs of Solomon' (Proverbs 1:1) concludes by celebrating a nonroyal figure."[8] This nonroyal figure is a woman who "fears the LORD" (31:30), whose wisdom is demonstrated in her everyday activities of being a wife to her husband and a mother to her children, providing for her family, managing her household, engaging in international trade in cloths and textiles, negotiating the purchase of fields, looking out for the poor, and more besides.

The passage draws on motifs from so-called "heroic" poetry which described the mighty deeds of warriors or heroes.[9] Verse 10 calls her "a wife of noble character" (see also 31:29). It could be translated "a woman of strength," or "excellence," but the word also carries military connotations, suggesting she is to be understood as "a valiant woman" or "a woman of valour." The line in 31:17 – "she sets about her work vigorously" – carries the sense of girding herself with strength, like a warrior putting on armour for a battle. The imagery is repeated in 31:25 where "she is clothed with strength and dignity," and can "laugh" (like a victorious warrior) "at the days to come." The woman's activities are thus celebrated in heroic terms. Here is a composition akin to a heroic poem about someone engaged in everyday labour.

Furthermore, in a book which begins with a portrayal of wisdom as a woman inviting people to come to her to receive insight and understanding from God, the woman of Proverbs 31:10–31 is arguably a picture of wisdom itself – and so is applicable to men as much as to women. It applies to all because it sets out the ideal of practical wisdom, involving words and deeds, operating in every sphere of life, embracing the daily rhythms of eating, drinking, working, sleeping. The book which begins with "the fear of the Lord" as the beginning of wisdom (1:7) concludes with a demonstration of what it looks like to fear the Lord in everyday life.

8. Davis, *Scripture, Culture, and Agriculture*, 148.
9. Bartholomew and O'Dowd, *Old Testament Wisdom Literature*, 105–106, 114.

Al Wolters has shown how the history of interpretation of this poem reflects broader currents in approaches to Scripture through the ages. Patristic and medieval views of grace standing apart from nature, or in tension with nature, meant that the woman tended to be allegorised as Mary or the church. The challenge to this unhelpful allegorical consensus came as the Reformation and Luther's doctrine of "calling" allowed the passage to be understood as a poem about the vocation of a wife and mother.[10] Wolters himself argues that "the woman's household activities are seen not as something opposed to, or even distinct from, her fear of the Lord, but rather as their external manifestation."[11]

From a whole-Bible perspective, this is what we might expect given what we know of the comprehensive supremacy of God and the lordship of Jesus, which is reflected in our second biblical portrait – that of the cosmic Christ in Colossians 1.

The Cosmic Christ (Colossians 1:15–20)

The apostle Paul wrote letters, not stories, but his letters can be seen to have a narrative substructure – the story of God's dealings with Israel and with the whole of humanity, indeed with the whole of creation, from the beginning of all things to the renewal of all things. Much of the time that story is implicit, and Paul can allude to it or refer to particular parts of it as he engages with the churches to whom he writes.

Sometimes a short summary of the story bubbles to the surface of his letters, as it does in Philippians 2:5–11 and Colossians 1:15–20. In the latter passage, Paul takes us from the creation of all things to the consummation of all things through the cross and the church in six verses! At the heart of that story is Jesus, the living Lord, the cosmic Christ. He is the one who embraces both beginning and end, who stands at the heart of God's plan for the ages, himself the image of the invisible God, the Lord of creation and redemption. Since all things were made through him and all things will be reconciled in him, there is nothing that does not come under his lordship. The creator, sustainer and reconciler of all is none other than Jesus, the Lord of all.

---

10. Wolters, *Song.*
11. Wolters, 25.

The cross is where Paul finishes this breathtaking paragraph. The death of Jesus is certainly the means of forgiveness (see Col 1:14; 2:13), but it also brings about the restoration of everything under Christ's lordship. The object of reconciliation is not just men and women but "all things" (1:20). Just as all things in heaven and on earth were created through Christ, so also all things in heaven and on earth are reconciled through his death on the cross. This, Paul goes on to say, is "the gospel that you heard and has been proclaimed to every creature under heaven" (1:23).

Howard Snyder notes that while "Paul begins with the fact of individual and corporate personal salvation through Christ," he "places personal salvation within a picture of cosmic transformation."[12] Christ deals with our sin through his death, restoring us to God, but also restoring God's order, bringing all things back to God. As Joseph Boot comments:

> God's work of redemption in these programmatic texts [Col 1 and Eph 1] is much wider than personal salvation and a place in heaven while "spiritual people" wait for the *parousia*. Instead, since all creation is implicated in the Fall, so all creation must be redeemed (Rom 8:18–25). Christ died to redeem everything that sin polluted. . . . The gospel sweeps up into its great symphony every movement of our daily work, our marriage and family, our vocations and callings. Everything that has been dominated by sin is now being transformed by the gospel.[13]

Indeed, this perspective is worked out in the rest of the letter to the Colossians, as Paul goes on to describe Christians as those who are being renewed in the image of their creator, who have taken off the "old self" and put on the "new self" (3:9–10), as those who, whatever they do, "whether in word or deed, do it all in the name of the Lord Jesus, giving thanks to God the Father through him" (3:17). Paul shows that our new standing in Christ makes a difference to how we live in the family and as slaves and masters (3:18–4:1), and how we speak to others about Jesus as and when we get the opportunity (4:2–6).

---

12. Snyder, *Salvation Means Creation Healed*, 99.
13. Boot, *Gospel Culture*, 95.

Here, then, is a powerful vision of the Christian life that embraces the whole of life, a compelling reminder of the deep and wide nature of the gospel. Here is a reminder that salvation isn't liberation from creation, but liberation from sin and its consequences. The God who created all things is the God who will restore all things, and who calls us to flourish in his liberating lordship in every aspect of life.[14]

> The God who created all things is the God who will restore all things, and who calls us to flourish in his liberating lordship in every aspect of life.

It is instructive to note that these two portraits are not isolated passages but are rooted in the argument and flow of the books in which they each sit. The portrayal of the wise woman in Proverbs 31:10–31 is not merely a poetic appendix to the book of Proverbs, but brings us back to the personification of wisdom in its opening sections, and provides a fitting crowning point to the teaching about wisdom in the book as a whole. The portrayal of the cosmic Christ in Colossians 1:15–20 is literarily and theologically stitched into the flow of the letter Paul writes, the scope of Christ's work in creation and reconciliation providing the ground and motive for the church's way of life, as Paul seeks to make good on his commitment to "present everyone fully mature in Christ" (1:29).

Even allowing for the significance of these two biblical portraits, it would be a mistake to imagine that a whole-life perspective is confined to a few "purple" passages in the Bible. As it happens, such a perspective is found throughout Scripture as a whole.

Two Biblical-Theological Strategies

At its best, the discipline of biblical theology is not merely a descriptive enterprise, allowing Christian interpreters to make sense of the Bible as a whole, but also a formative exercise, encouraging those same readers to be shaped by the Bible as a whole. We contend that there is no place in the Bible for a sacred-

---

14. There is a growing body of semi-popular literature which helpfully explores the comprehensive nature of salvation and its implications for the whole of life. As a sample, see Jethani, *Futureville*; Poythress, *Lordship of Christ*; Treat, *Seek First*; Wilson, *Story of Everything*; Wittmer, *Becoming Worldly Saints*.

secular divide as that phenomenon is commonly understood. But more than that can be claimed: the Bible which throughout its pages embraces the whole of life as an arena in which God works is the same Bible through which he speaks and shapes us in and for the whole of life. As Christopher Watkin observes, "We read the Bible not only as a set of ideas and stories to think about, but also as a set of patterns and dispositions through which we can think about everything and through which we live the whole of life."[15]

Space allows only a few, hopefully suggestive, observations on two strategies.

The Story the Bible Tells

The first strategy recognises that at the heart of Scripture is not a list of rules to be obeyed or a set of promises to be claimed or a collection of principles to be mined but a grand, sweeping story to be told. From the garden of Eden in Genesis to the city of the new Jerusalem in Revelation, the Bible begins with the creation of all things and ends with the renewal of all things, and at the centre of that story is Jesus, the one in whom God's purposes for all things will be completed.[16]

> The Bible which throughout its pages embraces the whole of life as an arena in which God works is the same Bible through which he speaks and shapes us in and for the whole of life.

Christians look to the biblical account of creation for their understanding of what it means to be human, created in the image of God. The opening sections of Genesis describe the place of humans in relationship to the world and to each other, as well as our capacity to relate with God. They affirm that the world was created good, that men and women were created good, that procreation is good, that work is good. Alas, the story goes on to show us that things don't stay good. Sin has tragic effects on our relationship with the world, with each other, with God and within ourselves. The Bible goes on to show the harsh reality of human existence under the rule of sin: men and women rebel against God and are unfaithful to each other;

---

15. Watkin, *Thinking through Creation*, 3.
16. Examples of this approach are now legion: Ashford and Thomas, *Gospel of Our King*, 11–96; Bartholomew and Goheen, *Drama of Scripture*; Wolters, *Creation Regained*.

they become alienated from others, relating through suspicion, envy, greed, pride and anger. Sin affects every aspect of life.

The biblical story goes on to show how God sets about his plan of restoration by making a covenant with a chosen people through whom he will bless all nations. It tells of God becoming flesh and living among us in Christ, rescuing us from sin and its consequences through his death and resurrection in order to bring about renewed relationship with God, with each other and ultimately with the rest of creation. Within the story, creation, incarnation and resurrection provide God's imprimatur on the whole of life, his "enthusiastic embrace of the material world."[17] Nor does the story end there, for Christians belong to the body of Christ, a people in whom God's spirit lives, which shapes our character and mission in distinctive ways. Meanwhile, we look forward to the consummation of all things, Jesus's return, the remaking of the universe, and new bodies. The Bible encourages us to look forwards to a comprehensive renovation, "a new heaven and a new earth, where righteousness dwells" (2 Pet 3:13; cf. Isa 65:17–25; Rom 8:18–25; Rev 21:1–4).[18]

The Bible tells us the way God's world really is and shapes us as disciples for living in it. And it does so for the whole of life – Monday to Saturday as well as Sunday, in public and in private, in culture as well as in church, in our "scattered" lives at work as much as when we are "gathered" together in worship. Moreover, this "whole-life" perspective is not limited to a few passages here and there but is woven through the story as a whole – from beginning to end. As Christians, we are incorporated into this ongoing drama which embraces every part of our lives, individually and together, for the sake of the world in which we are called to live.

> The Bible tells us the way God's world really is and shapes us as disciples for living in it. And it does so for the whole of life.

The Literature the Bible Contains

The whole-life dimension of the Bible is seen not just in the big story it tells but in the different kinds of writings it contains – stories and songs, laws and letters, proverbs and parables, poetry and prophecy.

---

17. Wittmer, *Becoming Worldly Saints*, 43.
18. See, for example, Middleton, *New Heaven*, and Smith, *Not Home Yet*.

Much of the Bible is made up of narrative, longer and shorter stories which show us who God is, what he is like, how he works in the world and through his people in every part of life – sometimes in dramatic ways as with Moses and David, sometimes behind the scenes as with Ruth and Boaz. These stories reveal God's unfolding purpose through covenant history, all the while inviting us to take our place in the forward movement of the story.

The biblical worldview is not dualist, but neither is it monist, collapsing the whole of reality into a single entity, denying the differentiation between God and his creation. Likewise, the various laws in Leviticus and elsewhere relating to holiness and purity do not reflect a sacred-secular divide so much as reinforce the distinction between God and his sinful people, and the necessity of sacrifice if we are to enjoy fellowship with him. Indeed, Morales states that the dominating concern of Leviticus is "YHWH's opening a way for humanity to dwell in the divine presence."[19] Hence, while laws about cleanliness and uncleanliness in Leviticus 11–15 may appear random at first glance, these sections describe what it means to be clean, or "fit for the presence of God," and what it means to be holy, or "belonging to God."[20]

More significantly for our purposes, while Leviticus addresses priestly and sacrificial concerns, it also posits what Jonathan Sacks has called "the democratisation of holiness."[21] Leviticus 19:1–2 dramatically (and unusually for the ancient world) embraces the people as a whole: "The LORD said to Moses, "Speak to the entire assembly of Israel and say to them: 'Be holy because I, the LORD your God, am holy.'" In addition, the call to holiness embraces the whole of life, as the rest of the section makes clear. As Sacks says,

> The book begins with an elite, the priests, sons of Aaron, a minority within a minority, one specific family within the tribe of Levi. It culminates in a call from God to the entire nation. It begins in the Sanctuary but ends in society. It democratises kedusha, holiness,

19. Morales, *Who Shall Ascend*, 23.
20. Morales, 155.
21. Sacks, *Leviticus*, 1–49.

the sign of God's presence, so that it becomes part of the ongoing
life of the people as a whole.[22]

Holiness is not only for the cult, its personnel and apparatus, but for the whole
community. In addition, Leviticus offers what Ellen Davis calls "a wholesome
materiality."[23] The sheer range of regulations in the law reminds us that the
holiness in view touches all areas of life – in working and resting, buying and
selling goods, looking after our parents, providing for the poor, in how we
work, in what we eat, in who we sleep with – living in the world but not living
like the world.

The poetry in the Psalms ignites our imagination and emotions and draws
a response from us through different seasons of life in praise and lament,
thanksgiving and confession, protest and celebration, bringing everything to
God in prayer. The Wisdom books help shape the everyday lives of those who
know that wisdom doesn't begin in human autonomy, but in relationship with
God, which is then worked out in different spheres of life – in our homes and
our workplaces, our neighbourhoods and communities – wherever God has
called us. Wisdom also encourages us to reflect on the deeper questions of life
when things don't go as we think they ought. The Prophets call God's people to
task not just for failure in the moral realm but the social and political realms
too, reminding them of the justice he requires, the sin he judges, the covenant
he keeps, the nations he includes and the restoration he promises.

The Gospels announce the good news that in Jesus's life, death and
resurrection, God's kingdom purpose has come to pass. They shape and
empower us as God's missional people as we follow the path of discipleship –
which turns out to be the way of the cross – in every part of life. Jesus's parables
in the Gospels reframe our expectations about how the kingdom of God works,
challenging our preconceptions, encouraging us to think about reality in a
different way, calling us to live in a different way. The Letters show us the
working out of the implications of what Christ has done to equip churches
to live faithfully and fruitfully in their different contexts scattered around the

---

22. Sacks, *Leviticus*, 4. See also Davis, *Scripture, Culture, and Agriculture*, 85: "Elsewhere in
Leviticus, holiness is the special characteristic of the sanctuary and the priests who attend it, but
here in the Holiness Code (sections 17–26), that notion is democratized and vastly extended."
23. Davis, *Scripture, Culture, and Agriculture*, 80–100.

Roman world. Then, the visionary, apocalyptic portions of Scripture shape the way we hope for what God will do in the future, and how we live meanwhile.

Through its different genres, Scripture not only explicitly and implicitly embraces the whole of life, but "disciples" us in how to think and feel and live: narrative tells of God's gracious plan being worked out through the ages and our part in it; laws disclose his will for how we should relate to him and to each other and how our life together might be ordered; wisdom shows what it is to fear him in all areas of life; prophecy challenges us to fulfil our responsibilities as his covenant people; gospels proclaim the centrality of Christ in God's plan of redemption, providing a kingdom-and-cross-shaped pattern for living; letters instruct those who are "in Christ" to grow up in him as we serve each other and live in the world; the apocalyptic trains us in how to hope as we look forward to the renewal of all things.

In these different ways – through the story it tells and the literature it contains – the Bible provides the perspective from which to view life as a seamless whole and equips us to live out the comprehensive salvation brought by Jesus: with no part of our existence held captive by the sacred-secular divide, no part of life sealed off from the lordship of Christ, and seeking in all things to honour him for the greater glory of God.

3

Naming the Issue Using the Key Historical Texts

Edwin E. M. Tay

Introduction

The prominence of secularization as a subject in the study of religion, including Christianity, has facilitated the widespread use of the sacred-secular binary.[1] Granting the legitimacy of this binary, this chapter introduces selected writings of five significant personalities from the history of the church. The contents of these writings help to address three specific forms of the sacred-secular divide (SSD) with which Christians in the past had to grapple in their discipleship. The first form of SSD is anthropological in nature: the mind/soul-body divide; the second, ethical: the contemplative-active divide; the third, vocational: the clergy-laity divide. These forms of SSD have not been described specifically as divisions between "the sacred" and "the secular" in the contexts in which they occur. Nevertheless, they do illustrate the problem of SSD in the challenges they present to Christian discipleship as the ensuing discussion will make clear.

In addition to the types of SSD identified, two preliminary comments are in order in view of the highly selective nature of the literature to be presented and the historical distance between it and us. First, the selection of a text

---

1. For specific examples, see Zitukawa and York, "Expanding Religious Studies," 78–97; Scherer, "Landmarks," 621–632; Fox, "Secularization," 306–322; Kim, McCalman, and Fisher, "Sacred/Secular Divide," 203–208; Buxton, *Celebrating Life*.

is based on the criteria of its representative and practical value. William Perkins's *A Treatise of the Vocations or Callings of Men*, for instance, is chosen since it encompasses not only the standard Puritan conception of callings but also invaluable material of practical significance. Likewise, Gregory of Nazianzus's "On Love for the Poor," a work that employs his anthropology in the context of practical relationships, is chosen over writings which are substantially theological or philosophical even if they directly address the SSD under consideration. Second, there are a host of texts that are helpful for our purposes, but only five have been chosen. This is to allow for more depth in their exposition so that the theological resources required for addressing the SSD identified may be better appreciated for their present application. The sequence of subsequent discussions is framed around the three SSDs in the order identified above and follows the general passage of history from the time of the church fathers to the Puritans in the late sixteenth and seventeenth centuries.[2]

Overcoming the Anthropological Divide

During the patristic period, the anthropological divide of mind and body or soul and body was a pervasive one within the religious pluralism and philosophical movements of the Greco-Roman world. Viewing the material world as the product of inferior deities, Gnosticism devalued it and operated with an anthropology in which the body functioned as the vehicle of the soul and mind but was not itself the subject of salvation.[3] Platonism posited a sharp division between two realms: the world of the divine in which true forms or ideas exist, and the world of sensible, changing realities which are but their shadows.[4] This cosmic divide has anthropological significance: the soul belongs to the former and is immortal; the body belongs to the latter and is impure. Against the backdrop of these anthropological dualisms, the church fathers

---

2. I am aware of the danger of anachronism in framing the section this way. Thus, I have supplied introductory paragraphs to each section that sets the SSDs in their historical contexts, along with longer expositions of each chosen text. These measures should provide sufficient materials for readers to appreciate the immediate and broader historical contexts of the five selected works.

3. Ferguson, *Encyclopedia of Early Christianity*, 186–187, 465–469.

4. Ferguson, 351, 923–928.

affirmed the goodness of God's creation, took seriously the effects of sin upon it, and expounded the implications these affirmations held for living a life of embodied existence in the pursuit of God.

The following works by Gregory of Nyssa (c. 335–395) and Gregory of Nazianzus (c. 329–390) are significant examples.

> The church fathers affirmed the goodness of God's creation, took seriously the effects of sin upon it, and expounded the implications these affirmations held for living a life of embodied existence in the pursuit of God.

Gregory of Nyssa, On Virginity

Although written in the context of monastic life in the fourth century, Gregory of Nyssa's *On Virginity* does not merely discuss the merits of celibacy as the title suggests. Reflections extend to that of marriage. Divided into twenty-eight sections, the intention of the encomium is explicitly expressed from the very start: "The aim of this discourse is to create in the reader a desire for a life of virtue. But because of the many distractions associated with what the divine apostle calls 'the married life,' the treatise suggests, as a kind of door or entrance into a nobler state, the life of virginity."[5]

At first reading, Gregory appears to be extolling a life of celibacy over that of marriage. Indeed, he has some harsh things to say about the married life.[6] However, he also warns his readers not to think that he is "disregarding the institution of marriage" and affirms that marriage "is not deprived of God's blessing."[7] Several things need to be borne in mind if readers are to make sense of Gregory's apparently opposing stances.

First, rhetorical devices have been deployed in Gregory's depiction of marriage and celibacy.[8] That he opens his work by praising virginity which

---

5. Gregory, preface to *On Virginity*, 6.

6. The title of chapter 4 is telling: "That everything wrong in life has its beginning in marriage which distracts one from the true life." Gregory, *On Virginity*, sec. 4, p. 20.

7. Gregory, sec. 7, p. 31.

8. From the translator's introduction to Gregory's *On Virginity*: "The form of the treatise is the protreptic address used by the philosophers to persuade their listeners to a certain course of action. The usual stylistic and rhetorical devices, e.g. contrasts, pathos, similes, and metaphors are skillfully employed in it" (p. 3).

he describes as "beyond praise" should alert us to at least the presence of irony.[9] Second, Gregory does not limit his understanding of virginity to a life of celibacy and abstinence from sexual pleasure. According to him, "When you speak of the pure and incorruptible, you are using another name for virginity."[10] Virginity is thus to be understood literally and metaphorically. Third, the aim to promote a life of virtue, as his opening comment makes clear, is the overriding concern of the work. In the hands of Gregory, virtue is, as Boersma explains, "a synonym for 'Christ' . . . a participation in the divine life . . . the anagogical progress itself."[11] Advance in virtue "is nothing but a description of the Christian life."[12]

When understood in the light of the above considerations, Gregory's view of the married and celibate lives from the standpoint of the soul-body relation is a balanced one. The person who has "purified the eye of his soul" is one who beholds material existence, and "forget[s] the matter in which the beauty is encased, and . . . uses what he sees as a kind of basis for his contemplation of intelligible beauty."[13] In other words, bodily existence is not intrinsically bad or evil regardless of whether one is married or celibate but is capable of participation in divine pursuits. The crux of the matter is the inner dynamic of the embodied life. The foolish person "hands his soul over to the pleasures of the body . . . considering nothing else to be good than pleasing the body."[14] However, one who lives a life of virtue in and through the body strives to "see" God through the eyes of the soul as "the goal of true virginity."[15]

Thus, Gregory's negative presentation of marriage is not a rejection or degradation of marriage *per se*, but of the failure to live a life of moderation and virtue in pursuit of God in the context of marriage. This failure is the explanation for the vices peculiar to married life. He is equally critical of the lives of those who pursue celibacy for its own sake rather than pursuing the *telos*

---

9. Gregory, *On Virginity*, sec. 1, p. 9. For Gregory's use of irony, see Hart, "Reconciliation of Body," 450–478.

10. Gregory, *On Virginity*, sec. 2, p. 10.

11. Boersma, *Embodiment and Virtue*, 4.

12. Boersma, 4; cf. Boersma, 117–127.

13. Gregory, *On Virginity*, sec. 11, p. 39.

14. Gregory, sec. 4, p. 24.

15. Gregory, sec. 11, p. 42.

of the Christian life.[16] In Hart's assessment of Gregory's theology of marriage, "the needs of the body and the soul are ultimately compatible and thus provide a nondualistic understanding of the goal of asceticism, grounding asceticism in overcoming the illusions about the body rather than in the spirited struggle against the body."[17]

Gregory of Nazianzus, "On Love for the Poor" (Oration 14)

An anthropology that does not denigrate materiality but takes seriously the progress of the Christian life in the physical body will be concerned with the care of both soul and body in the practice of discipleship. Under the leadership of Basil who became bishop of Caesarea, the church in fourth-century Cappadocia engaged in the construction of the Basileias, the first Christian hospital in the ancient world built for the care of the poor, sick and dying.[18] Prompted by the crisis of a famine and its devastating impact on the marginalized in society, the building project was supported by the preaching of the Cappadocian Fathers that emphasized acts of benevolence and Christian philanthropy.[19]

Within the social setting enunciated above, Gregory, bishop of Nazianzus, composed one of his most moving and lengthiest orations, "On Love for the Poor."[20] The sermon opens with a plea to love the poor "not grudgingly but generously," so that his hearers "may become rich in the kingdom."[21] Presenting the challenge to love the poor as the *sine qua non* of Christian discipleship, Gregory argues his case in several ways, aided by the use of powerful rhetoric.

First, Gregory argues that among the virtues exemplified in Holy Scripture, love is the greatest, and among the forms of its expression, love for the poor is the most excellent.[22] Second, there exists a solidarity between the church and the poor so that caring for the poor and sick is tantamount to loving Christ

---

16. Gregory, *On Virginity*, sec. 8, pp. 33–34; cf. Hart, "Reconciliation of Body," 462.

17. Hart, "Reconciliation of Body," 476.

18. Ferngren, *Medicine and Health Care*, 124–130.

19. Daley, "Cappadocian Fathers," 431–461.

20. For helpful expositions of "Oration 14," see Matz, *Gregory of Nazianzus*, 113–126, and Beeley, *Gregory of Nazianzus*, 254–258.

21. Gregory of Nazianzus, "Oration 14," sec. 1, p. 39.

22. Gregory, sec. 2–5, pp. 39–42.

and the members of his body.[23] Third, we are most God-like in his overflowing generosity when we love the poor, especially before assistance is requested.[24] Evident here is the theme of deification that is prominent among the Greek Fathers and central to Gregory's soteriology. Fourth, Gregory warns that love for the poor is a key consideration for the administration of divine judgement at the eschaton.[25]

Interwoven into Gregory's biblical, theological and rhetorical appeals is his anthropology. He views the human person as "the image of God" and "concocted of clay."[26] The human body is to be cherished as our "fellow servant" and evaded as our "enemy"; respected as our "fellow heir" and escaped from as our "chain."[27] This hybrid nature has a pedagogical function that serves the greater end of our salvation in the school of humility. Making the point rhetorically, Gregory comments:

> What is this wisdom that I embody? What is this great mystery . . . that we may know that we are at once most exalted and most humble, earthly and celestial, ephemeral and immortal, heirs of light and fire – or of darkness – depending on which way we turn? Such is our hybrid nature which . . . takes this form so that whenever we feel exalted because of our likeness to God's image, we may be brought down because of our clay.[28]

Gregory acknowledges that although weak, the human body is our "helper" in the pursuit of God.[29] Whether rich or poor, our neighbours are God's image bearers whose physical needs are to be cared for since the union of body and soul is of God.[30] What matters in our discipleship is the health of the soul as it seeks after God through the body. He warns that the failure to love the lepers in whom poverty is epitomized is symptomatic of a diseased soul that is "far

---

23. Gregory, sec. 8, p. 44.
24. Gregory, sec. 22–27, pp. 55–61.
25. Gregory, sec. 39, p. 70.
26. Gregory, sec. 6, p. 43.
27. Gregory, sec. 6, p. 43.
28. Gregory, sec. 7, pp. 43–44.
29. Gregory, sec. 6, p. 43.
30. Gregory, sec. 8, 14, pp. 44, 48–49.

worse than any in the body."[31] However, demonstrating love for the poor in their bodily suffering is to imitate Christ who became poor in order to redeem us from spiritual poverty.[32] The nature of the soul-body relation for Gregory is not one of division but union in the light of his soteriology as illustrated in his concern for the poor.

Overcoming the Ethical Divide

The distinction between a life focused on active service and one that consists largely in the contemplation of truth has a long history of discussion in the church. Reflections on "the two lives" as Augustine termed them, characterized by action and contemplation respectively, are evident in the history of exegesis that compares Mary with Martha, Rachel with Leah, and Peter with John.[33] Tracing the exegetical developments of the Mary-Martha relationship in Luke 10:38–42 and John 12:1–8, Constable has observed the passage from the complementarity of the two women and what they represent in the time of the fathers to their distinction and separation in medieval exegesis.[34] Venerable Bede (672–735), whom Lynch described as "the most learned Westerner in the eighth century," is a medieval exegete who maintained a complementary view of action and contemplation.[35]

Bede, Homilies on the Gospels (1.9 and 2.17)

Reputed as "one of the masterpieces of monastic literature," Bede's *Homilies on the Gospels* consists of fifty homilies, all of which were delivered in the Wearmouth-Jarrow monastery.[36] Arranged according to the liturgical calendar, they reveal Bede's concern for a Christian discipleship that emphasizes the necessity of active service even in expositions that relate to prayer and

---

31. Gregory, sec. 18, pp. 51–52.

32. Gregory, sec. 1, 15, pp. 39, 49–50.

33. Augustine, "Sermon LIV," sec. 4, p. 430.

34. Constable, *Three Studies*, 1–141.

35. Lynch, *Medieval Church*, 55. Rakoczy identifies Catherine of Sienna (1347–1380) as a medieval example among other non-medieval ones who take the complementary view. Rakoczy, *Great Mystics*.

36. Bede, *Homilies*, xi.

contemplation.[37] Bede's fullest discussion of the relationship between action and contemplation is found in homily 1.9 on John 21:19–24. Peter's question to Jesus about John ("Lord, what about this man?"), along with Jesus's prophecies concerning both their lives, supply the platform for reflections on "the two ways of life in the Church which are carried out in the present, namely the active and the contemplative."[38]

According to Bede, the active life is common to all Christians. It consists of "righteous labors" that keep us from sin and engage us in the service of God and love of neighbour.[39] Action prepares the believer for contemplation, while the blessing of contemplation is proleptically experienced as the believer pursues hard after its object. Bede explains:

> The contemplative life . . . is [lived] when one who has been taught by the long practice of good actions . . . direct[s] the eye of his mind towards love alone; and he begins, even in the present life, to gain a foretaste of the joy of the perpetual blessedness which he is to attain in the future, by ardently desiring it, and even sometimes, insofar as is permitted to mortals, by contemplating it sublimely in mental ecstasy.[40]

Bede does not confine his reflections on the interaction of the two lives in the here and now but also takes the future into account. In homily 2.17, he elaborates on their relationship with an eschatological perspective: "When the labors and hardships of this age come to an end, and our debts, [that is] our faults, have been forgiven, the entire people of the elect will rejoice eternally in the sole contemplation of the divine vision."[41] In other words, the active life ends with death, but the contemplative life continues after death. Until the fullness of the eschaton arrives, Christian discipleship involves our labours for Christ in obedience to his commandments and the concomitant enjoyment

---

37. DeGregorio, "Venerable Bede," 1–39.
38. Bede, *Homilies*, 1:85–95.
39. Bede, 1:91.
40. Bede, 1:91.
41. Bede, 2:174.

of "some image of the future tranquility" even in the present.[42] In the words of DeGregorio: "Bede's unifying message was that, for Christians in this life, contemplation must embrace action, and action contemplation."[43] What unites both is the person of Christ. He is the one we imitate in action and on whom our eyes are fixed in contemplation.[44]

Overcoming the Vocational Divide

A significant development in the European Reformation of the sixteenth century is the doctrine of the general priesthood, commonly known as the priesthood of all believers. Examining the relationship between the general priesthood that pertains to all Christians, and the special priesthood that is confined to ordained clergy, Bulley has shown that in the third century the participation of the laity in ministry was significantly diminished by the rise of the clergy's specialized priesthood.[45] This clergy-laity divide persisted into the Middle Ages so that, by the twelfth and thirteenth centuries, the ideal church was thought to be "a society of disciplined and organized clergy directing the thoughts and activities of an obedient and receptive laity – kings, magnates, and peasants alike."[46] The Protestant Reformation brought significant changes to this state of affairs in the way the doctrine of the priesthood and vocation were understood.

Martin Luther, Address to the Christian Nobility of the German Nation

An Address to the Christian Nobility of the German Nation by Martin Luther (1483–1546) is the first of three reforming treatises published in 1520.[47] Written at a time of escalating controversy over the nature of papal authority, Luther's

---

42. Bede, 2:176.

43. DeGregorio, "Venerable Bede," 33–34.

44. For Bede, "the perfection of the active way of life" is the life of Christ which Peter is to imitate, while "contemplative happiness" is made perfect when we see Christ face to face. Bede, *Homilies*, 1:92.

45. See Bulley, *Priesthood of Some Believers*.

46. Southern, *Western Society*, 38; cf. Maddix, "Biblical Model," 214–228.

47. Luther, *Christian in Society*, 115–217.

tract sought the support of the German princes for his reforming efforts. Against the notion that it is not the laity but clergy who have authority over religious matters, he argued that every believer is a priest through baptism and established the difference between clergy and laity on the basis of their distinct responsibilities.

In the first section of the tract, Luther sought to demolish "three walls" that secured the authority of the medieval Catholic church. The first "wall" concerns the inferior status of "temporal power" to "spiritual power," the subjection of laity to clergy.[48] Appealing to 1 Corinthians 12:12–13, 1 Peter 2:9 and Revelation 5:9–10, Luther counters the divide: "There is no true, basic difference between laymen and priests, princes and bishops, between religious and secular, except for the sake of office and work, but not for the sake of status. They are all of the spiritual estate, all are truly priests, bishops, and popes. But they do not all have the same work to do."[49]

Having removed the clergy-laity divide on the grounds of the general priesthood, Luther went on to demolish the second and third "walls" by drawing out the implications of that priesthood. Against the second "wall" that confines the authority to interpret Scripture to the pope, Luther asserts rhetorically, "If we are all priests . . . and all have one faith, one gospel, one sacrament, why should we not also have the power to test and judge what is right and wrong in matters of faith?"[50] In Luther's judgment, the third wall – that only the pope has authority to convene church councils – will crumble when the first two are destroyed.[51]

While Luther's doctrine of the general priesthood "effectively demolished the ecclesiology of his day," as Trueman notes, it did leave room for the special priesthood.[52] Luther acknowledges the legitimacy of the clergy's office for the sake of good order in the church.[53] However, he conceived of office in terms of

---

48. Luther, 127–133.

49. Luther, 129.

50. Luther, 135.

51. Luther, 136.

52. Trueman, *Luther*, 74.

53. Due to the threat of doctrinal errors and the violence that erupted in the Peasants' War, the maintenance of good order through the special priesthood was increasingly stressed by Luther after 1520. See Rogers, "Dangerous Idea?," 120–127.

responsibility, not spiritual status. Thus, the clergy "are neither different from other Christians nor superior to them, except that they are charged with the administration of the word of God and the sacraments," just as "a cobbler, a smith, a peasant – each has the work and office of his trade, and yet they are all alike consecrated priests and bishops."[54] Luther makes clear that the formal office of priest is to be located within and derived from the general priesthood, while the general priesthood is founded upon the priesthood of Christ.[55]

The implications of Luther's address could not have been clearer for the Christian nobility. Since they are "fellow-Christians, fellow-priests, fellow-members of the spiritual estate, fellow-lords over all," they should "when necessity demands it," do what they can "to bring about a truly free council."[56] What Luther secures with the doctrine of the general priesthood is the liberation of the laity from the chains of a clergy-laity divide for ecclesial and political reforms. Once the connection between the general priesthood and the social responsibility of the laity was made, the subject of the Christian's vocation in society became increasingly significant in Reformation and post-Reformation literature.

William Perkins, A Treatise of the Vocations or Callings of Men

Building upon the doctrine of the general priesthood, the Puritans in the sixteenth and seventeenth centuries engaged in substantial reflections on the implications of that doctrine for life in the family, church and society through the lens of vocation.[57] While statements on the sanctity of work and vocation were evident in the writings of leading Reformers such as Luther and Calvin, they were incidental occurrences.[58] Within the Protestant tradition, it was the Puritans who first expounded on the subject substantially in their preaching and writings.

---

54. Luther, *Christian in* Society, 130.
55. Althaus, *Theology of Martin Luther*, 313–315, 323–332.
56. Luther, *Christian in Society*, 137.
57. See Ryken, "Some Kind of Life," 45–66; Ryken, *Worldly Saints*.
58. For Luther on vocation, see the classic discussion in Wingren, *Luther on Vocation*. Cf. Calvin, *Institutes*, sec. 3.10.6, pp. 1:724–725.

Among Puritan writings on vocation, *A Treatise of the Vocations or Callings of Men, with the Sorts and Kinds of Them and the Right Use of Them* by William Perkins (1558–1602) is arguably the most significant from the standpoint of theological synthesis.[59] Published posthumously in 1603, its contents are set within the biblical framework of God's redemptive work in Christ in the light of humanity's fall into sin. God's assignment of various vocations is a crucial aspect of the way fallen humanity is to be "fitted and framed" to recover and live as God has intended "for the honor and glory of His name."[60] Based on the key text of 1 Corinthians 7:20, "Let every man abide in that calling wherein he was called," Perkins's treatise has three main sections: "What Vocation or Calling Is"; "The Parts and Kinds Thereof"; "The Holy and Lawful Use of Every Man's Particular Calling."[61]

Vocation is defined by Perkins as "*a certain kind of life, ordained and imposed on man by God for the common good.*"[62] He has in mind various stations in life and their related responsibilities, such as kings in their rule, ministers in their preaching and heads of households in their governance. These are not simply occupations but callings, from the Latin *vocare* ("to call"), because God is the author of vocations and "every man is to live as he is called by God."[63]

Having defined vocation in general, Perkins distinguished between two types of callings: general and personal or particular. General calling is "that whereby a man is called out of the world to be a child of God, a member of Christ, and an heir of the kingdom of heaven."[64] Personal calling refers to "the execution of some particular office, arising of that distinction which God maketh between man and man in every society."[65] The former applies to all Christians while the latter pertains to the specific positions, roles and responsibilities in the home, church and society to which a person is divinely appointed. A man could have multiple callings. Be it the vocation of a father,

---

59. Perkins, *Treatise*. Subsequent citations from this edition have been modernized in font type and spelling. Cf. Patterson, *William Perkins*, 140–146.

60. Perkins, "The Epistle Dedicatorie," in *Treatise*, § 3.

61. Perkins, *Treatise*, 1–2.

62. Perkins, 2. Italics original.

63. Perkins, 2–3.

64. Perkins, 13.

65. Perkins, 22.

doctor or soldier to which the same person is called, the end of every one of them is to serve "the common good."[66]

When lived in the way prescribed by God, personal callings are the means by which the world is shaped according to God's redemptive purposes. This involves the union of the general and particular callings in the practice of Christian discipleship. Perkins explains, "Every particular calling must be practiced in, and with the general calling of a Christian . . . both callings must be joined as body and soul are joined in a living man."[67] The practical implications of this rule are far-reaching. A magistrate is not only a Christian by virtue of the general calling, but "he must be a Christian Magistrate in executing the office of a Magistrate in bearing the sword."[68] When practiced across the whole of life, service to God is rendered and "marvelous contentation" (i.e. great satisfaction) obtained, "though it be but to sweep the house, or keep sheep."[69]

> When lived in the way prescribed by God, personal callings are the means by which the world is shaped according to God's redemptive purposes.

Perkins's integrated view of the two callings dignifies even the lowliest of work and occupations. Thus, he affirms, "the action of a shepherd in keeping sheep . . . is as good a work before God, as is the action of a judge in giving sentence, or of a magistrate in ruling, or a minister in preaching."[70] Discharging the responsibilities peculiar to our callings requires us to "cleave to our surety Christ Jesus," for it is the mediation of Christ on our behalf that enables us "to make a good account before the Lord, at the last day of judgment."[71] Perkins's doctrine of vocation is but the Reformation doctrine of the general priesthood applied to Christian ethics.

---

66. Perkins, 6.
67. Perkins, 31–33.
68. Perkins, 32.
69. Perkins, 34.
70. Perkins, 39.
71. Perkins, 133, 136.

According to Ryken, the distinction of vocation into the two types of callings is "the greatest Puritan contribution" to our understanding of vocation.[72]

Conclusion

Our creedal confession of belief in the communion of saints means, among other things, that we listen to and learn from those before us who have struggled with the Scriptures and walked the path of Christian discipleship.[73] This chapter is an exercise in listening to the past for present instruction. The voices heard are those of two Cappadocian Fathers, one English monk, one German reformer and one leading Puritan. Ordered according to three types of SSD, expositions of the five chosen texts have been offered with an eye to the way they provide theological resources for addressing the mind-body/ soul-body, contemplative-active and clergy-laity divides. I would like to offer one observation and draw one implication by way of conclusion.

The theological resources that have been brought to bear upon the three SSDs are immediately soteriological in nature and christologically grounded. Thus, in the context of the anthropological divide of soul and body or mind and body, the two Cappadocian Fathers affirmed the necessity of an embodied existence that aims at union with God in a life lived after the example of Christ. Against the ethical divide of contemplation and action, Bede understands discipleship as an eschatologically oriented life that embraces "the two lives" where the object of both is Christ. Luther rejects the vocational divide of clergy and laity on the grounds of the general priesthood by virtue of Christ's priestly mediation. Perkins works out the implications of the general priesthood in a doctrine of vocation where "cleaving to Christ" is key to the eschatological vindication of the way our callings are lived out.

If attempts at overcoming SSD require the theological resources of Christology and soteriology, it follows that the origin of SSD may well lie in the problem these resources are ultimately meant to address. Kim, McCalman and Fisher locate SSD's origin to the rise of modernism.[74] Stevens traces it to

---

72. Ryken, "Some Kind of Life," 49.
73. See Holmes, *Listening to the Past*, 18–36.
74. Kim, McCalman, and Fisher, "Sacred/Secular Divide," 205–206.

the rise of universities with their adoption of an Aristotelian model of thinking that separates theology from practical living.[75] Buxton traces its origin to the dualisms in Greek philosophy while Lind locates it even earlier to before 500 BC.[76] From the theological standpoint, these proposals are but symptoms of an underlying cause. SSD is a systemic problem and global phenomenon that is to be traced theologically to the effect of sin upon humanity. Sin fragments life, divides what God has joined together and impedes human flourishing. It is only in Christ that "all things hold together" (Col 1:17). Dealing with SSD will consequently require theological resources that offer a whole-life view of salvation in Christ and a doctrine of sin that accounts for its disintegrating effects upon God's creation and image bearers.

---

75. Stevens, *Other Six Days*, 9–16.

76. Buxton, *Celebrating Life*, 6–9, 12–17; Lind, "Origins," 23–40.

4

Naming the Issue Using the Key Contemporary Texts

Antony Billington

As Edwin Tay notes in the previous chapter, the sacred-secular divide has manifested itself in various forms through the history of the church – whether as anthropological (the mind/soul-body divide), ethical (the contemplative-active divide) or vocational (the clergy-laity divide). Even where these have not been explicitly labelled as divisions between "sacred" and "secular" perspectives, they nonetheless reflect that disjunction.

The purpose of this chapter, in tandem with the previous one, is to show how – contrary to what is sometimes imagined to be the case – many Christians through the ages have operated with a comprehensive, whole-life perspective on God, humanity, sin, salvation and the mission to which God calls his people. The overall stance the contributors to this volume are taking and encouraging others to adopt in the task of theological education is not new to the pages of Christian history but stands in healthy continuity with those who have gone before us.

> Many Christians through the ages have operated with a comprehensive, whole-life perspective on God, humanity, sin, salvation and the mission to which God calls his people.

The brief discussion that follows gathers together several key figures, texts and movements into specific areas, even while recognizing inevitable overlap between several of the categories. With it comes the encouragement for others to retrieve the best from what their own traditions say about the significance of the topic.

A This-Worldly Spirituality

In their "archaeology of contemporary culture," Bob Goudzwaard and Craig Bartholomew begin with the contrasts between the medieval period and the factors which gave rise to "the classical modern worldview" – a perspective that privatized religion while asserting faith in progress and rationality.[1] There can be no doubt it was all too easy for Christians to capitulate to the reigning set of worldviews dominating the so-called Enlightenment, to reduce faith to the personal matter of an individual's relationship with God. Others, however, pursued alternative tracks.

Even where one might demur with the finer details of his analysis, David Bebbington's suggestion that evangelicalism can be characterized by a quadrilateral of priorities that transcend particular eras or contexts remains a significant starting point for understanding its theological and practical basis. One of those four identifying characteristics, alongside conversionism, biblicism, and crucicentrism, is activism.[2] While much of evangelical activism has been about winning new converts for Christ, Bebbington acknowledges it has frequently gone beyond that into the social and political realms.

In his treatment of the age of Jonathan Edwards, George Whitefield, and John and Charles Wesley, Mark Noll notes that evangelicalism was "overwhelmingly a movement of spiritual renewal," and "yet the otherworldliness of self-conscious evangelical piety was never by any means the whole story."[3] So it is, for example, that "John Wesley encouraged Methodists to seek holiness of heart and life in ways that also transformed their secular vocations."[4]

Covering a later era, John Wolffe provides a reminder of the influential role evangelicals have played in politics, as men and women who were strong in

---

1. Goudzwaard and Bartholomew, *Beyond the Modern Age*, 15–36.
2. Bebbington, *Evangelicalism in Modern Britain*.
3. Noll, *Rise of Evangelicalism*, 221.
4. See Armstrong, "About God's Business," 32.

their personal faith but were also salt and light in the public arena.[5] A notable example is William Wilberforce. As a twenty-six-year-old and rising politician, Wilberforce had suffered several months of anguish following conviction about his sinfulness and was contemplating withdrawal from politics in order to cultivate his relationship with God. He was urged by several, including John Newton, to remain in politics, encouraging him to see it "as a sphere for the exercise of his Christian vocation, rather than a distraction from it."[6] As Wolffe notes, Wilberforce's agenda of the suppression of the slave trade and the reformation of manners "did not supersede the overriding evangelical imperative to preach the gospel, but was a recognition that his own gifts and opportunities gave him different and more specific tasks."[7]

William Carey, one of the first Western missionaries to India, often seen as a pioneer of the modern Christian missionary movement, not only served as a missionary (as we commonly understand that word) but also as a botanist, economist, medical humanitarian, media pioneer, agriculturalist, translator and educator, astronomer, library pioneer, forest conservationist, crusader for women's rights, public servant, moral reformer and cultural transformer.[8]

In a treatment of the era of C. H. Spurgeon and Dwight L. Moody, David Bebbington makes it clear that, while a commitment to winning people for Christ made the evangelical movement numerically large, a commitment to activism meant they weren't sitting passively in pews but were out and about seeking to make a difference in the world.[9] Hannah More, writer and philanthropist, provides a summary of the prevailing attitude of many:

> Let me not be suspected of intending to insinuate that religion encourages men to fly from society, and hide themselves in solitudes; to renounce the generous and important duties of active life for the visionary, cold, and fruitless virtues of an hermitage or a cloister. No: the mischief arises not from our living in the world, but from the world living in us; occupying our hearts, and

---

5. Wolffe, *Expansion of Evangelicalism.*

6. Wolffe, 152.

7. Wolffe, 152.

8. Vishal and Mangalwadi, *Legacy of William Carey*, 18–25.

9. Bebbington, *Dominance of Evangelicalism.*

monopolizing our affections. Action is the life of virtue; and the world is the theatre of action.[10]

The accusation of narrowness clearly holds good at particular times and in particular branches of evangelicalism, especially when there has been a withdrawal from matters considered "worldly" in a negative sense. Moreover, activism in and of itself does not necessarily tackle the sacred-secular divide at its root. Even so, for the most part, evangelicals have, throughout history, encouraged activity in social and political life and have been genuinely affirming of the significance of a "this-worldly" spirituality.

A Comprehensive Worldview

Christian philosopher James K. A. Smith has called for a "temporary moratorium" on the notion of "worldview."[11] The language of worldview, he argues, reflects an understanding of humans as primarily rational creatures, and it targets only one aspect of our humanity, our mind, with the assumption that if we think like Christians we will act like Christians. In this view, education (including theological education) is largely about the dissemination of certain content on how to think about the world. In truth, Smith's argument is not that the idea of worldview is wrong so much as that it is inadequate because it fails to account for the precognitive, embodied nature of human beings who are formed by worship of God, not merely informed by teaching about God.[12] His criticisms about the potential pitfalls of worldview are well taken, even if they don't entail a rejection of the concept. Indeed, worldview has long provided a significant way for Christians to reflect on "the comprehensive framework of one's basic beliefs about things."[13]

Scottish theologian James Orr (1844–1913) was the first to speak of the Christian faith as a *Weltanschauung* (a worldview):

---

10. More, *Works of Hannah More*, 283.
11. Smith, *Desiring the Kingdom*, 65.
12. Smith, "Worldview," 15–24.
13. Wolters, *Creation Regained*, 2. For a full treatment, see Naugle, *Worldview*.

He who with his whole heart believes in Jesus as the Son of God is thereby committed to much else besides. He is committed to a view of God, to a view of man, to a view of sin, to a view of Redemption, to a view of the purpose of God in creation and history, to a view of human destiny, found only in Christianity. This forms a "Weltanschauung," or "Christian view of the world," which stands in marked contrast with theories wrought out from a purely philosophical or scientific standpoint.[14]

Abraham Kuyper (1837–1920), theologian, newspaper editor and founder of the Free University in Amsterdam, who served in parliament and as prime minister of the Netherlands, acknowledged his indebtedness to James Orr. Kuyper took seriously the lordship of Christ over every aspect of life, shown not least in the range of his own activities.[15] The line with which he is most often associated, and which sums up his own perspective, was first delivered in his speech at the inauguration of the Free University of Amsterdam in 1880: "There is not a square inch in the whole domain of our human existence over which Christ, who is Sovereign over all, does not cry: Mine!"[16]

Kuyper argued that God had appointed distinct social spheres – family, church, state – with different responsibilities, but which find unity in their dependence on God. This key idea of "sphere sovereignty" came to expression in his *Lectures on Calvinism*, based on six lectures he gave at Princeton University in 1898.[17] For Kuyper, Calvinism's root principle "was not, soteriologically, justification by faith, but in the widest sense, cosmologically, the Sovereignty of the Triune God over the whole Cosmos, in all its spheres and kingdoms, visible and invisible."[18] As such, Calvinism "created a life- and world-view, and such a one as was, and still is, able to fit itself to the needs of every stage of human development in every department of life."[19]

---

14. Orr, *Christian View*, 4.

15. For introductions to Kuyper, see Bartholomew, *Contours*; Mouw, *Abraham Kuyper*; Wagenman, *Engaging the World*.

16. Kuyper, "Souvereiniteit in Eigen Kring," 488.

17. Kuyper, *Lectures on Calvinism*; see also Heslam, *Creating a Christian Worldview*.

18. Kuyper, 79.

19. Kuyper, 171.

The term "neo-Calvinism" is sometimes used to refer to the tradition of thinking inspired by Kuyper. One of the features of this movement is a comprehensive understanding of creation, fall and redemption. A Christian worldview requires all three: so great was the creation, so radical was the fall, so complete is Christ's work of redemption, that it encompasses nothing less than the whole of creation. One way of expressing this is to say that grace restores nature, where the redemption that comes through Jesus is the restoration of an original good creation, discounting dualistic worldviews which delimit the scope of redemption to a "sacred" realm.[20] Herman Bavinck, a younger contemporary of Kuyper, was also clear that "grace does not abolish nature, but affirms and restores it."[21]

Francis Schaeffer (1912–1984) belongs to this neo-Calvinist stream. Schaeffer was an American theologian and pastor most famous for his writings and the establishment of the L'Abri (meaning "shelter") community in Switzerland. He believed the Christian faith could answer the issues of the age and was concerned to address the larger questions of meaning, purpose and identity from the contours of a biblical worldview embracing the totality of reality.[22]

How Now Shall We Live? by Charles Colson and Nancy Pearcey self-consciously reflects the approach of Francis Schaeffer.[23] Pearcey's own significant work, *Total Truth*, argues that the major elements of the biblical story of creation, fall and redemption are formative for how Christians should understand the world and engage with alternative views on offer.[24] In particular, Pearcey tackles the public-private distinction, which assigns faith and moral values to the private realm and insists these are to be kept separate from matters such as science, politics, economics, education and so on, which belong to the public realm. This two-storey perspective, she claims, has permeated the thinking of Christians, resulting in the compartmentalization of faith. By contrast, a biblical worldview approach to every aspect of life insists

---

20. Wolters, *Creation Regained*, 12.
21. See Bartholomew, *Contours*, 45–75.
22. See Schaeffer, *Complete Works*.
23. Colson and Pearcey, *How Now*.
24. Pearcey, *Total Truth*.

that Christianity is "true truth" – Mondays to Saturdays as much as it is on Sundays.[25]

A Liberated Laity

"It is only possible for the Gospel to reach the whole population through the active co-operation of all church people. We are convinced that England will never be converted until the laity use the opportunities for evangelism daily afforded by their various professions, crafts and occupations."[26] This is part of a report by the Church of England Commission on Evangelism, published in 1945. What was needed, according to the report, was a recovery of "the Apostolate of the whole Church," where all – clergy and laity alike – are to witness to their Lord, and where such witness is seen as "the very essence of the Christian calling."[27]

Reflections on the significance of the laity have waxed and waned throughout Christian history, but the period following the Second World War saw a growing interest, with several major denominations – Roman Catholic as well as Protestant – rediscovering the importance of laypeople. In an early volume in this period, Hendrik Kraemer drew attention to their significance, arguing that "the specific place of the laity is at the frontiers, where the real dialogue between Church and World becomes an event."[28] As Robert Banks notes, Kraemer's book "crystalized the concerns underlying the formation of various institutions in Europe after World War II," which "sought to give laypeople a theological understanding of their responsibilities in church and world and to equip them better for service in both."[29]

Richard Mouw's *Called to Worldly Holiness* captured something of the shifts that took place over the following twenty years.[30] Mouw noted the need not only for a theology of the laity (as in the title of Kraemer's book), but also "a theology

---

25. See also Ashford and Thomas, *Gospel of Our King*; Goheen and Bartholomew, *Living at the Crossroads*; Walsh and Middleton, *Transforming Vision*.

26. Church of England, *Towards the Conversion*, 58.

27. Church of England, 40.

28. Kraemer, *Theology of the Laity*, 172.

29. Banks, *Redeeming the Routines*, 157.

30. Mouw, *Called to Worldly Holiness*.

for the laity" and "a theology by the laity."[31] Mouw's book was the first in a Laity Exchange Books series, published by Fortress Press.[32] Mark Gibbs wrote in the editor's introduction that the series was "intended to stimulate and to help the Christian laity in the exercise of their ministry today, particularly in the secular world outside the walls and structures of the institutional churches."[33] Gibbs himself had become an international spokesperson for the ministry of the laity, and subsequently wrote of Christians with responsibilities in secular society as having particular "ministries in the secular world."[34] Likewise, in *The Liberation of the Laity*, Anne Rowthorn wrote of the laity as the "prime ministers" of the church in the world, through which the church "is present in every area of human activity."[35]

As far back as 1969, John Stott published *One People: Clergy and Laity in God's Church*.[36] While Stott believed there was a role for ordained ministry in the church, the book criticizes clericalism, the domination of the laity by the clergy, and calls us instead to see the whole church as the laity, with certain leaders "appointed to serve them, to seek to equip them to be what God intends them to be."[37] Through a study of four New Testament words associated with the church, Stott notes the lack of distinction between leaders and laity, pastor and people, such that "the overwhelming preoccupation of the New Testament is not with the status of the clergy, nor with clergy-laity relations, but with the whole people of God in their relations to Him and to each other."[38] On the final page, he writes: "Living and working in the midst of the secular world, the layman is in the frontline of the Church's testimony. . . . To this work of witness all God's people are summoned."[39]

---

31. Mouw, 19–20.

32. Others included Gibbs, *Christians with Secular Power*; Diehl, *Thank God*; Leckey, *Laity Stirring the Church*.

33. Gibbs, "Editor's Introduction," in Diehl, *Thank God*, vii.

34. Gibbs and Morton, *God's Frozen People*; Gibbs and Morton, *God's Lively People*; Gibbs, *Christians with Secular Power*, 5.

35. Rowthorn, *Liberation of the Laity*, 5.

36. Stott, *One People*.

37. Stott, 42.

38. Stott, 20.

39. Stott, 92.

Over seventy years after the publication of *Towards the Conversion of England*, the Church of England report *Setting God's People Free* was published, debated and ratified by synod. It speaks about us being "summoned . . . to a common vocation," where "the whole people of God, clergy and laity, gathered and sent, are charged with continuing Christ's priestly work of blessing, mediation and reconciliation on behalf of the whole of humanity, to bear witness to, and participate in the mission of God."[40]

As Robert Banks has made clear in a number of publications over the years, the liberation of the laity has implications for those concerned about theological education.[41] Commending the need for an "everyday theology," he notes the gap between belief and daily life, where "few of us apply or know how to apply our belief to our work, or lack of work"; where "we have little sense of a Christian approach to regular activities"; where "our everyday concerns receive little attention in the church."[42]

The Missional Church

The term "missional" has become commonplace in recent popular and academic literature, though its meaning is frequently left undefined. Most often, it signals a shift away from seeing mission as something which some members of the church do to seeing mission as something which God does through the church as a whole. Just as the Father sends the Son, and as Father and Son together send the Spirit, so Father, Son and Spirit send the church into the world. This shift has involved a move from seeing mission as something that happens "over there" to seeing mission as being "from everywhere to everywhere" and as involving every one of God's people, in every situation of life.

This can result in seeing mission as an expression of God's love and purpose for the world more broadly – as any activity which anyone might do which contributes to human wellbeing, including revolutionary movements or ecological activism, because they reflect God's "liberating" purposes for the world. Others are critical of that broad approach because of its tendency

---

40. Lay Leadership Task Group, *Setting God's People Free*, 1.

41. See Banks, *Theology*; *Redeeming the Routines*; and *Reenvisioning Theological Education*.

42. Banks, *Redeeming the Routines*, 50–66.

to ignore the significance of human sin and the call for repentance and faith. Even so, some evangelicals who hold to the centrality of verbal evangelism still want to set that within a broader understanding of mission.

Chris Wright defines mission as "our committed participation as God's people, at God's invitation and command, in God's own mission within the history of the world for the redemption of God's creation."[43] This more comprehensive understanding of mission includes not just proclamation of the good news of the kingdom but also teaching, baptizing and nurturing new believers, responding to human need in loving service, seeking to transform unjust structures of society, safeguarding the integrity of creation and sustaining life on earth.[44]

Those unsure how to negotiate between maximal definitions of mission (which seem to suggest that everything is mission) and minimal definitions of mission (which limit mission to verbal proclamation of the gospel) might want to note Lesslie Newbigin's helpful distinction between missional dimension and missional intention. There are intentional activities we do, such as evangelism, church planting, works of mercy and so on, that have the specific purpose of making known the gospel in word and deed. And yet, even when we're not doing those activities, all our lives have a missional dimension because of being caught up in God's good plan for all things. As Michael Goheen puts it: "Every aspect of the believer's and the believing community's life has a missional dimension. However, not all of the church's life has a missional intention. Not every activity is deliberately aimed at inviting people to believe the gospel and submit to the Lordship of Jesus Christ."[45]

Newbigin himself served four decades in India before returning to England in 1974. His experience in a non-Western country provided him with insights into the ways in which the gospel had become assimilated into Western assumptions, and he spent the next two decades publishing articles and books outlining how an authentic encounter between the gospel and Western culture could take place. Newbigin was in no doubt that all Christians find themselves in a "missionary" situation, with the need to take on the posture and practices

---

43. Wright, *Mission of God*, 22–23.
44. See Wright, *Mission of God's People*.
45. Goheen, *Introducing Christian Mission Today*, 83.

of missionaries in order to engage others with the good news about Jesus.[46] Seen this way, evangelism is not a "bolt on" Christian activity but is organically connected to the whole of life: a fusion of presence and proclamation, the message of our lips matching the message of our lives. It is the outflow of who we are in Christ, equipped and sent by him as witnesses in his ongoing mission to the world.

Increasing numbers have argued that theological education needs to be overhauled along these lines. What might theological education look like if we took seriously the centrality of mission to the church's identity? Not the study of mission as a separate discipline, but the task of theological education itself reframed through a missional lens. In one recent discussion, Michael Goheen notes:

> A missional curriculum does not mean merely adding more courses on mission and evangelism or world religions or other subjects traditionally associated with missiology. Rather, it explores how mission will reframe biblical studies, systematic theology, church history, and congregational theology to equip the church for its mission.[47]

Applying Newbigin's distinction, some – but not all – subjects in the curriculum intentionally deal with various issues of mission. Yet all theological subjects can have a missional dimension. What would biblical studies, systematic theology and church history look like if a whole-life, missional dimension was integral to the different disciplines? How might theological educators reframe the curriculum of core modules – Old Testament, New Testament, hermeneutics, doctrine, ethics, church history – through a whole-life lens in a way that equips disciples to be missionary followers of Jesus in their contexts? The later sections in this book show how this can be done and indeed *is* being done by a number of theological educators.

---

46. For a way in to Newbigin's work, see Goheen, *Church and Its Vocation*.
47. Goheen, "Missional," 314.

A Developing Evangelicalism

The Lausanne movement – with its congresses, working groups, and forums – has been one of the most significant expressions of evangelicalism over the past four and a half decades.[48]

Spearheaded by Billy Graham and John Stott, the First International Congress on World Evangelization met in Lausanne in July 1974 with the theme "Let the Earth Hear His Voice." Two notable moments were Ralph Winter's redefinition of "all nations" as ethnolinguistic groups instead of political nations and C. René Padilla's advocacy for *misión integral* (holistic mission). The most influential outcome of the congress was the creation of *The Lausanne Covenant*.[49] C. René Padilla commented on what made the document significant:

> That a 2,700-word statement on evangelism should deal with such a wide range of subjects [fifteen] is in itself a proof that Evangelicalism on the whole is no longer willing to be identified as a movement characterized by a tendency to isolate evangelism, in both theory and practice, from the wider context represented by the nature of the Gospel and the life and mission of the Church.[50]

In October 2010, the Third International Congress on World Evangelization (or the Third Lausanne Congress) was held in Cape Town, with 4,200 delegates from 198 nations and hundreds of Protestant denominations, along with 350 observers from Roman Catholic, Orthodox and other traditions. The notion of an "integral gospel" or "holistic gospel" has become increasingly common parlance, although intramural debates continue about the relationship between evangelism and social responsibility. Even so, something more than that is at stake when it comes to tackling the sacred-secular divide, which is the working out of the implications of the gospel in all aspects of life – in the home and at work, in the hospital and at school, in the art gallery and the sports arena, in business and in politics.

---

48. See Cameron, *Lausanne Legacy*; Dahle, Dahle, and Jørgensen, *Lausanne Movement*; Stanley, *Global Diffusion*, 151–179; Yeh, *Polycentric Missiology*, 122–161.
49. See First Lausanne Congress, *Lausanne Covenant*.
50. Padilla, *New Face of Evangelicalism*, 10–11.

"The Cape Town Commitment" was put together following the 2010 Lausanne Congress on World Evangelization. One section points towards the importance of mission being worked out in the whole of life and the significance of that for theological education:

> The mission of the Church on earth is to serve the mission of God, and the mission of theological education is to strengthen and accompany the mission of the Church. Theological education serves first to train those who lead the Church as pastor-teachers, equipping them to teach the truth of God's Word with faithfulness, relevance and clarity; and second, to equip all God's people for the missional task of understanding and relevantly communicating God's truth in every cultural context.[51]

It goes on to say:

> Those of us who lead churches and mission agencies need to acknowledge that theological education is intrinsically missional. Those of us who provide theological education need to ensure that it is intentionally missional, since its place within the academy is not an end in itself, but to serve the mission of the Church in the world.[52]

The final end of theological education is not the church, but the world, with church leaders trained to mobilize the people of God for their missional call in the world. Hence, "We urge that institutions and programmes of theological education conduct a 'missional audit' of their curricula, structures and ethos, to ensure that they truly serve the needs and opportunities facing the Church in their cultures."[53]

---

51. Third Lausanne Congress, *Cape Town Commitment*, sec. 2F.4.
52. Third Lausanne Congress, sec. 2F.4.
53. Third Lausanne Congress, sec. 2F.4.

A Whole Gospel

Recent years have seen an encouraging renaissance of interest in theological reflection on the nature and significance of the gospel.[54]

It is often tempting to reduce the gospel to a personal transaction between me and God in which Jesus dies for me, I repent and God forgives my sin. Certainly, the gospel is not less than that. But it is much more, involving not only the rescue of men and women from judgement but the renewal of God's relationship with his people and the restoration of creation itself. The good news of what God has done in Jesus carries zoom-lens implications for the redemption of individual sinners and wide-angle implications for the ultimate reconciliation of all things.[55]

The gospel announces that, supremely through the death and resurrection of Christ, God is restoring men and women to himself, forgiving their sin, reconciling the alienated, redeeming the enslaved. The gospel says that God is restoring humans, giving them new life and beginning the work of recreating them in the image of Christ, remaking a new humanity in the body of Christ. The gospel declares that God has set in motion the restoration of the world itself, the reconciliation of all things in heaven and on earth, so that nothing will be left untouched by its expansive scope. On this understanding, a commitment to the gospel is significant for the whole of life. At home and at work, in the art gallery and the sports arena, in business and in politics, walking the dog and washing the dishes,[56] there is no place the gospel does not touch with its implications because of the comprehensive nature of God's saving work in Christ, his rule over every aspect of life.

> The good news of what God has done in Jesus carries zoom-lens implications for the redemption of individual sinners and wide-angle implications for the ultimate reconciliation of all things.

---

54. For some representative treatments, see Bates, *Gospel Allegiance*; Horton, *Gospel-Driven Life*; Keller, *Shaped by the Gospel*; McKnight, *King Jesus Gospel*; Wright, *Simply Good News*.
55. This "zoom" and "wide-angle" lens analogy is borrowed from DeYoung and Gilbert, *What Is the Mission*, 91–113, and Snyder, *Salvation Means Creation Healed*, 99.
56. See Chester, *Everyday Gospel*.

A Restored Vocation

Development of the doctrine of vocation was a major feature of the Lutheran and Reformed wings of the Protestant Reformation, encouraging Christians to see all spheres of life as significant places to respond to the call to love God and serve neighbours. Due largely to the forces of capitalism and secularism, that perspective was slowly eroded. The division and specialization of labour, the capitalist reduction of value to exchange value, the secular neglect or denial of religious or supernatural reality, and a relativizing of public expressions of Christian faith all contributed to a weakened understanding of vocation.[57] For a while, we were living in what Paul Stevens called a "post-vocational world":

> Without any theology of vocation, we lapse into debilitating alternatives: fatalism (doing what is required by "the forces" and "the powers"); luck (which denies purposefulness in life and reduces our life to a bundle of accidents); karma (which ties performance to future rewards); nihilism (which denies that there is any good end to which the travail of history might lead); and, the most common alternative today, self-actualization (in which we invent the meaning and purpose of our lives, making us magicians). In contrast the biblical doctrine of vocation proposes that the whole of our lives finds meaning in relation to the sweet summons of a good God.[58]

Alongside a desire to affirm the comprehensive scope of the gospel and its implications has gone an encouraging recovery of interest in the nature of vocation. In one treatment, Douglas Schuurman writes that "Christians must recover anew the language, meaning, and reality of life as vocation," and that a "central task of pastoral ministry" is to remind Christians that "God calls them into their homes, neighborhoods, workplaces, and civic and political communities to serve God and neighbor."[59]

The general call of God in Christ takes specific form in each of our lives, in which all spheres are places for service to God and neighbour:

---

57. Schuurman, *Vocation*, 48.

58. Stevens, *Abolition of the Laity*, 72.

59. Schuurman, *Vocation*, xii–xiii.

> One is not called to be a Christian "in general"; one is called to be a Christian in the concrete social locations one presently occupies, as this mother to these children, this citizen of this country, and so on. . . . Particular duties are callings or vocations insofar as the vocation or calling to be a Christian is expressed through them.[60]

Since Christ's lordship extends to the whole of life, "true calling is experienced inside the ordinary, mundane world, not outside of it."[61] Schuurman concludes that "if Christians are to become faithful participants in the purposes and processes of creation and redemption, it is essential that they hold together both the 'sacred' and the 'secular,' the 'religious' and 'non-religious' aspects of experience, and that they do so in a way that affirms the importance and integrity of each."[62]

As John Stackhouse puts it, vocation "stretches out to encompass everything we are and do," and is applicable to "everyone, everything, everywhere, in every moment."[63] Our human calling is to make shalom, our Christian calling is to make disciples and the sphere in which we work out those callings is, as Stackhouse reminds us, the "real world."

For theological educators, the key challenge is how to integrate these principles into the culture and practice of training Christian leaders so that they not only avoid the great divide themselves, but also liberate their congregations into being whole-life missionary disciples.

---

60. Schuurman, 29; see Schuurman, 17–47, for the relationship between "general" calling and "special" calling.

61. Schuurman, 137.

62. Schuurman, 52; cf. Helm, *Callings*, 22–43, on "the dangers of a double mind."

63. Stackhouse, *Why You're Here*, 5.

5

Naming the Issue in Contemporary Contexts

Part 1: Latin America
Dinorah B. Méndez

The phenomenon of the sacred-secular divide is recognized across the Christian world in current global societies. It has probably been a permanent challenge for the Christian faith. Consistency is required between personal conviction in everyday life and social transformation. It is necessary for inner faith to be expressed in external behaviour. However, the sad situation is that many Christians as individuals, and many churches as a community, are living in a dual reality in which a spiritual realm affected by faith and focused mainly at an individual level exists separately from a material or secular realm, which is related to this world at the social level. In Latin America, as elsewhere, the key questions are "How is this divide affecting the church and society today?" and "How can the church overcome this situation and make a positive contribution to its social context?"

In the Latin American context, since its inception around the mid-nineteenth century, evangelical faith and churches have demonstrated a strong social conscience and devoted much effort toward social transformation in all its forms. During the first decades of evangelicalism's presence on this continent, many churches, mission agencies and NGOs carried out important work in education (especially in improving literacy and in Christian schools), health, agriculture, personal and family ethics, and helping drug addicts. However, at that time, evangelicals were a small minority of the population and had little influence on the structures of Latin American societies. In addition, those earlier evangelicals had a rather individualistic perspective of the gospel, which kept them silenced in the public sphere, failing to contribute to or influence, in any significant way, the social transformation of their countries. Their impact was mainly focused on a local or personal level, bringing transformation to the lives of individuals and their families but not to the community on a social level.[1]

Some Reasons for the Lack of Social Impact

Evidently, there have been different trends among evangelicals in Latin America with more or less social commitment, but in general terms a lack of positive impact on social transformation in the continent has predominated.

In the opinion of some theologians such as Samuel Escobar and Emilio Antonio Núñez, the evangelical faith in Latin America had strong Pietistic roots. As such, mission was mainly understood in terms of individual conversion. Furthermore, some of the earlier missionaries had a premillennial eschatology and a separatist ecclesiology both towards other confessional bodies and towards society in general. All of this, accentuated by the need to stand out against Catholicism, the continent's predominant church, could lie behind the limited involvement of evangelicals in meaningful social transformation.[2] Thus, some of the causes may be theological and missiological. At the beginning, evangelical believers were able to live as a minority whose personal conversion and behaviour helped them to achieve social transformation for themselves and their families in a hostile environment. But, in the long term, excessive individualism and the lack of institutional cohesion have caused division, competition and disunity rather than co-operation and unity in raising a common voice against social and political problems in the Latin American context.

---

1. See several works, such as Bastian, *Historia del Protestantismo*; Bastian, *Protestantismo y Sociedad*; Méndez, "La Esfera Socio-Religiosa"; Scott, *Los Evangélicos Mexicanos*.
2. Escobar, "It's Your Turn," 19–21.

In the same vein, Gálvez adds that non-historical evangelical denominations, such as some Pentecostals, have never considered the social aspect of their communities as most social activists typically do. He asserts that they have a different approach to social concern. They care for the poor and are eager to assist them, but they see it as part of God's redemptive plan for them. Pentecostals are focused on the salvation of the poor in preparation for the imminent return of

> Excessive individualism and the lack of institutional cohesion have caused division, competition and disunity rather than co-operation and unity in raising a common voice against social and political problems in the Latin American context.

Christ, part of their dispensationalist teachings. For them it is very important to separate the sacred and the profane. Therefore, they do not have theological teaching on social action alone, but as a part and a result of evangelism, and they are not involved in political participation in civil life. Thus, they do not show interest in "mundane" issues that interest the rest of society. In the view of Gálvez, Pentecostals do not tend to pay attention to culture, politics, social issues, globalization or religious pluralism.[3]

Bullón sees the summary of Escobar's perceptions of the history of the Protestant and evangelical missions and social transformation in Latin America as one of contrast between promise and precariousness. Promise, because of the large number of examples of social commitment by evangelicals in different areas of need, as well as specific interventions in the secular (including political) sphere. But precariousness because of the limitations of evangelicals, their failures and small impact, especially compared to the scale of the needs and social challenges in the context. This analysis provides another reason for the lack of impact and social transformation in this continent: the relative newness and minority of the Protestant and evangelical movements in Latin America, compared to the strength and presence of the Catholic ones for more than five centuries.[4]

---

3. Gálvez, "Guatemalan Perspective," 146–151.
4. Bullón, *Protestant Social Thought*, 27.

Evidence of the Sacred-Secular Divide in Latin America

One difficult issue to be resolved by Latin American Christian movements is the imbalance between numerical growth and human transformation. In many nations, despite the church's numerical growth, poverty, corruption and other social evils remain unsolved. Even though churches have invested significant energy in social work, many of these social evils remain.[5]

The numerical growth of the evangelical church is desirable. However, in Guatemala and the Central American region, there are worries about such growth. Clearly, the expansion of the gospel is always a blessing. But the point to highlight here is that this growth has had no significant impact within the social structures. This is a valid observation, since Guatemala continues to be an underdeveloped nation and continues to be beset by many social problems. It has a high poverty rate; it holds second place in social inequality; corruption contributes to low collection of taxes; and the country is one of the most violent in the region. Thus the sacred-secular divide is evident in that context.[6]

> In many nations, despite the church's numerical growth, poverty, corruption and other social evils remain unsolved.

Therefore, the numerical factor does not assure a qualitative presence, and faith can easily become a refuge for the masses, manifested as a religiosity free of social commitment, or even a conglomeration that has no social impact in the community. In the 1980s, Gonzálo Báez-Camargo, a Mexican leader, argued that the new generation of Mexican evangelicals had to be a creative minority willing to live the gospel within their context. He emphasized that the challenge of influencing the life of our nations does not depend on numerical presence, but on the transforming power of the gospel, coupled with the qualitative presence of churches within society.[7] These cases are representative of the general situation across the continent.

Further evidence is the case of countries such as Chile, Brazil, Peru and Guatemala, where politicians identifying with the evangelical faith have been

---

5. See Ortiz, "Beyond Numerical Growth."
6. Ortiz, 162–163.
7. Báez-Camargo, "Tiempo de Saltar," 15.

elected to public office and have ended their careers with very little evidence of success, or even in scandalous cases of corruption. This seems to reveal that, for achieving social transformation, the political path followed by evangelicals has not been satisfactory thus far, especially because they have reproduced the cultural style of leadership predominant in Latin America: the *caudillo* (strongman) type, with some outbreaks of authoritarianism. In addition, the problem is that the practice of this model of leadership is very strong, not only in society but sadly also in many of the evangelical churches.[8]

> The challenge of influencing the life of our nations does not depend on numerical presence, but on the transforming power of the gospel, coupled with the qualitative presence of churches within society.

In Mexico, the case that this author knows best, the socio-economic and political situation is another reality that demands a response from evangelicals. The socio-economic circumstances have been critical for decades. Mexico, as well as the entire South American continent, has been marked by the presence of scandalous poverty and inequality. This situation is accompanied by a political reality of turmoil. In response, the governing elite has tried out one model of governance after another with little success. Neither five centuries of Catholic Christianity nor various waves of different Christian movements have improved the reality of misery and injustice.[9]

Another example of the sacred-secular divide in Latin American church and society is the new trend of neo-Pentecostal movements, especially with their focus on the "prosperity gospel." Because their theology is not compatible with the existence of the poor, poverty is seen as evidence of sin. Then they need to find a spiritual rationalization for the reality before them, generating a significant frustration for many followers.[10]

---

8. Méndez, "Evangelical Mission," 141.

9. Méndez, 140–141.

10. See Gálvez, "Guatemalan Perspective," 154–157.

Suggestions for Further Study

Another topic for further study which reflects this compartmentalization of life is the situation of people who have a deep religiosity and are nominally affiliated with the Catholic church, or even, socially, with an evangelical church, but who have pro-abortion views and are sexually promiscuous, who use alcohol, drugs and pornography, and who have low moral standards in family, work and community issues (reflected in occurrences of adultery, bribery or simple idleness). In addition there are new challenges, such as environmental stewardship, new "ecclesiologies," gender issues, bioethical advancements, immigration, political refugees and displacement.[11]

Today, spiritual need and religious confusion is a common reality all over the world, including Latin America. People are looking for answers that are not only material but also spiritual, for refuge, for restoration, and even for rehabilitation to continue living or to make sense of life. So this is the perfect time to take the challenge and opportunity of sharing the gospel in an integrated way. This means to live the whole gospel with all its implications for the whole person in this context, avoiding the temptation of proclaiming a gospel of fast consumption, without solid discipleship, and without social commitment.

Part 2: Africa
Bernard Boyo

The sacred-secular divide is rife not only in Kenya, which is a predominantly Christian country, but in other parts of the continent as well. The debate has elicited diverse views with "serious questioning and rethinking . . . occurring not only from the sacred side of the divide, but from the secular side as well."[12] The sacred-secular divide debate has, primarily, been a Western construct where religion and family issues are relegated to the private realm. There are, however, voices such as Stuart Kaufmann in *Reinventing the Sacred: A New View of Science, Reason, and Religion* (2010) who propose a deep connection between the natural world and religion, as well as partnership between the realm of

---

11. See Salinas, *Taking Up the Mantle*, 184.
12. Kim, McCalman, and Fisher, "Sacred/Secular Divide," 204.

science and religious values, thus indicating as unwarranted the simplistic and reductionist understanding of the division between the two.[13]

Traditionally, among many African cultures, the dichotomy between the sacred and the secular is untenable since life is viewed as a whole – intertwined intrinsically in all its diverse facets. As observed by Gregg Okesson,

> The "sacred" or spiritual presents one of the predominant ways many Africans think about and/or shape their world. Traditional religion(s) were often oriented around the divine, or sacred, and permeated all facets of life. They focused on how the spiritual affects such "mundane" realities as agricultural cycles, birth, death, and developments within the community.[14]

This wholeness of life is, in part, a depiction of the African philosophy of life. In general, Africans hold dearly the centrality of communalism which indicates the high sense of value of the individual within the community. Ostensibly, the importance and value of the individual is intricately intertwined with the whole community or society. The identity of the individual can only be conceived in the confines of the whole community, an idea supported by John Mbiti, arguably the father of African religion, who says, "I am because we are and because we are therefore I am."[15]

> Traditionally, among many African cultures, the dichotomy between the sacred and the secular is untenable since life is viewed as a whole.

Africans are generally pragmatic not theoretical, and thus it is what works to alleviate one's current situation of need that matters, particularly in the context of poverty and sustenance, which entails the whole community. This is so because life is viewed as a whole with every aspect being interrelated. The question of God is not an academic venture – it is caught, not learnt. The question of the existence of God is embedded in society and, as such, a high sense of the reality of the spiritual realm and its interaction with the human

13. Kim, McCalman, and Fisher, 204.
14. Okesson, "Sacred and Secular Currents," 40.
15. Mbiti, *African Religions and Philosophy*, 108–109.

sphere is a common phenomenon. The realms of the physical and spiritual can be distinguished but not separated.

The education sector, particularly Christian institutions of higher learning, bears the major task of promoting a holistic approach to education in the context of the dichotomized worldview that characterizes postmodern Africa. This calls for a decisive and continued review and evaluation of university courses to ensure relevance and compliance with regional and national regulatory bodies. A number of liberal arts universities, such as Daystar University in Nairobi, Kenya, endeavour to maintain their unique Christian niche and distinctiveness by ensuring that Bible and theology courses form the core of all the programmes offered at the university. The intent is to help in addressing the sacred-secular dichotomy by ensuring that each program at the undergraduate level includes a minimum threshold of the integrated courses in their curriculum as a requirement. This is an essential task since Bible courses give a basic understanding and foundation of what the Christian faith and belief entails, as well as creating relevance and practical application of faith in all disciplines.

In order to address the sacred-secular divide in the context of African academia, Daystar University has adopted and maintained a liberal arts approach to education which seeks "to develop well-rounded individuals with general knowledge of a wide range of subjects and with mastery of a range of transferable skills . . . 'global citizens,' with the capacity to pursue lifelong learning and become valuable members of their communities."[16]

The intent is to inculcate an integrated approach to education where the biblical view is embedded in each academic discipline. What is envisaged is that all students graduating in the disciplines at the university are released into society to work in various sectors based on their individual areas of specialization. In this way, they will be prepared to bring about the necessary transformation of society with a biblical mindset that does not dichotomize the secular and the sacred. In essence, they live out their faith in the context of their day-to-day work, irrespective of the sector of society in which they find work – be it the public or private sector – as employees or employers.

---

16. Haidar, "What Is Liberal Arts."

Due to the diversity of individual disciplines at different levels, the core courses are mainly structured for each level. At the undergraduate level, for instance, core integrated courses can cover at least thirty credit hours of the one-hundred-and-thirty credit hours required for the program. Integration at the postgraduate level may take a different tangent due to the specialized nature and brevity of the program. One of the approaches at Daystar University is a common core course titled Biblical Foundations of Christian Service whose objective is to prepare students to render effective service based on the motif of the kingdom of God. This course is premised on the essence that "all truth is God's truth" and as such all work is service rendered to God. The students are required to relate the course material to current affairs related to their discipline or area of work in view of the issues and challenges facing their contemporary context. This emphasis is embedded within the philosophy that integrates faith and life which is true to the African cosmology.

In order for the aforesaid approach of education to be realized, the ethos of the academic institution must be deeply embedded in its faculty and staff. As the carriers of such a philosophy, the employees are expected to be Christians who are thoroughly committed to the integration of faith and work. Since few have worked this out before, the need for their training is essential. In order to aid this kind of preparation, Daystar University has embarked on carrying out annual training on theology of work (TOW), the objective of which is to establish a biblical understanding of work in relation to one's role and responsibilities in the workplace. This week-long intensive training enables the participants to develop a biblical theology of work as stewards entrusted with the responsibility of managing all aspects of creation in its diversity. While the training is received with eagerness and enthusiasm, and participants receive a certificate of attendance, ongoing work is always needed to stop employees slipping back into the sacred-secular divide.

In the light of the diversity of religious affiliations among the members of any given university, the approach of addressing the sacred-secular approach becomes an ongoing challenge. It is always a challenge to explain to students, and even staff members, who may not be well acquainted with this philosophy of education, why core courses not in a student's field of study are required. However, the feedback received from alumni quite often indicates that such courses have become the cornerstone of their engagement in their places of work.

Yet another challenge is the non-denominational aspect of Christian institutions of higher learning required to admit qualified students without discrimination on religious grounds. Mechanisms of ensuring that the integration of faith and learning is maintained without breaching the regulations governing religious inclusivity are necessary. Daystar University ensures, as part of the admission process, that all students sign a code of conduct form endorsed by their guardian or sponsor, indicating their commitment to adhere to the university academic structure as well as participate in the spiritual disciplines of the university. These include a day of prayer each semester, weekly one-hour chapels on Tuesdays, and small Bible study group attendance on Thursdays. This is also required of all staff and faculty, who are expected to take a lead as student mentors, and for individual career progression and promotion within the university. During these hours, the university closes for business. All the measures of instilling Christian values in the education process at the university are indicative of the need to continually address the sacred-secular divide within the African context.

Part 3: Asia

Theresa Roco-Lua

Asia is the home of the world's oldest religions, and these religions have shaped the worldview and way of life of the vast majority of Asians. According to Saphir Athyal, "In Asia, cultural and religious aspects of life are very closely linked together, and therefore thought patterns and words already have certain religious overtones."[17] There is a "cosmological fusion" of religious phenomena with politics, society, knowledge and even technology.[18]

The Asian way of thinking is more inclusive and integrated ("both/and") than the Western way of thinking, which is more dualistic ("either/or"). Ken Gnanakan explains that the Western dualistic approach has clashed with the

---

17. Athyal, "Toward," 78.
18. Duara, "East Asian Perspective," 4.

more holistic Asian understanding of life where wholeness is part of life. The indigenous Asian spirituality was based on human experience as a whole, and therefore outward expressions and inward feelings were all seen to belong to one another.[19]

Filipino anthropologist and pastor Ed Lapiz points out that the Western concept of secular and sacred has done a lot of damage. Now there are "divisions that did not exist before in the Oriental mind. . . . The eastern mind is usually wholistic – it does not impose boundaries."[20]

While the sacred-secular divide (SSD) is considered an externally imposed reality to Asia, elements of the divide were already present in the animistic worldview of many Asian countries. There were sacred grounds, sacred things and sacred people. Religious leaders were regarded as far more holy than the ordinary people. This deep-seated mindset influences Christian faith and practice.

Dichotomies in Asia

At the SSD consultation in Asia, the participants pointed out that the dichotomies in Asia articulate the tension between "what is" and "what should be" in a situation in which the dominant religions or the pre-Christian religions continue to influence Christian faith and practice. The great divide is within the Christians, in the dual identity they live with.[21]

The following are examples of undesirable divides/dichotomies in Asia identified by the consultation participants:[22]

- From a Buddhist-dominated ethos, a spiritual/worldly divide: renunciation of/withdrawal from the world is seen as the highest calling, and engagement with the world as undesirable and evil (Ivor Poobalan, Sri Lanka).
- From Hinduism-influenced Indian Christianity, a power-based/ egalitarian divide: the uncritical transfer of the socio-religious

---

19. Gnanakan, *Whole Gospel*, 309.
20. Lapiz, *Pagpapahiyang*, 66–67.
21. The consultation was held at Trinity Theological College in Singapore on 24–27 February 2018.
22. This list was outlined by Finny Philip, one of the consultation's participants.

hierarchy of the caste-system into church structures (Havilah Dharamraj, India).

- From the Filipino folk religion ethos, a faith/practice divide: continuing to practice magic/the occult while affirming the Christian faith (Timoteo Gener, Philippines).
- The state/church divide: the view that, for a Christian, politics and Christian faith are incompatible (Bernard Wong, Hong Kong).
- A sub-culture in which the cultural identity predominates over the Christian identity in social relationships (Sylvia Soeherman, Indonesia).
- A classroom practice in which the teacher-student dynamic is informed by a defectively traditional paradigm rather than by the model of Jesus as teacher (Mona Bias, Philippines).
- A church structure informed by an authoritarian use of power, rather than by the use of power for service (Clement Chia, Singapore).

These unhealthy divides must be challenged by biblical principles and bridged through whole-life discipleship.

Symptoms of SSD in Asian Churches

The SSD is evident in Asian churches. Many Christians equate the Christian life with "spiritual activities" such as attending worship, prayer and Bible study, and separate their ordinary day-to-day life and work from their Christian walk. Thus, there is a deep disconnect between faith and life, making them ineffective witnesses for Christ. One example is how Christians accept corruption as a way of life and even bribe officials to achieve their purposes. Corruption is rampant even in many churches today. Jeyaraj sees this as a growing problem in India.[23]

> There is a deep disconnect between faith and life, making them ineffective witnesses for Christ.

---

23. Jeyaraj, "Revitalizing the Churches," 297, 301.

Another symptom is that ministry is confined to serving in church-related activities, so members are equipped mainly for involvement in the church. Thus, Christians think that what they do in church is more sacred than what they do at home or at work. There is also the wrong concept of "calling" and "full-time ministry" as referring to the work of the "clergy." Chang comments that to be a pastor is often seen as a higher calling, a spiritual ministry, while business people, for example, are often viewed as not serving God but serving mammon. He sees the need to emphasize the priesthood of all believers and to promote the intrinsic value of work; there should be no divide between sacred and secular vocations.[24]

> To be a pastor is often seen as a higher calling while business people are often viewed as not serving God but serving mammon.

The divide is also manifested in the concept of Christian mission, often limited to doing evangelism and church planting. Churches confine their ministries to the "spiritual development" of people. They lack engagement with societal issues, thus failing to impact society. The Philippines, for example, is considered a Christian country but is also characterized by massive poverty, corruption, criminality, and social injustice. Churches are not equipped to engage with these issues or to serve as agents of transformation in society. Part of the problem is the lack of integration in the training of pastors and Christian leaders. Datuk Denison Jayasooria, a human rights commissioner in Malaysia, emphasizes the important role of theological education:

> Theological colleges need to provide an enabling environment for Christian thinking that will deal better with contemporary issues affecting Asian societies. As theological institutions prepare workers for the kingdom, these storehouses of knowledge are rich sources for expounding the Word of God. How do we develop tools for a greater understanding of the Word that will relate to the real issues of the day, especially those which affect the ordinary members of the local church?

---

24. Chang, "Business as Mission in Asia," 12, 15.

Theological colleges must enlarge their scope and review their curricula to address these community and national concerns. Otherwise our church leaders will be insular and parochial. We must broaden our theological horizons to apply a Christian mind to the pressing contemporary issues of our time.[25]

Whole-Life Discipleship

The sacred-secular divide affects the witness of the church in Asia. It must be overcome through intentional whole-life discipleship. Gnanakan calls for the development of holistic spirituality which should drive us closer to the whole life lived in interconnectedness rather than in isolation. "We are whole people, living as witnesses of the whole church in a real and interconnected world."[26] Theological education needs to equip leaders who can lead churches in whole-life disciple-making.

Part 4: The Indian Sub-Continent
Ivor Poobalan

South Asia is the most populous and religiously diverse region in the world. Hinduism has by far the most adherents, making up nearly 60 percent of the total population of the eight countries of South Asia: Afghanistan, Bangladesh, Bhutan, India, Maldives, Nepal, Pakistan and Sri Lanka. Over 30 percent of South Asians are Muslim, which makes up the second largest religious grouping. Buddhism has its roots in Hindu philosophy and is the predominant religion in Sri Lanka and Bhutan. The worldview of South Asians is therefore deeply informed by these influential religious movements. Christians constitute less than 2 percent of the population.

Hinduism and Buddhism are the predominant religions of India and Sri Lanka respectively. Hindus make up nearly 80 percent of all Indians and

---

25. Jayasooria, "Human Rights," 81.
26. Gnanakan, *Whole Gospel*, 309.

13 percent of Sri Lankans. Buddhists, though an insignificant minority in India, constitute 70 percent of the population of Sri Lanka. Though these philosophies are quite different, both systems of thought share a fundamental belief in the superiority of a transcendent state. They describe material existence in terms of *samsāra*, the concept of an endless cycle of births and rebirths, and they both propose ways to escape *samsāra*.

Hinduism describes this process of escape as *moksha*, or spiritual liberation, whereby the individual soul (*atman*) is released from its material existence and merges with *Brahman*, the ultimate, infinite, genderless and pervasive reality. *Moksha*, however, is not independent from the three other mutually non-exclusive *purusārthas*, or aims of life – *dharma* (moral responsibility), *artha* (worldly success), and *kāma* (love, pleasure and passions).

This way of conceptualizing life may counter the notion of a sacred-secular divide (SSD), because in a typically Hindu manner all these aspects of one's life circumstances are included and incorporated into a harmonious whole. In the Western experience of SSD, the various activities and spheres of life pertaining to the individual – such as worship, religious duties, work, family and leisure – are categorized as either "sacred" or "secular/worldly" based primarily on the Greek philosophical scheme of spirit and matter. In a Hindu culture, an individual experiences no religious or psychological conflict in simultaneously pursuing morality and duty, wealth-creation and prosperity, love and passion, and spiritual disciplines and liberation.

Hindu cultures, however, manifest significant societal fragmentation based on the Brahmin ideology of social hierarchy. This scheme divides society into four castes based on colour and race, and an implicit fifth caste of "non-Hindus" or outcastes (tribals, *Dalits*, other religious groupings and foreigners) that fall *outside and below* the recognized castes. A person's caste, whether *Brahmin* (priestly), *Kshatriya* (warrior), *Vaishya* (merchant) or *Shudra* (labourer), is determined at birth and cannot be changed by any means. Although social intercourse is permitted between castes, strict rules and rituals related to space, food, marriage customs and work ensure that caste purity is maintained by non-mixing. Interaction with outcastes has stricter regulations. Consequently, it is in the arena of human relations and association that the sacred-secular divide operates within a Hindu society. A biblical parallel is easily found in the evidence for the Jew/Samaritan or Jew/Gentile divide in the literature of the New Testament (see John 4:9; Acts 10:28). The feudal system that was maintained for centuries in Europe also provides an apt parallel.

As a result of this form of SSD, Indian society may be described as fundamentally and intrinsically fragmented, the root cause for the perpetuation of poverty, discrimination and exploitation. This thinking has been uncritically carried into some Christian traditions, which has in turn dealt a significant blow to the credibility and transformational power of the gospel. A recent example of this contradiction within Christianity in India is seen in the aftermath of the mass conversions of *Dalits* to Christianity within the last century. *Dalits* had assumed that Christianity was egalitarian and would enable them to escape caste. They discovered, to their disappointment, that the churches practised caste-consciousness too: at times explicitly – asking lower castes to sit on the floor or stand outside the sanctuary during worship – but mostly implicitly, like disallowing marriage or jobs to a lower caste, or refusing to share in fellowship meals and hospitality, or restricting entry to the ordained ministry.

> As a result of this form of SSD, Indian society may be described as fundamentally and intrinsically fragmented, the root cause for the perpetuation of poverty, discrimination and exploitation.

Buddhism was founded by Siddhartha Gautama as a protest against the social inequality and consequent injustices that had been propagated by the Brahmins and their caste ideology. Although it originated in India, Buddhism flourished in neighbouring Sri Lanka, Tibet, Bhutan and Myanmar. The Buddha, as he was later known, rejected the caste scheme and argued that an individual's stage in *samsāra* was not based on the caste one belonged to but was a consequence of a person's desire (*thanha*) for attachment or clinging (*upādāna*) to sense-experience. The essence of Buddha's teaching is contained in the Four Noble Truths. These speak of the existence of suffering, the arising of suffering, the cessation of suffering and the way leading to the cessation of suffering. Liberation from *dukkha* (suffering) is to be achieved not by the four *purusārthas* (aims of life) of Hinduism but by following the Noble Eightfold Path: right speech, right action, right livelihood, right effort, right mindfulness, right concentration, right understanding and right thoughts. Buddhism is a non-theistic religious system and places the full onus for liberation from *samsāra* on the individual adherent. The pathway to *nirvāna* or non-being is dependent on successfully ridding oneself of every impulse towards sense-attachment.

Because of the predominantly Buddhist culture, Sri Lankans instinctively equate mundane life concerns as arising out of the negative characteristic of worldly attachment and suspect any and every pleasurable experience as unmeritorious in itself. Like the Nazirites of ancient Israel, the 15,000 Buddhist monks are revered for modelling the religion's highest ideals. A monk is a renouncer: one who is venerated by the public for demonstrating an utter disinterest in every cause of existential concern and attachment.

This underlying worldview presses into the church. Finding resonance in the dualistic language of the New Testament – flesh and spirit, this world and the world to come, sin and holiness – Sri Lankan Christians find it natural to shape discipleship by the dualistic values of our surrounding culture. Thus the "full-time worker" is thought to hold the higher moral ground over the "lay believer"; "spiritual" activities such as prayer, retreats, fasting and preaching are honoured more than farming, journalism, cyber-security or homemaking. And, like the *sangha* (the Buddhist monastic order), some sections of the church will only concern themselves with purely ecclesiastical activities, leaving the problems of society, politics, and the environment to the care of the church's more "worldly" people.

It is this cultural value of SSD that makes the Roman Catholic and traditional Protestant division of the clergy from the laity more respectable. It may also be the reason for the ready acceptance of mandatory celibacy for ministry workers in the fully indigenous Ceylon Pentecostal Mission and its dubious teaching on "consecrated ministry" (where married couples permanently separate from each other). Now known as the Pentecostal Mission, this church movement has branches in over sixty countries.

> Some sections of the church will only concern themselves with purely ecclesiastical activities, leaving the problems of society, politics, and the environment to the care of the church's more "worldly" people.

Part 5: Eastern Europe
Marcel V. Măcelaru

Eastern Europe is a complex place,[27] home to a rich variety of cultures, diverse religious groups, conflicting ethno-religious identities and a long record of unique church-state symbioses that have shaped the being and doing of "national" churches in this part of the world. It is also the place where Christians of various convictions have had to face for decades the opposition of Marxist-based totalitarian communist regimes that ruled the countries in the region during the second part of the twentieth century. Although to some extent tolerated at an individual level, within the communist worldview Christian practice was denied space as a social reality. Consequently, during the communist decades the sacred-secular divide has developed deep roots in the region.

The 1989–1990 collapse of communism brought significant changes on the Eastern European arena. Most significantly, the newly gained freedom of religion made Christian engagement at all levels within the society possible. Needless to say, this raised the hope of many in the early nineties that a genuine Christian revival would take place in the region. The immediate reaction from the international Christian community came in the form of hundreds of missionaries and mission agencies that were sent to "bring Christ" to Eastern European "godless" lands.[28] Similarly, the indigenous evangelical churches, which previously were forbidden to proclaim the gospel and minister to non-believers, became engaged in all forms of evangelistic actions; all this to the point that voices from within the "national" historical churches began accusing evangelical Protestant Christianity of ineffective proselytism, patterned after

---

27. Since scholars offer various definitions of the region and disagree on its geographical contours, the designation "Eastern Europe" is unavoidably imprecise. Here it is used in a political sense to include the former Communist Bloc countries of Albania, Belarus, Bosnia-Herzegovina, Bulgaria, Croatia, the Czech Republic, Estonia, Hungary, Latvia, Lithuania, Macedonia, Moldova, Montenegro, Poland, Romania, Serbia, Slovakia and Ukraine. For more on Eastern Europe, see Frucht, *Encyclopedia of Eastern Europe*, and Kuzmič, "Christianity in Eastern Europe," 77–90.

28. On the fallacious premises for western missions in the region during the nineties, see Peterlin, "Wrong Kind of Missionary," 164–174.

Western models of mission.[29] Unfortunately, however, the concerns in most such ministries were "the salvation of the soul" of individual non-believers and "the spiritual wellbeing" of church members, without this ever translating into a larger vision of Christian life. As such, the connection between one's faith and the "secular" – that is, holistic Christian engagement within the society – was and continues to be neglected.

Sacred-Secular Divide in Eastern Europe

In the light of all the above, I propose to describe the current situation of the church in the context of Eastern Europe as "transition(ism)." By this I have in view the "ideologization" of a prolongated "in-between" that continues to characterize evangelical Christian thinking and being in the region and permits the perpetuation of the detrimental dichotomic worldview that took shape during the decades-long oppressive opposition to Christianity by communist totalitarian regimes (before 1989) and is now justified as faithfulness to the old, "tested" ways of being and doing church. The dominant feature of this dual worldview is the isolation of religious belonging and practice (the sacred) from other areas of life (the secular) – work, education, civic participation, entertainment, etc.

This dualism is fuelled by unjustified, as well as justified, fears of that which is new and different, and it is maintained by dissatisfaction with harsh persisting socio-economic realities, which leads to discouragement, and the never-ending catch-up race in which former communist societies became engaged once they entered the world of free-market economy, which leads to despair. The hermeneutic that makes such ideologization possible offers a utopian view of history, within which the here and now is but a transition toward something better – a focus on the future that makes compromises in the present possible and acceptable.

I propose that transition(ism) is the fertile ground within which a spirituality of withdrawal, reinforced by escapist eschatologies, has flourished. The net result has been missional idleness and a lack of will-power within

---

29. See Elliott, "East European Missions," 9–19, and Volf, "Fishing," 26–31.

Christian communities in the region to address the urgent issues facing church and society.[30] At least four characteristics of transition(ism) come to mind:

First, there is the tendency of Christian churches in the region to focus inwardly, to the detriment of active participation in the life of their respective communities. This not only makes the witness of the church ineffective, but also reinforces the sacred-secular divide that marks the believers' worldview and consequently their existence.

Second, there is still much theological illiteracy and consequently confusion in terms of what genuine (gospel-shaped) identity and true Christian ethos are about. The significant growth in numbers that has occurred in some cases[31] has not been accompanied by true *metanoia*. This leads to the believers' uncritical identification with the world and the adoption of non-Christian mentalities in regard to aspects of life that are perceived as "neutral," less Christian or plainly "secular."

Third, there is widespread suspicion in regard to initiatives that presuppose change, especially within the more established evangelical denominations. As such, there is little attention given to the development of biblical models of Christian leadership, both in terms of community structures and in terms of personal ministry intelligence. Programmes for training and discipling believers are seldomly available; and even when present, they are often about the perpetuation of old, outdated hierarchical models that replicate within the church the formerly surrounding communist structures, rather than about serving the other in love or empowering others as whole-life missionary disciples.

Fourth, there is significant ecclesial fragmentation (denominational, generational and theological) and a tendency towards isolated expressions of Christian ministry, as opposed to dialogue and co-operation. These have perpetuated underdeveloped ecclesial personae, within which Christian communities and individual believers are envisioned in terms of divisive socio-cultural and ethno-national identity markers rather than as members within the universal, unified body of Christ. Consequently, inter-ecclesial collaboration is often replaced by unhealthy inter-ecclesial competition. This

---

30. On these issues, see "Findings Report," 1–4.
31. For example, Măcearu, "Holistic Mission," 305–322

focuses the attention and directs the efforts of congregations and individual believers toward liturgical sophistication to the detriment of genuine fellowship and holistic Christian praxis. It propagates misleading notions of Christian life as Sunday-practiced church-bound events, to the detriment of a holistic understanding of Christianity as an existence that integrates faith with all dimensions of life: the spiritual, the physical, the intellectual, the emotional, the aesthetic and the social. Ultimately, the lacunae noted undermine the very truth that Christ is Lord over the entire reality, including all aspects of human existence, whether perceived as sacred or as secular.

> The sacred-secular divide survived after the fall of communism due to the continuation of an underdeveloped understanding of Christian existence within the churches in the region.

Conclusion

Within Eastern Europe the sacred-secular divide has deep roots and specific manifestations. It flourished during the long decades of communist obstruction of Christian praxis prior to 1989 and it survived after the fall of communism due to the continuation of an underdeveloped understanding of Christian existence within the churches in the region. Its expression, specific to the context, includes the propagation of an eschatology of withdrawal, the lack of effective discipleship, the shortage of genuine Christian leadership and a confused ecclesial identity. I suggest that for churches in the region breaking free from sacred-secular dichotomous thinking and practice requires re-thinking what Christian existence entails. It requires the following:

- The practice of a spirituality that takes into account contemporary socio-ethical concerns.
- The development of discipling models that endorse an excellence-oriented culture of learning.
- The offer of qualitative community service, characterized by care for the other and concern for truth, equality and freedom.

- The promotion of a holistic view of Christian identity, both personal and ecclesial, within which commitment to Christ impinges upon life in its entirety.

Part 6: North America
Greg Forster

The broad outlines of the SSD challenge are the same in North America (defined in this volume as the US and Canada) as they are everywhere else. But the unique history of North America has produced some unique forms in which the problem manifests itself, and recent cultural developments are changing the form in which we find SSD in North America. Thankfully, enormous growth in the faith and work movement is helping drive new approaches to tackling SSD; in particular, the movement is developing stronger bonds with local churches and seminaries, with encouraging implications for the future.

Historical Factors Shaping SSD in North America

The United States and Canada were founded by colonists from England, France and other European nations. These populations self-selected into the trans-Atlantic migration for a variety of reasons, but the most common motives were religious mission – dissenters seeking both freedom and the opportunity to build a new community on their distinct beliefs – and a desire for economic self-betterment. After some early experiments with illiberal religious communities were repudiated, North American political traditions emerged with central commitments to liberal democracy and to natural human rights – especially rights to free religious belief and practice and to the pursuit of happiness through property and commerce.

Thus, religious exercise and economic work have both, historically, been highly valued in North American culture. At the same time, the emphasis on natural human rights necessarily prevents the emergence of a public, shared integration or synthesis of these activities. If a nation's sense of identity and belonging centres on something like "this is a place where Anglicans, Presbyterians and Baptists don't tell one another what to do," that same sense of national identity cannot also incorporate much of an account of how our faith should inform our work – that would preclude the right of Anglicans, Presbyterians and Baptists to find their own diverse solutions to the problem. But where people are free to work out their own solutions to the problem, they are also free *not* to work out solutions to the problem. The gradual introduction of ever-greater religious diversity, rightly embraced as the natural consequence of the fundamental commitment to religious freedom, has only made this challenge more acute.

The legacy of slavery is also relevant, especially in the United States, where the domestic economy was long dependent upon enslaved labour to a greater degree than was the case either in Canada or Europe. In a culture that so highly valued both freedom and economic self-betterment – not on the basis of particular laws and traditions but of avowedly universal natural human rights – to deny a large portion of the population both freedom and the fruits of its labour was a moral disorder of the first magnitude. Such disorders do not fade quickly – or quietly.

The bleeding has been staunched but the wounds have not healed. All discussion of economic work in the United States – very much including the faith and work and SSD conversations – is haunted by unresolved questions and doubts about the fundamental fairness of a marketplace ordered by the traditional American commitments to freedom and natural rights, and about what does or does not constitute "racism" or "white supremacy." The same unresolved questions haunt discussions of work in the context of immigration, where the proper way to implement and protect the principles of our natural-rights tradition is highly contested.

Finally, the twentieth-century decline of "mainline" churches and growth of "evangelical" churches is significant. The mainline churches – large and longstanding denominations – have always felt a responsibility for guiding the way people live in public spaces such as the workplace. This grows in part out of their historically recognized role as leading institutions in American culture. Whatever their other problems, they were not theologically prone to SSD. Evangelicals, by contrast, inherit a legacy in which SSD is a larger problem. This arises partly from a sense of alienation from the culture (which arises partly from memories of persecution by the mainline churches and their cultural allies) and partly from a felt need to dissociate themselves theologically from the mainline.

The Classic SSD Problem

Recent developments in North America have changed the picture so much that it makes sense to draw a distinction between "the classic SSD problem" in North America – meaning the problem as it existed for most of the twentieth century – and the changing form of the problem we see emerging today. The basic problem is the same, but the form has changed in big ways. This distinction is of particular importance because almost all leaders in the faith and work movement were formed in the days of the classic problem, and continue to operate on its assumptions, even as the ground has shifted dramatically under their feet (in many cases without their realizing it).

The classic problem is defined by a relatively stable and familiar cultural environment in which different kinds of activities (job, home, church, school, etc.) are largely compartmentalized from one another. Overcoming SSD is thus primarily a matter of overcoming compartmentalization – helping people take something (their faith) that they are accustomed to putting in one of the boxes (church) and instead put it into all the boxes.

The relative stability and familiarity of the cultural environment is a key factor in the formulation of the classic SSD problem. Obviously the existence of the sociological "boxes" into which our activities are divided depends upon the cultural environment being relatively stable; if the boundaries that keep the boxes compartmentalized were constantly moving around, or if there were no boundaries, there would be no "boxes" at all. There would be at best a buzzing swarm of moving targets, at worst a mere cloud of chaos.

The solutions to SSD that predominate in North America were designed with this relatively stable and familiar environment in mind. The assumption is that we know what "work" is and we know what "faith" is, and the only problem is to connect them. Integration and wholeness are achieved by having an authoritative speaker (such as a pastor or movement leader) describe people's work activities to them in ways that reveal these activities to be manifestations of faith (carrying out the creation mandate, bringing the love of God to the world) and then assigning people tasks to perform or qualities to manifest in their work (diligence, excellence, generosity, honesty, witness).

The Changing Form of the SSD Problem

A variety of factors is transforming the SSD problem in North America. Chief among these is a rapid increase in the pace and scale of social change. The cultural environment in North America was always, in most respects, more prone to ambiguity and change than most global cultures. However, recent generations have seen this tendency taken to the nth degree. The problem now is not that "faith" and "work" are kept in separate boxes; the problem now is that there are no boxes. The classic strategy of having leaders describe people's work to them and assign them tasks to perform in their work loses effectiveness in a chaotic environment where no one description or assignment will be widely applicable.

> The problem now is not that "faith" and "work" are kept in separate boxes; the problem now is that there are no boxes.

The difference is especially observable in those in the millennial generation or younger, whose lives were never shaped by the old environment of relative stability and familiarity. An advantage of their experience, typically, is that the need for integration and wholeness is already palpably felt. There is no need to tell them that God cares about their whole lives and they must strive to find modes of Christ-centred completeness. They know this all too well. The corresponding disadvantage is that these generations typically find it harder to find a sense of authentic meaning and purpose in "ordinary" work than do we older folks. In the classic mode of the problem, if people could be brought to realize that they need wholeness and that God cares about their work, statements like "when you make good products at a good price, you are bringing the love of God to the world" were readily accepted. The essential moral legitimacy and social importance of "ordinary" economic work had a strong plausibility structure in the stable and familiar culture, and only required integration with faith. With younger folks today, while there is no need to bring them to see a need for wholeness when they already feel that need severely, there is no stable and familiar culture to provide a plausibility structure for the moral legitimacy and social importance of "ordinary" economic work.

In the United States, a prominent response to cultural chaos has been the effort to impose cultural order by force. This is the origin of the "culture war" between the political Right and Left, which has become a filter through which

> With younger folks today, while there is no need to bring them to see a need for wholeness when they already feel that need severely, there is no stable and familiar culture to provide a plausibility structure for the moral legitimacy and social importance of "ordinary" economic work.

almost every aspect of American life must pass. Both sides feel entitled to dictate their interpretations of the nation's foundational moral principles as the only valid or authentic interpretation, understanding the other side to represent the invasion of alien, illiberal political principles that are diametrically opposed to liberal democracy and natural human rights.

This polarization is as much present inside the church as outside it. The lines between the religious right churches and religious left churches are sharp and obvious to all. While a growing number of churches strive to transcend the culture war, most strategies for doing so involve withdrawing the church from teaching anything substantive on issues like sexuality or justice – which surrenders the public discourse on these issues to the extreme voices that dominate the culture war. Faith and work and SSD issues are, for many churches, a welcome opportunity to say something about people's life outside the church without falling afoul of the culture war. But there is an increasing felt need among these churches to say something about the social structures that shape and interpret our work, so the problem of the culture war looms over the movement's future.

Growing Movements and New Solutions to SSD

The faith and work movement has been growing explosively for the last decade in North America, in both scope and depth. The movement's history reaches back to the early twentieth century, and has had two earlier "waves" of major activity.[32] Legacies of these earlier waves include Regent College in Vancouver, where the application of theology in all of life is a founding value. We are now experiencing a third and very impressive wave of major activity.

One sign of the movement's maturity is the founding of new institutions and the re-founding or repurposing of old institutions. Organizations with

---

32. See Miller, *God at Work*.

names like Center for Faith and Work (in New York) and Institute for Faith and Work (Denver and Nashville) are drawing together city-based networks of Christian leaders. Large "para-church" organizations founded to serve youth, finding that their original missions are now largely covered by youth pastors in local churches, are making large investments in faith and work guidance as a service they can provide to young people. Christian study centres at colleges and universities, most of them modelled on the Center for Christian Study at the University of Virginia, are also taking up the theme.

Christian thought leaders, like the think tank Cardus, are discerning the importance of faith and work and SSD issues for the future of Christian identity in a pluralistic culture. The Theology of Work Project, which draws scholars and workplace leaders globally but is headquartered in North America, has produced a Bible commentary on faith and work in every book of the Bible. Economic development ministries, such as those represented in the Christian Community Development Association, increasingly echo these themes as well.

The movement is also making new connections to churches and seminaries. A pastor's network called Made to Flourish has built local networks of churches dedicated to faith and work in twenty-seven cities. I am privileged to serve a network of evangelical seminaries, the Oikonomia Network, with twenty-one partner schools raising up leaders for churches to preach and practice a vocationally whole gospel. Among other efforts, we hope to help the movement escape the culture war trap through our Economic Wisdom Project resources, produced by years of collaboration among theological faculty concerned to speak into the cultural structures of work in a way that avoids ideological captivity.[33]

Many new and renewed organizations in the movement have formed strong bonds with local churches or are even based out of them. These and many other efforts are helping thousands of congregations fulfil the gospel promise that the Lord will build up and bless his people for everything they do all week through the ministry of the local church.

The movement is also producing new approaches to SSD for the emerging challenge of a more chaotic cultural environment. A recent proposal by the executive director of Made to Flourish, Matt Rusten, illustrates the movement away from the old model where a leader describes your work to you and then

---

33. See economicwisdom.org.

tells you what to do in your work. On a quarterly conference call with North American faith and work leaders in February 2019, Rusten suggested four things every church should consider doing in the area of faith and work, and none of them fit the old model of "let me tell you about your work then tell you how to do it." They were:

1. Ensure the workplace is included in weekly liturgical/congregational prayer, and also set aside specific occasions for focused vocational prayers.
2. Have pastors visit people in their workplaces to learn their context first-hand; if possible, participate in the work itself.
3. Allow congregants to tell their own stories of work; ask questions about their challenges and hopes that catalyze reflection without dictating answers.
4. Perform an annual "asset mapping" survey of the congregation so leaders have accurate and up-to-date information about the vocational and other resources the congregation can use to bless the community in a variety of ways.

The days of the "sage on the stage" are over for the faith and work movement in North America. The Lord makes disciples through fruitful co-operation, in a collaborative kingdom where everyone is equal under our king.

These new directions – and, indeed, the faith and work movement itself – have not yet reached the majority of North American churches. But their progress is greater than I ever could have expected when I first entered the movement eleven years ago. The Holy Spirit is moving to build this movement. We are not owed success, but as the old and tired ways continue to lose credibility, I am optimistic about what is brewing in so many churches here.

> The days of the "sage on the stage" are over for the faith and work movement in North America. The Lord makes disciples through fruitful co-operation, in a collaborative kingdom where everyone is equal under our king.

6

Naming the Issue in
Our Seminaries

Ian Shaw

The four global consultations held by the Langham/LICC project into overcoming the sacred-secular divide were marked by a remarkable spirit of openness, co-operation and inter-institutional understanding and support on the part of those who participated. Where there was a recognition that certain contexts and institutions faced significant issues, and change was needed, there was no desire to hide this, or to pretend all was always well. This brought a clarity and focus to the discussions, and a strong emphasis on mutual support and encouragement. There was a deep commitment to learn what best practice was, to implement it, and to do everything to help others work towards the same goals. This chapter includes reflections from participants both during the consultations and afterwards about the situations they were facing. They have largely been given without names attributed so that the focus remains the issues raised, rather than who said them or where they worked. Giving the comments without attributing them to specific sources honours the integrity and openness with which they were given and allows a measure of confidentiality.

As we undertook the four global consultations, the participants reported a range of levels of awareness on the issue.[1] After listening to a presentation

---

1. For the comments and observations in this section, particular thanks are due to the more than thirty global seminary leaders from four continents who contributed to the discussion.

and discussion on the nature and widespread influence of the sacred-secular divide, one African seminary leader observed, "We are sleepwalking on this issue." Some had undertaken studies in the area, others were confronting the problem for the first time. But even those who had made it a specific field of study and research had their understanding and appreciation deepened.

The degree of awareness of the issue of the sacred-secular divide in the seminary was often linked to the level of awareness of the problem in the wider social context. While one participant commented, "there was not as such much awareness," another reported, "I was not very much aware of the issue and I had not given much thought to it until after attending the consultation." Another frankly admitted an awareness that the issue existed, but added, "I had never formulated it as an issue to be addressed." It was so much a part of the fabric of culture and society that the idea that there could be a specific Christian response to it was not part of local theological discourse.

> It was so much a part of the fabric of culture and society that the idea that there could be a specific Christian response to it was not part of local theological discourse.

Others spoke of a greater recognition of the problem as significant in their context. This was particularly apparent in Asia and Africa. For some this was significantly shaped by culture. One leader from Southeast Asia commented, "I am quite aware of the sacred-secular divide in the church setting and Christian life in our region, particularly in the Chinese Christian world." Another leader from South Asia noted the influence of other Asian religions on this: "New converts from Buddhist and Hindu backgrounds might view the church premises and the pastoral staff as 'spiritual' and everything that happens outside as 'sensual,' in keeping with the worldview they are already used to." Local churches then perpetuate the sacred-secular divide in terms of the priesthood, church-architecture, etc.

Others felt that the problem was exacerbated by theological perspectives within certain churches. In Asia it was noted that the newer Pentecostal and charismatic churches emphasized church-related activities such as Bible studies, prayer, and tithing as implicitly (and at times explicitly) "sacred," and alongside that indicated that family life, work, commerce, and social and political engagement were considered "worldly" involvements. To others, ecclesiastical structures compounded the problem – this was reflected in the divide between the full-time pastors and lay people in the denominational churches in terms of the authority of leadership.

In Africa, the challenge faced by some Christians in separating themselves from other religious and cultural practices was apparent, creating an unhelpful dual identity. One leader noted the phenomenon of "Christians worshiping in the church in the morning and then seeking further help from other 'unchristian spiritual' sources, for example, diviners and witchdoctors in the evening or some other times." This was, to him, evidence of a "dichotomizing" tendency among Christians, which remains a challenge in the church and which was carried over into all areas of life.

Many participants observed, and were surprised by, "the seemingly little amount of Christian ethos that is carried over in the day-by-day living of church-goers," which again reflects this duality. There was noted to be "quite a discrepancy between the ethical discourse and the actual ethical standards practiced by many church members." One African seminary lecturer reported a widespread "dichotomy of life for many people between their public life and their religious life." This "dichotomizing" was especially noted when it came to business practice. Many Christians maintained "pious habits" when in religious circles, "while in the marketplace they do not think that their spirituality has anything to do with the way they conduct business." Although Ethiopia is a predominantly Christian country, it was observed, "most Ethiopians do not see their business as a calling from God."

The problem of corruption was an issue frequently commented upon, "in all areas of society at all levels," as one leader put it. Yet, incongruously, side by side with this, the tendency was "to show a great popular religiosity." In Latin America, one of the most Christian countries in the region, with an evangelical Christian as President, was also one of the most corrupt countries in the world. Corruption was observed, and lamented, across the spectrum – in politics, the workplace, and business dealings. A seminary leader from Latin America recounted the story of a Christian being approached by a street robber, who forced him to stop in the road. When the person stopped and put their hands up the robber saw the intended victim had a Bible in his hand. "Oh," he said, "I won't rob you because I'm also a Christian!" One of the leaders participating in the consultations, who had undertaken doctoral research at Stellenbosch

University into the Christian response to corruption, again attributed the problem of corrupt practices to the division between the secular and sacred, the public and private, creating a "dualistic thought." This had in turn created a barrier for the church in developing solutions to the problem of corruption.

The consultations were not only designed to highlight the issue, but to encourage thinking that would signpost ways forward. One African leader commented, "I was reminded that the church lives both in this world and in the kingdom of God – meaning that both governments/states and the church are ordained by God, but the church and Christians do point toward the ultimate kingdom of Christ." He commented, "However I must say, the LICC/Langham project clarified the matter even further." Those working in Latin America felt there was more awareness of issues because of the emphasis on integral mission among some evangelicals. This emphasis leads to a recognition of the need to preach the gospel not just to save the soul, but to bring transformation of the full self and all of society. However, as a participant from Latin America noted, even with this, the recognition is "only partial," and there is only a low level of "conscious practice."

What was observed in society was often repeated in theological institutions. One participant reported that "there was and still is an invisible separation among the goals of different subjects in the programmes of the seminary. There are not integrative goals."

The problem of the sacred-secular divide seen in local churches was repeated in the students they sent to seminary for training, and even in their teachers: "Students and some members of the faculty see no or limited connection between the secular and sacred, public and private. They tend to see Christian faith as that which is only limited to formal acts of devotion and piety, but, outside the church, their everyday life and behaviour remains untransformed."

In some institutions, where there were professional training tracks, the issue was of particular concern. One seminary leader reported the struggles of some to connect professional training to Scripture: "Faculty and students think they do not need to study the Bible in their professional programs." In other institutions, students ascribed "more value to professional courses as opposed to Bible-related courses."

Another significant dichotomy was observed in the clear separation of programmes and degrees for full-time pastors/ministers from those programmes for laypeople. In particular, one leader commented on "the privileging of the MDiv program over other programs for lay Christians." A very different model had been attempted at a seminary in South Asia which had been founded in 1994 to address the theological education needs of what were then called the "lay" persons of the churches in the region of the capital city. While it was recognised that persons in vocational ministry ("full-time church-paid workers") would benefit, the focus of the training was on people in the marketplace and those who played an auxiliary role in local church ministry. This intention led this Asian seminary to a curriculum and delivery design that attempted to minimize SSD. Over the years there has been a conscious effort to structure courses to engage "head, heart and hand," and expose students to contextual realities and the importance of the application of biblical values to life.

This was somewhat exceptional. Elsewhere, there was a widespread recognition that "many courses were only concerned with their core content without any connection to bridging the sacred-secular divide." One leader sadly summed this up:

> Although it remains a fact that some church leaders in my country have tended, and others continue to hold on to the dualistic theology of a sacred-secular divide, this fact is also reflected in the way students and even staff behave and work. In almost every sphere of service and work, there seem to be a sense of dividing things and issues in two areas – secular and sacred.

In the consultations, our groups of leaders were very open about the challenges in their own teaching in these areas. One commented, "I seldom touched on the other six days of Christian living in a concrete sense." Another reported a tendency in their teaching to solely "orientate toward 'church life.'" For some, the culture of the institution actually worked against challenging the sacred-secular divide. As one leader observed, "Due to the nature of my institution, I thought it was a 'virtue' to not openly show the connections between what I was teaching with general Christian behaviour."

For others, there was a recognition of the problem, but not of the potential for theological education to challenge it: "Though I understood that the sacred-secular divide was an unnecessary division, I was not intentional in my teaching to bridge the divide." Others had begun to make some progress but had found the practical applications of this harder: "I addressed the issue of the 'public' role of theology – the idea that theology ought to impact life outside of the church, but never concretely discussed what that would look like."

Others were more conscious of the potential for theological education to challenge the sacred-secular divide issue. For one leader it was a natural part of their role: "I have always bridged the sacred-secular divide in my teaching by relating what I teach and its implications to the day-to-day life of my students." For another, it was a new emphasis, and one they sought to encourage and train others to address: "I have been making every effort to bridge the gap in my teaching since I was aware of the challenge. I have also organized and helped facilitate the theology of work seminar for staff in the last three years."

One leader recognized that challenging the sacred-secular divide came more easily in some disciplines than others: "Some of the subjects are more difficult to manage with a more integrative way of teaching, but many of my subjects such as Christian heritage, systematic theology, Baptist identity, Latin American religious heritage, and research of the socio-religious context are easy to teach in a way to make application to daily life, personally, as a church, and socially."

The nature of the institution, and even each class, contributed positively or negatively to how the teacher could respond. If the class was "a mix of Christians serving primarily in local church ministries and those who are primarily engaged as marketplace workers and homemakers," the connections between theological study and whole-life discipleship were easier to make. A strong driver to seeking to bring change was personal; as one leader reported, "My own longstanding conviction of the unhelpfulness of SSD, I believe, has made it more natural for me to teach differently."

The above examples demonstrate the openness and honesty of those who attended the consultations as to the challenges their seminaries faced, as well as their strong points, in overcoming the sacred-secular divide. This created an atmosphere in which there was no desire to hide issues or pretend things were well when they weren't. In fact, if things were reported as not going well, the mutual support and encouragement of the group was strong, with a desire to learn from each other and to promote best practice. As we shall see in chapter

14, there has already been fruit from this as participants have returned to their contexts and begun deploying ideas they had gained.

How Whole-Life Is Your Institution?

In the light of encouraging such a spirit of openness about the issue, below is a short exercise that encourages an evaluation of how whole-life your own institution is and the degree to which it is affected by the sacred-secular divide. It's obviously not exhaustive, nor intended to be, but it can help to assess what may need to change and how that might be done in your own context.

Questionnaire	Yes	No
1. The faculty regularly reflect on how Christians integrate faith to the whole of life and intentionally pass on those principles of integration to the students.	☐	☐
2. We have a clear understanding of what a disciple-making community looks like both at our seminary and in a local church, and we equip our students to assess their context in the light of that framework.	☐	☐
3. Teaching in all subject areas is applied into a full range of life contexts – at home and at work, in the church and beyond – reflecting the issues students will face themselves and will be called on to help others handle.	☐	☐
4. Our seminary is a safe place where students honestly wrestle with big issues, valuing them as an opportunity to learn and grow in faith.	☐	☐
5. Our seminary life encourages faculty and students to take local, national and global citizenship seriously and to relate the Christian gospel to the totality of Christian living.	☐	☐
6. We teach our students a theology of work so that they can apply it in a range of post-study contexts and, as leaders, help others to do so.	☐	☐
7. We help students to handle key questions that non-Christians pose in such a way that they can help other Christians do the same.	☐	☐
8. We invite Christians to speak and teach at seminary who are from the "workplace" as well as in ministry and mission.	☐	☐
9. We have identified the core competencies of a disciple-maker and we train our students in these and in how to pass these on.	☐	☐

	Yes	No
10. Our prayer life at seminary reflects the fact that we value all the contexts for which we seek to equip students – church ministry, home and overseas mission, academia, para-church organisations, the marketplace.	☐	☐
11. The faculty models whole-life disciple-making to the students in such a way that they are able to do likewise.	☐	☐
12. The seminary uses examples from contemporary culture – things such as films, work experiences, news – to learn more about what it means to follow Jesus today.	☐	☐
13. We regularly encourage the whole seminary to reflect on what they are learning.	☐	☐
14. Our commissioning or graduation services reflect the range of influence that we believe our students will have in and beyond the church.	☐	☐
15. We help students to grasp the breadth and depth of salvation, giving them a foundation on which to build whole-life Christianity.	☐	☐
16. We train students to preach in a way that clearly reflects the challenges of living as a Christian in today's world that their congregations will experience.	☐	☐
17. Our seminary is a place where creativity flourishes.	☐	☐
18. The faculty recognizes the role of church leaders in developing whole disciple-making church communities, and we reflect on how we might equip them better to do that in today's world.	☐	☐
19. The way that we teach missiology will help future leaders equip Christians to be missional disciples wherever God has called them.	☐	☐
20. Our seminary helps students handle the tensions of suffering as well as joy, of failure as well as success.	☐	☐
Total:	**Yes**	**No**

Section 2

Addressing the Issue through Theological Education

7

Overcoming the SSD through Institutional Change

Part 1: An Introduction
Ian Shaw

What happens in theological colleges significantly impacts not only our students, but also the churches and ministries in which they go on to serve. Theological education is a crucial part of the *missio Dei* in which Christians are called to participate. Too often, success in theological education has been measured by whether students pass their qualifications, rather than by the impact they have as a result of their ministries after they have completed their studies. If the intention of theological education is to create students who not only *are* whole-life missionary disciples but who also, through their ministries, *make* whole-life missionary disciples, that needs to be reflected at all levels of the institution's structure and activities. It should be woven into the DNA of the institution.

The vital connection between the seminary and the church was stressed by John Stott, who wrote: "The health of a congregation depends largely on its pastor, the pastor on his seminary, and the seminary on its faculty. . . . There is an urgent need for more seminary teachers who combine faith, personal godliness, and academic excellence."[1]

In the light of this crucial, deeply influential relationship between the seminary and local churches, seminary leaders and teachers must model what they want to see formed in their students. The impact of their efforts will be seen years later in churches and Christian ministries, the congregations they serve and the people they go on to work with. Failure to give due attention to this has sadly resulted in many church members seeing little connection between their everyday Christian living and what goes on in the seminary. Theological institutions can often be seen as irrelevant to the needs of churches and their members, and some reject the necessity of their work altogether because of this.

Change is never easy: maintaining the *status quo* tends to be the easiest option. As we discussed the problem of the SSD during the Langham/LICC project consultations, one Kenyan Christian leader commented, "Some prefer to keep the discontinuity between the Christian faith and everyday living. It makes life easier, fewer issues and challenges are faced." So let's not pretend that addressing the issue of the SSD through theological education is going to be easy.

Asking Fundamental Questions

At the outset, we need to deal with some significant questions:

- Why does theological education exist and why is it necessary?
- How has what we do in the seminary actually contributed to the sacred-secular divide problem?
- How do we help the Christian leaders we train in seminary to empower their congregations as whole-life missionary disciples?
- What do we need to change, and how can we do this?

In order to seriously tackle this issue, theological educators need to think through some important questions about what theological education is about,

---

1. John Stott, personal statement about the Langham Trust scholarships with advert for post of administrator for Langham Trust, April 1989, quoted in Shaw, "John Stott," 310.

and what the seminary is there for. Is the primary aim of the seminary leader to keep the board or the denomination happy, keep student numbers up or pay the bills? We need to have far clearer and greater missional goals than these, even if those issues preoccupy the seminary leader most days. We need to recognize the fundamental principle asserted by René Padilla, of which a participant in one consultation reminded us: "The seminary does not exist for itself but for the sake of the church."

This problem of discontinuity between the seminary and the church, and between what Christians profess and how they live in everyday life, not only raises deep questions about why we have theological education but also about the way we do it. Much theological education has been shaped around dealing with the internal issues and debates within the academy, which are undoubtedly important and interesting. However, in making theology an end in itself, there is a serious danger of losing the missiological intent of theological education. The South African missiologist David Bosch argued that "the church ceases to be the church if it is not missionary, theology ceases to be theology if it loses its missionary character. . . . Theology rightly understood *has no reason to exist* other than crucially to accompany the *missio Dei*."[2]

So mission is the reason for the theological enterprise: theological education is the handmaiden of mission. "If theological education has no missiological orientation towards the world, is theological education actually theological?"[3] The missiological dimension gives theological education its purpose and direction. Sadly, many theological colleges appear to have lost this understanding of their crucial role in the *missio Dei* and, as a result, are unable to equip students to overcome the SSD. They don't see their mission as being to equip others for mission. Much teaching is delivered without explicitly helping students to see its connection to the everyday realities of Christian living. This leaves students who are studying theology because they feel called into Christian ministry unsure of the reasons they are studying

> In making theology an end in itself, there is a serious danger of losing the missiological intent of theological education.

---

2. Bosch, *Transforming Mission*, 494.

3. Bosch, 494.

what they are asked to study in seminary. The often quoted figures produced by Robert Banks in his research into theological education in the United States in the late 1990s were disturbing. They showed that some 50 percent of MDiv students had left the Christian ministry for which they had been trained within five years of leaving seminary.[4]

Theological educators should instead embrace the challenge of envisioning and empowering future church leaders to fulfil the biblical imperative to make whole-life missionary discipleship central in their congregations. The problem of the sacred-secular divide needs to be tackled across the seminary, in all our programmes and at all levels. It involves a re-orientation in the understanding of the nature of, and preparation for, the pastoral ministry. Many in our churches are convinced that their primary role in the Christian life is to support the leadership of the church in their mission. The pastor or evangelist or youth worker is on the frontline – they are the ones doing mission.

> The problem of the sacred-secular divide needs to be tackled across the seminary, in all our programmes and at all levels.

After all, they have gone to theological seminary to be trained for that mission. After graduation, other Christians earn money to pay the minister to fulfil that mission. Maybe the members of the congregation have a few opportunities for witness to their friends, neighbours or work colleagues, but the real work is done by the theologically trained "professionals."

This misconception needs to be reversed. Ephesians 4:12 clearly teaches that the role of the Christian leader is to prepare God's people for works of service. So those on the frontline are the church members, and it is the role of the Christian leader to prepare them, train them and support them in that ministry on the frontline. So, in the church there may be fifty, one hundred, five hundred or many more wholly engaged as whole-life missionary disciples. The task of theological education is therefore to train Christian leaders so that they can facilitate and support the work of others in mission. That is the reason why they need to be well-trained: to act as resource people, and trainers, for others. The marked dichotomy between professional clergy and the laity – one

---

4. Banks, *Re-envisioning Theological Education*, 200.

group engaged in mission and the others not – was identified by participants in the Langham/LICC consultations as a significant contributor to perpetuating the SSD.

> The task of theological education is to train Christian leaders so that they can facilitate and support the work of others in mission.

This weakness in much theological education is a systemic problem and affects all fields. It cannot be addressed by changing the teaching in just one subject, such as missiology. Instead it must be specifically addressed across the institution and its curriculum, right through the teaching of core subjects like Bible, hermeneutics and doctrine.

The whole of Scripture is all about "whole-life," so responding to the challenge of using theological education to train whole-life missionary disciples and whole-life missionary disciple-makers involves having a whole-life approach to the study of Scripture and theology. As Antony Billington from LICC put it during one of the Langham/LICC consultations, "We need a 'whole life-whole Bible' approach in theological education."

Re-orientating theological education so that a key goal is the issue of the SSD requires change. But change does not come easily (see chapter 13 in this book). There may be resistance from denominational leaders, board members, other colleagues or even students. So, in the following sections, we are going to look at possible one-degree shifts in curriculum, programme, individual course and lecture levels.

But first we will look at three examples of how the issue has been addressed at an institutional level.

The rest of this chapter considers three examples, one each from South America, Africa, and South Asia, of seminaries where there has been an institutional attempt to be missional and overcome the SSD.

Across global theological education, seminary leaders are working to ensure that the SSD is challenged. The process is not easy, and there are challenges, but important work is being done that others can learn from. Here are three examples from participants in the Langham/LICC global consultations that help point a way forward. They are from Brazil, Sri Lanka and Kenya.

Part 2: Overcoming the SSD at South American Theological Seminary

Antonio Carlos Barro, President

The question that the issue of the sacred-secular divide (SSD) poses is one of the most important, demanding answers and reflections not only from the church worldwide but also from religious institutions such as NGOs, missions organizations and especially theological schools.

I stress the importance of theological schools because they are at the vanguard of Christian ideas and, as such, should be able to work closely with the church in pursuing better ways to meet the needs of society, regardless of geographical location. However, in order to move toward creating whole-life missionary disciples, one must understand what SSD is. The definition is quite simple if we think about people living in two separate worlds: "the private world of family and church where they can express their faith freely and the public world where religious expression is strongly discouraged."[5]

For centuries theological schools have been training or preparing leaders to serve within the confines of the church and making this service the most important aspect of Christian ministry.

It is then no surprise when one surveys the curriculum taught by theological schools to find that the majority of courses focus on Christian people and how they can be better Christians in the private world of family and church.

It is rare to find courses in any discipline that teach students how to lead the church to cross the bridge from church to society, from faith expressed privately to faith expressed publicly. As a result, people get themselves busy within the confines of the church. In this sense, society does not receive the impact of the Christian faith.

---

5. D. Kim, D. McCalman, D. Fisher, "The Sacred/Secular Divide and the Christian Worldview," *Journal of Business Ethics* 109, no. 2 (2012): 203.

The SATS Perspective on SSD

If the division between secular and sacred exists in the church and in the Christian way of life, it is most probably because the curricula of our theological institutions are not systemically integrated with the mission of God in the world!

At the South American Theological Seminary (SATS) we recognized that the curriculum needed to embrace and express the concept known as *missio Dei*.[6] The courses we teach must show the student both how to read the Bible and how to read society.

SATS prioritizes the methodology of the hermeneutic circle in our teaching. The challenges of contemporary realities, contexts and situations call us to new questions and biblical reflection. This process of a new biblical reading from these concrete situations must nevertheless take into account the origins and history of Christianity, crystallized in diverse theological traditions. In this way, systematic and contemporary theology has a new purpose and function, which is the effective preparation of students not only for thinking in theological ways but also for engaging in missional practice. Such practice takes place amidst the demand for consistent, practical and relevant responses that will transform lived situations. It is here that practical and missiological theology contributes so powerfully by robustly connecting contextual, biblical and Christian reflection in an interdisciplinary way to daily practice. This is the rationale behind the hermeneutic circle that SATS uses.

> The courses we teach must show the student both how to read the Bible and how to read society.

To summarize: the mission of God (*missio Dei*) takes place in the most varied contexts (reality) that require intentional effort to interpret their codes (analysis of reality) in order to make the word of God powerfully relevant (biblical and theological reflection) through the manifestation of his kingdom in words and deeds (praxis) in the hope that lives will be saved, and situations and realities will be transformed (transformed reality).

---

6. "Mission is not first something the church does, but describes the being of God. The triune God is in and for Godself missionary." Flett, "Theology of *Missio Dei*," 69.

In this way we believe that SATS is giving our future leaders the necessary tools to pastor and lead their congregations to be relevant in whatever context the members of the church are living.

Collaborative Formation

In order to accomplish our task, it is important for every faculty member to understand this concept and work together to fulfil our mission.

In our early days, we decided that each faculty member would work in a collaborative way to better guide our students. In the five-day pedagogical meeting that takes place at the beginning of each semester, each professor brings the syllabus of the classes they will teach. That syllabus is shared amongst the faculty members who are teaching the same group of students.

We then review the objective of each course and we see if that objective is in line with the objective of the semester for that particular group of students. We also review the amount of work each professor requires, and we confer to see if that amount is appropriate or not. Professors are then open to considering suggestions on how to improve their classes and their reading lists. This is also a time to review whether there is any duplication, and so on.

Our faculty are now very used to this system and are very open to receiving comments or suggestions about a syllabus. By the end of the week, we are confident that the students will profit from our teaching.

Conclusion

Since the mission of God, not the mission of the church, is the umbrella for our teaching, we then request that our faculty members ask a simple question: How will my teaching contribute to the fulfillment of the *missio Dei*? In this regard, it does not matter what the discipline is. Each one will point to the mission of God. As an illustration: how does the study of homiletics help the students lead the church toward society in mission?

> We request that our faculty members ask a simple question: How will my teaching contribute to the fulfillment of the *missio Dei*?

In this sense, we try to comply with Wolters as he states, "All of these 'two-realm' theories, as they are called, are variations of a basically dualistic worldview, as opposed to the integral perspective of the reformational worldview, which does not accept a distinction between sacred and secular 'realms' in the cosmos."[7]

Finally, as faculty members we understand that the ultimate goal of our theological training is to bring all honour and glory to God.

Part 3: Overcoming the SSD at Colombo Theological Seminary
Ivor Poobalan, Principal

Colombo Theological Seminary (CTS) was founded in 1994 by the collaboration of national Christian leaders representing a large spectrum of the Sri Lankan church. Their desire was to see the formation of a new generation of leaders who would live by evangelical values and guide the church by an integrated vision of the gospel that would overcome the normative, but unhelpful, SSD.

The biblical underpinnings of this endeavour are found in the way John introduces Jesus the Saviour in his prologue (John 1:1–18). The Word that was with God in the beginning, and was God, says John, *became flesh and lived among us*. Incarnation, then, is the paradigm that shapes the seminary's sense of mission and *modus operandi*. CTS must maintain a firm commitment to the evangelical faith and, at the same time, be engaged in the mission of the church in a way that is relevant to contemporary concerns.

Theological Education for *All* Christian People: Challenging the Clergy-Laity Divide

From the outset CTS was designed to teach and equip all serious Christians committed to serve God as witnesses within the church and out in the world. It was thereby envisioned that while several seminary students would be

---

7. Wolters, *Creation Regained*, 11.

clergy or vocational church workers, the majority would either be homemakers or professionals from the marketplace. The idea was to find a way to empower this larger body of students with sound theology that could be applied in multiple contexts, whether church ministry, the mission field or the marketplace.

> By members of faculty modelling the way, students are able to appreciate the importance of an integrated Christian lifestyle.

For this reason, CTS based itself in the capital city, Colombo, ensuring accessibility to believers working in the Greater Colombo area. The programmes are non-residential, enabling the students to remain actively engaged in their local contexts. Classes are scheduled six days a week, from 9 a.m. to 8 p.m. on weekdays. The graduate programme is scheduled for late evenings and all day Saturday to ensure that church workers and office workers together may be educated for competence in biblical studies or missions or Christian education.

> The idea was to find a way to empower this larger body of students with sound theology that could be applied in multiple contexts, whether church ministry, the mission field or the marketplace.

CTS collaborates closely with the local church that recommends the student, to ensure a more effective formation. The student is supervised and supported by the pastor or an elder of the church during the period of studentship. The local church mentors the student on the distinctive denominational emphases and frees the seminary to major on the essential doctrines and practices shared across denominations.

The approach has worked reasonably well. The ability to provide a programme that invited the participation of all denominations, coupled with a flexible and user-friendly delivery, has resulted in an average of 700–800 Christians in leadership enrolling in seminary courses every year from a relatively small Christian demographic. After twenty-five years of seminary ministry, CTS alumni are found in diverse contexts, serving their Master faithfully and with greater competence in the church and in the world.

Curriculum Design That Is Responsive to Context: Challenging the Traditional-Contextual Divide

CTS began with the distinct advantage of being conceptualized and pioneered by national Christians who intimately understood the challenges of the South Asian region. Consequently, while traditional theological curricula were carefully consulted, the particular needs of the local context also drove the shape of the various programmes.

Syllabi were determined with the end in mind. Religious pluralism, an ongoing civil war, social injustice, a church uninterested in world missions, militant Buddhism and the struggles of indigenization became vital considerations in identifying the subjects to be included and the pedagogy required. By a process of "double-listening" the seminary has endeavoured to recognize the value of both *traditional content* such as biblical exegesis, theology, history and mission, and *contextual priorities* such as peace-making, science, contemporary ideologies, politics and trauma counselling.

In addition, the seminary curriculum has been reviewed and revised every seven years, both in terms of evangelical faith and missional relevance. This has ensured that the theological curriculum is as rooted in conviction as it is responsive to context.

Teaching Faculty Engaged in Local Church and Missions Ministry: Challenging the Academic-Praxis Divide

In Sri Lankan culture, religious leaders are thought to be above mundane concerns. Their role is viewed as more esoteric: to pursue spirituality through study and meditation and remain "unpolluted" by worldly involvements. Much like the philosophers of the Greco-Roman world, religious figures are afforded a higher status in the public eye and their material, physical needs are met by the loyal, hard-working laity. Because of this way of thinking, believers may see Christian leadership as a "higher calling" and consequently undervalue the praxis of ministry. In addition, the theological teacher may easily be positioned as a "pure academic" who is not expected to engage, whether pastorally or missionally.

To combat this dangerous dichotomy between academics and praxis, all teachers at the seminary are deeply involved in their local church communities and bear a reputation of practical commitment to ministry and mission. During its brief period of existence, faculty at CTS have consistently demonstrated the sheer importance of hands-on ministry by championing church planting, pastoral work, Christian education, preaching, children's and youth work, and counselling. By members of faculty modelling the way, students are able to appreciate the importance of an integrated Christian lifestyle: faith and works, academics and praxis, family and ministry – head, heart and hands.

A study done in 2016 showed that of 388 alumni, only 7 were no longer found in active, recognized positions of Christian leadership. This is less than a 2 percent dropout rate from the profession, a statistic that radically contrasts with the international average.

Part 4: Overcoming the SSD at Daystar University

Bernard Boyo, Dean

In Kenya, which is a predominantly Christian country, the presence of the sacred-secular divide phenomenon is rife in all sectors of society. At Daystar University, a Christian University which "aspires to be a distinguished, Christ-centred African institution of higher learning for the transformation of church and society," we are seeking to develop holistic educational approaches to address this. The mission of the University is "to develop managers, professionals, researchers and scholars to be effective, Christian servant leaders through the integration of Christian faith and holistic learning for the transformation of church and society in Africa and the world."[8] In its endeavour to offer Christian education and communication for excellence in servant leadership, Daystar's core ideals are "Christian Values, Education, Effective Communication, Excellence and Servant Leadership."[9]

---

8. Daystar University, *Catalogue 2017–2021*, iv.
9. Daystar University, https://www.daystar.ac.ke/vision&mission.htm.

In addressing the SSD, the university endeavours to include its values in the teaching process by adopting and maintaining a liberal arts approach to education. This approach seeks "to develop well-rounded individuals with general knowledge of a wide range of subjects and with mastery of a range of transferable skills as 'global citizens,' with the capacity to pursue lifelong learning and become valuable members of their communities."[10] In keeping with its Christian philosophy, the university has general courses in Bible and integrated studies as required core courses at all levels, from certificate to doctoral level programmes.

At the undergraduate level, for instance, each programme is required to cover at least thirty credit hours of general courses. Key to the master's study level is a common core course titled Biblical Foundations of Christian Service whose objective is to prepare students to render effective service based on the biblical foundation of the kingdom of God motif. This course is premised on the conviction that "all truth is God's truth," with a clear focus that sees all work as service rendered to God. At the PhD level there is a course on integration of faith and life which seeks to enable students to reach their full potential as Christians by integrating faith and life, irrespective of their specific areas of academic disciplines, lives and careers. The question of the SSD is critical in theological education in Africa, since, as Okesson argues, "The curriculum of African theological institutions should reflect a creative and flexible relationship between these elements in the formation of ministerial leadership for today's Africa."[11]

> This course is premised on the conviction that "all truth is God's truth," with a clear focus that sees all work as service rendered to God.

In order to maintain its Christian ethos, all members of the University are well informed, at the point of entry, of the Christian philosophy that defines Daystar. All members of staff and faculty are expected to profess the Christian faith. While maintaining an open admission to students of all faiths, one of the admission requirements for all students is the signing of a code of conduct

10. Haidar, "What Is Liberal Arts."
11. Okesson, "Sacred and Secular," 41.

form endorsed by their guardian or sponsor indicating their agreement to adhere to Daystar's Christian values and their commitment to participate in the spiritual disciplines of the university.

In keeping with the higher education regulations in Kenya, Daystar continues to review and harmonize all its courses as it maintains the significance of general courses in Bible and theology. This process seeks to give a minimum threshold that each programme at the undergraduate level will have to include in their curriculum as required core courses of the university. By so doing the university is guided by the philosophy that Bible courses give a basic understanding and foundation of what Christian faith and belief entails, as well as creating relevance and practical application of faith in all disciplines. In this sense, then, the centrality of Christian faith is thus entrenched in all disciplines and all programmes offered at the university, thereby combating the unwarranted sacred-secular dichotomy.

All students, staff and faculty are also expected to attend weekly chapel and small group Bible study which take place on Tuesdays and Thursdays respectively. Daystar also dedicates one day each semester for prayer where all the functions of the university are halted and everyone assembles for prayers, culminating with the sharing of communion (Lord's Table). These activities are intended to create opportunities for communal spiritual enrichment and personal and corporate spiritual disciplines.

Among the challenges facing the institution is the diversity of religious and theological perspectives represented by members of our students, staff and faculty. The main issue rests with the perceived view that Daystar's core courses in Bible and theology are often deemed to be an additional course load for students not majoring in the Bible. There are students who tend to think that these courses are not core to their majors or subject areas and, as such, need not be part of the curriculum. Likewise, some members of faculty, particularly in disciplines other than the Bible and theology, feel that the Bible courses are unnecessarily forced into the curriculum.

The attendance of chapel and Bible study groups is often met with myriads of questions from members of staff and faculty whose attendance is also required as part of individual career progression and promotion within the university. The danger is that staff may think they just have to attend as routine because it is a requirement.

The material impact of this requirement, especially for students, is also a continuing challenge as most do not see the need for mandatory chapel attendance. Since they are required to sign in as they get into the chapel, some just attend to fill in the sign-in sheet and then leave.

Daystar has endeavoured to instruct all faculty and staff in the integration of faith and work and has introduced a one-week intensive on the theology of work aimed at, over time, giving all faculty and staff a biblical understanding of work as it relates to their role and responsibilities in the workplace. At the end of the course, the participants are given a certificate of attendance. We are not yet fully able to assess the impact of this, since almost three-quarters of staff have yet to participate in the training. Similarly, we recognize that there is a further challenge: to ensure that the changed mindset and worldview of faculty works its way into the delivery and assessment of courses and offers students a holistic, integrated biblical understanding across the full range of subjects we offer. We have begun the journey but there is much still to be done.

> Daystar has introduced a one-week intensive on the theology of work aimed at giving all faculty and staff a biblical understanding of work as it relates to their role and responsibilities in the workplace.

8

Overcoming the SSD through Curriculum Change

Ian Shaw

In this book we are wrestling with this major issue: How can theological educators envision and empower future church leaders to fulfil the biblical imperative to make whole-life missionary discipleship central in their congregations?

We have established that what happens in theological seminaries significantly impacts not only our students but also the churches and ministries in which they go on to serve. Theological education is a crucial part of the *missio Dei* in which Christians are called to participate. Therefore, we should make the central, missiological aim of theological education to be the training of people who will make whole-life missionary disciples. This needs to be woven into the DNA of the institution. The previous chapter considered how the issue can be addressed at the institutional level and explored some examples of how this has been done. We need to overcome the irrelevance and redundancy many perceive to exist in theological education.

> Therefore, we should make the central, missiological aim of theological education to be the training of people who will make whole-life missionary disciples.

We need to start with the end goal in mind, and then design back from there. As Søren Kierkegaard once famously observed, the tragedy of life is that one can only understand it backwards, but one must live it forwards.[1] In the same way, curricula need to be designed backwards but delivered forwards. So, if those trained in our seminaries are to fulfil the Ephesians 4:12 mandate of preparing God's "people for works of service, so that the body of Christ may be built up," this aim needs to be reflected throughout the institution and the curriculum. Whole-life missionary disciple-making must be the stated learning intention across all programmes: it cannot simply be fixed by adding a single module on the subject. Indeed, that would only perpetuate the division. It needs to be integrated into all our subject areas, at all levels: the institution (as we have seen), curriculum, programme, module and individual lecture. It must permeate all subject areas: Biblical studies, theology, church history, missiology, practical theology. If it is not woven into the DNA of the institution and its curriculum, it will be marginalized. Because this is a systemic problem, it needs to be comprehensively addressed.

So, we turn now to the issue of how shaping the curriculum can contribute to the issue of overcoming the sacred-secular divide.

Defining "Curriculum"

The traditional way of defining the curriculum has been to see it as the syllabus that is taught. This includes the programmes in the institution, the subjects covered and all the teaching and learning resources that lie behind it. In reality, that is just the "explicit curriculum": that which is publicly known and stated at the outset. It is found in publications like the prospectus, the programme handbooks, and course and module outlines. These are all fundamental to theological education, but there is a danger in suggesting that theological education is simply about delivering content, repeating it back in assignments and offering grades based on how successful this has been done.

Formally, a curriculum is an explicit plan tied to certain goals and objectives. This emphasizes the need for there to be deliberate intentions and for there to be an assessment of whether these have been achieved. In this it has been observed that curriculum operates at three levels:

---

1. S. Kierkegaard, "Journal: 167 (1843)," in *Works of Søren Kierkegaard, Vol. 18* (Copenhagen: Søren Kierkegaard Research Center, 1997), 306.

1.   Curriculum intended – what was "meant."
2.   Curriculum implemented – what was "taught."
3.   Curriculum achieved – what was learned.[2]

However, there is now a growing recognition of the need for an even wider definition of curriculum.

In theological education, curriculum should embrace the totality of the experience of being at the seminary. The learning and personal development activities of the school range from classes taught to meals eaten together, worship times and informal time together over coffee or conversing in the corridors. Curriculum includes co-curricular and extra-curricular activities, which can be done on the campus or off it, and all of which can be significantly formative. Going with faculty on a mission trip together or to lead services in local churches on a Sunday can significantly shape the student's experience.

In what follows we will look at this broader definition of curriculum, including not only the explicit curriculum but also the "hidden" curriculum and the "null" curriculum.

The Explicit Curriculum

In his book *Leading Curriculum Development*, John Wiles states that the curriculum "represents a set of desired goals or values that are activated through a development process and culminate in successful learning for students."[3] This helpful definition establishes the intentionality and coherence of curriculum. It is not teachers sitting in a room and saying, "So what do we want to teach?" That approach would only create a curriculum which is a patchwork of the different interest areas of the lecturers, with little coherence or integration. Instead, the curriculum is a design for learning, like the blueprint for a machine, or the plans for building a house. It involves a "development process." This takes time, thought, planning, discussion. Underlying the curriculum are "desired goals or values." These give the curriculum its purpose and its shape. So, if the aim of an institution is to get students to challenge the SSD, this is where that process needs to start. Creating students who are whole-life missionary

---

2. Bauersfeld, "Research Related," 204.
3. Wiles, *Leading Curriculum Development*, 5.

disciples and also whole-life missionary disciple-makers are goals and values that need to be woven into the DNA of the programme. But curriculum also has an outcome – the successful learning of students. This book takes the view that such "successful learning" does not end with the summative essay or examination, but success should be measured in future ministry and how graduates, after they have left seminary, replicate that ministry in the lives of the people they work among.

Curriculum Development

John Wiles describes the curriculum development process as "a matter of choosing from many possibilities the set of goals or values to be promoted in the classroom."[4] Therefore, it is vital that the institution establishes the "set of values" that the curriculum seeks to promote. So, if the goal is creating whole-life missionary disciple-makers, what are the values that are needed to achieve that? These will include values like integration, application and missional focus. The goals will be shaped by the type of graduates the institution, and its programmes, are designed to create. The emphasis in these values will not just be the students' output in terms of their studies and qualifications but the outcomes in their ministry and the impact it has on the ministry of their congregants.[5] For more on this, see chapter 15 in this book.

> If the goal is creating whole-life missionary disciple-makers, what are the values that are needed to achieve that?

Once the key values have been established, curriculum development leaders then need to establish a defined plan of what is intended of students during their period of studies – the specific programmes to be delivered, their learning outcomes, key content (areas), even lesson plans. Experienced teachers generally make good curriculum developers because they have learned effective practice in all these areas. To overcome the SSD, the teachers involved in this curriculum development should be those who understand the nature and work of whole-life missionary disciple-making and, ideally, have experience with it.

---

4. Wiles, 6.

5. For a very helpful discussion on this, see Shaw, *Transforming Theological Education*, 51–61.

The curriculum development stage needs to begin with an analysis of needs. What knowledge, understanding, skills and experience are required of students in order to achieve these goals and values? This informs the vision of what is going to be done. If the SSD is to be overcome, these "needs" should be shaped by the overall vision. Armed with a needs analysis, which will enable the students to achieve the intended goals and values, the curriculum plan, or map, can be created.

The team, involved in the design, implementation and outcomes of the curriculum should not lose sight of the desired "goals and values" which should drive their concerted efforts. Curriculum developers need to ensure the curriculum is built around these, rather than the specific subject interests of the teaching team. There is always a temptation to begin with the question "What can we teach?," or even "What would we like to teach?," rather than "What do students need to know in order to achieve our stated goals and values?" This does not mean that the wider faculty have no say in the process; indeed, they should be involved in this development work. However, their contributions are more in terms of "What is it that I can bring from my subject area in order to achieve the institution's goals and values, primarily training whole-life missionary disciple-makers?"

Once the curriculum outline has been established, it needs to be fleshed out in terms of specific courses or modules (see chapter 9), each of which include learning activities that contribute to the goals and values and meet the learning needs of students to achieve these (see chapter 10). The type of assessments used in the curriculum can also break down the cognitive-behavioural divide that has characterized much theological education. The key need is to match the style and approach taken in teaching and assessment to learning intentions (see chapter 12).

After it has been developed and implemented, the new or revised curriculum's integrity then needs to be maintained. This involves the teaching of the curriculum, the learning experience of students and the assessment of their work. The success of the institution in delivering the curriculum and achieving its outcomes should be kept under review. With a focus on equipping students to overcome the SSD, the review should assess whether this goal has been met. This is the role for the curriculum leader or manager, a senior figure in the seminary. Generally, those with extensive teaching experience make the best curriculum leaders. They are aware of what works, and why, although they too should be open to innovation and change.

In their curriculum maintenance role, the curriculum leader should make sure that, as well as maintaining a focus on goals and values, the latest thinking and research is regularly introduced to teachers, so that best practice is constantly being introduced. They also need to ensure that the requirements of governmental bodies, accrediting associations, professional bodies, etc., are regularly reviewed and compliance maintained. This should be drawn together into a curriculum management plan, and key stakeholders should be able to see and comment on this.

Finally, in this process of curriculum development, implementation and management, the curriculum needs to be evaluated. This means the establishment of clear and assessable outcomes to enable monitoring of whether what was planned is actually being delivered. Regular review of these outcomes establishes a culture of enhancement, which gives a dynamism to the process, such that curriculum is never truly static.

Student feedback is therefore very important. Often the results of student feedback reflect the popularity of the lecturer and their style, or of the subject area, rather than whether students have successfully mastered the subject material and attained the skills they need for future ministry. So, student feedback at a curriculum/programme level should not just be directed at the effectiveness of the individual teachers in class but also at whether the overall curriculum is achieving its intended aims. In this way, feedback from the institution's alumni also becomes extremely important: have the institution's curriculum goals and values been achieved by giving its graduates the theological tools and ministry skills needed for the work they are doing three or five years after graduation? Feedback from alumni can be fed into the reflective cycle of curriculum renewal and development.

> Student feedback at a curriculum/programme level should not just be directed at the effectiveness of the individual teachers in class but also at whether the overall curriculum is achieving its intended aims.

Sadly, there are indications that some curriculum approaches have not only been unsuccessful in equipping students for overcoming the sacred-secular divide but may in fact have increased it.

Learning Approaches That Help to Build Overcoming the Sacred-Secular Divide into Curriculum

In his book *The Future in Education* (1941), Sir Richard Livingstone, president of Corpus Christi College, Oxford, famously stated:

> The test of successful education is not the amount of knowledge that a pupil takes away from school, but his appetite to know and his capacity to learn. If the school sends out children with the desire for knowledge and some idea of how to acquire it, it will have done its work. Too many leave school with the appetite killed and the mind loaded with undigested lumps of information.[6]

So, good theological education should inspire a thirst for learning, and then inculcate the skills by which learners will spend a life satisfying that thirst.

In establishing the curriculum, it is important to work out the learning approaches that should be adopted to instil that thirst. There are a range of options available, from inquiry-based learning to workplace-based learning or problem-based learning, or a combination of all of these. There are also choices about what to decide not to teach – there is only limited space in any curriculum.

> Good theological education should inspire a thirst for learning, and then inculcate the skills by which learners will spend a life satisfying that thirst.

Inquiry-based learning

In this, students are set challenges to explore and assess key issues, with an onus on them collecting a range of evidence and resources in order to produce a meaningful response. The onus is not just on getting the correct answers but on using the right methods and doing the correct analysis upon which those answers are based. Students can be encouraged to undertake small

---

6. Livingstone, *Future in Education*, 29.

research projects that relate specific theological topics to the issue of whole-life missionary disciple-making.

Workplace-based learning

Programmes that include workplace learning opportunities (such as placements) allow learners to practice and develop the skills they have gained. Learners can be given the opportunity to see the development of whole-life missionary discipleship in action or deploy the skills of doing such discipleship themselves. To achieve this, part of a course could be delivered "on site" in a work context or through placements, short internships or a period of full-time or part-time work (paid or unpaid) for which credit can be given. A traditional "sandwich course" includes a lengthy placement in another context, such as a period working with a future employer or learning a language in another country. Knowledge and skills have to be deployed in real and meaningful situations away from the classroom. This type of experience can only serve to enhance the training for a future ministry free of the SSD. A 2010 study of pastors in SE Asia found that 45 percent felt stress early in their ministries because of inadequacies in their theological training, especially in the area of practical skills.[7]

Problem-based learning

This places a heavy emphasis on pastoral realities, and the application of theological reflection to these. Much emphasis is placed on case studies or reflections on pastoral experience. It shows that Christian ministry is complex, requiring the deployment of a variety of skills in different contexts. Theological issues are rarely simple and are often interrelated. The issue of the SSD between personal faith and the everyday application of it is a problem worth studying in itself, to enable learners to develop an understanding of its nature and strategies for how to overcome it.

Non-fragmented curriculum

Over the years the increasing focus in theological education has been on rational reflection. Historically, theological education gradually moved from

---

7. Cited in Burke, "Time to Leave," 263–284.

the cathedral cloisters into the university, with more emphasis on detailed analysis of theological issues, rather than reflection on theological issues in pastoral contexts. Heavily influenced by the approach of Aristotle, the dominant mode of study was to break issues down into their constituent parts in order to understand the whole.[8] The legacy of this is that theological disciplines have been compartmentalized: Biblical studies is often taught separately from preaching, pastoral care separate from Christian doctrine. The curriculum becomes fragmented: each subject rests in a separate silo, creating a series of distinct courses that do not connect together. Students are left to "join up the dots" between subject areas, but without significant guidance, they find this very difficult to do. And if they cannot make the connections during their studies, their future ministries will repeat this lack of connection between theological thought and practice. It is little surprise, then, that their congregations are unable to see the connection between Christian teaching and the business of everyday living. Avoiding fragmentation in the curriculum is an initial step in training students who do not perpetuate the sacred-secular divide.

> Students are left to "join up the dots" between subject areas, but without significant guidance, they find this very difficult to do.

Integration should be emphasized

Intentionality is needed in curriculum design to ensure integration. Indeed, whole-seminary curriculum integration is needed to create whole-life missionary disciple-makers. This will help avoid the apparent dichotomy between cognitive and affective strands in theological education, as well as between cognitive and behavioural. Integration lessens the risk of perpetuating the SSD within the seminary with the inevitable result that the divide will be repeated when students leave seminary.

Strong efforts need to be made to create a curriculum that is internally coherent. I remember well a very sharp question asked by an educationalist who was evaluating a programme I had been part of a development team for. "Well," he said, "is this a programme, or just a collection of modules?" We

---

8. This is fully discussed in Cannell, *Theological Education Matters*, 126–237.

In *The Future in Education*, Sir Richard Livingstone also noted, "The good schoolmaster is known by the number of valuable subjects which he declines to teach."

Curriculum should also be lean, clearly focused on what is necessary, and leave out what is of marginal importance. There are tough choices. Valuable but not essential material may have to be laid aside. There are difficult discussions to be had, but the curriculum should be pruned in such a way that the fruit it produces is whole-life missionary disciples. Students should be able to develop skills across the theological disciplines without the coherence of the goals and values of the curriculum being lost.

> Students should be able to develop skills across the theological disciplines without the coherence of the goals and values of the curriculum being lost.

The "Hidden" or "Implicit" Curriculum

There is more to the curriculum than what is visible in institutional and programme documents. Sometimes institutions and educators are unaware of the hidden, or implicit, curriculum, but that doesn't mean it is not strongly present. It informs the ethos, culture and values of the institution. It shapes the whole atmosphere in which students, lecturers, administrators and support staff work and learn, share experiences, knowledge and attitudes together. These are the wider sociological and psychological dimensions of learning. We sometimes say something is "caught rather than taught." That is the dimension of the hidden curriculum. While much time and effort can go into defining and developing the explicit curriculum, the hidden curriculum is often neglected.

Based on his studies of high school students, Fyock argued that the attitude and behaviour of educators plays a more significant role in the formation of students' beliefs, values, and attitudes – their worldviews – than the explicit curriculum.[11] Sometimes the implicit messages given are positive, sometimes negative. A very structured approach to learning activities, in which students

---

11. Fyock, "Effect."

are told exactly what to do and think about every issue reduces their ownership of learning and reduces the tendency to integration and creativity.[12]

In nearly ten years of working with Langham Partnership, I visited over 150 seminaries in Asia, Africa, Europe, the Middle East, Australasia, and North and South America. It was possible to learn a great deal about them from their websites, prospectuses, and promotional material, but until you walked through the door, you did not have a full sense of what sort of seminary it really was. From how you are welcomed, the posters on the walls, how the students and faculty dress, and how they conduct themselves, you quickly learn a great deal about the real nature of institutional culture.

The implicit curriculum is also about what you don't see, as well as what you do see. There may be no students from a particular racial, ethnic or tribal background, or students may all share the same social group. The culture, the way the seminary does things, is as powerful in the learning experience of students as the formal statements of its purpose and intent, sometimes more so. The attitudes of faculty, administrative staff, library staff and support staff such as janitors, all powerfully reflect the culture. If there is no tangible sense of connection between what the seminary is doing, and the life and ministry of churches and Christian organizations where graduates will work, SSD is already being perpetuated.

> From how you are welcomed, the posters on the walls, how the students and faculty dress, and how they conduct themselves, you quickly learn a great deal about the real nature of institutional culture.

There is a danger of curricular dissonance. Lecturers and staff fail to practice what they preach. This significantly undermines the explicit curriculum, and students are likely to repeat the negative modelling they witness. If the SSD is to be overcome, the values and approaches necessary to do this will need to be reflected in the hidden curriculum. As Mark Greene commented during one of the Langham/LICC consultations, "a lecturer's asides reveal their true heart." Their unscripted comments betray what is really motivating or gripping them. If their love is for philosophy, or ethics, or pastoral ministry or mission, that will come out in their comments outside the formal lecture notes. If those

---

12. On the "hidden" curriculum, see Shaw, *Transforming Theological Education*, 81–90.

comments are filled with allusions to the making of whole-life missionary disciples, or student success in disciple-making after graduation, current students will be captured by that vision.

The Null Curriculum

But there is another aspect of curriculum. Sometimes called the "null" curriculum: that which we do not teach or choose not to teach. Obviously, we can't teach everything, but what we choose to emphasize and what we choose to pass over is significant. In some seminaries, there is much less teaching of biblical languages, if at all. There may be strong reasons for this, but does this omission send a signal about how the biblical text and its authority is viewed? Other programmes have few practical elements, or, where they are included, they are not assessed. Some emphasize management approaches and sociological perspectives. Again, what does what is not taught reveal about the institution's approach to theological study and ministry outcomes?

> What does what is not taught reveal about the institution's approach to theological study and ministry outcomes?

It is worth reflecting on your own institution to see that which is deliberately, unintentionally, or unavoidably excluded. We have recognized that tough choices need to be made – not everything can be covered in curriculum. What is missing from your curriculum, and why? What signals do those omissions give? Specifically, in relation to training whole-life missionary disciple-makers, is that stated anywhere, or does it feature even in the hidden curriculum?

Curriculum Delivery

Students learn not just from what they are taught, but also how they are taught. This profoundly shapes learning. What may seem abstruse or uninteresting subjects can come alive through committed and inspirational teachers. Highly important and fascinating topics can become dreary and boring with poor teaching. Overcoming the SSD should be woven into the delivery approach of teachers.

The way classrooms are set up can emphasize integration or lack of it. Although there may be a need for visibility to assist communication with the class, the teacher at the front, maybe raised on a platform, maybe even wearing an academic gown, can give the impression that she/he knows it all, is the expert or "guru" at whose feet students sit. This tends towards a "banking" form of theological learning in which students just store away large amounts of information from the expert; information that is learned rather than understood and applied. This is then replicated when the trained pastor arrives in the church. There they take the role of the "expert," the "professional," who seeks to deploy that expertise and assert status and distance, rather than as a servant deploying that knowledge to train others. Often in teaching there is a sole emphasis on the meaning of a text, rather than a corresponding desire to apply the understanding of that text to help people in ministry situations. Students need to love the application of scholarship to ministry as well as loving the scholarship itself. We need to give students opportunities to think critically and in scholarly ways about theological matters, but also help them to know how theological matters play out in life and ministry.

It is important for students to have opportunity to develop the interpersonal skills that will be essential to their ministry of creating whole-life missionary disciples. Students need to be able to discuss and work together through disagreements or different perspectives towards mutually agreed conclusions or strategies. Teaching strategies can contribute significantly to creating contexts for the successful formation of these skills.

> We need to give students opportunities to think critically and in scholarly ways about theological matters, but also help them to know how theological matters play out in life and ministry.

In delivering the curriculum there needs to be a collaboration – *koinonia* – between students and faculty, creating a community of learning, not just of the teachers and the taught. Community should be the dominant model, not competition, when seeking to train whole-life missionary disciple-makers. Striving solely for the highest grades does not always produce the best Christian practitioners.

Integration of Spiritual and Academic Formation

Training students for ministries that will equip people for whole-life missionary discipleship requires a whole-curriculum approach. It should be embodied in both the explicit and implicit curriculum, what is written and what is embodied. Curricular and extra-curricular activities should reflect these values. This takes thoughtful, detailed planning and regular review.

Most theological schools include a time of corporate worship during the week, and sometimes daily. This certainly fosters integration between different members of the community, and between study and worship. In 1999, Banks quoted evidence from a survey of theological education in the USA which found that less than 40 percent of theological students believed that theological education had helped them to grow spiritually. So, an astonishingly high 60 percent did not feel that they had grown spiritually as a result of several years of theological study.[13] This is a major concern.

Maybe it reflects something of the "Great Divide" that has crept into theological education. If there is a break from class to go to some community devotional activity, we should avoid saying "now we will go to worship." If we are living out the commandment to "love the Lord your God with all your heart and soul and mind," then we will also be worshipping as we study. Wherever possible, worship should be brought into the classroom, so that students learn to feel no discontinuity between that and community devotions. It is important in lectures, seminars and tutorials to take time often to let students pause and ponder, praise and pray. John Stott regularly quoted Bishop Handley Moule's aphorism: "Beware of an undevotional theology and an untheological devotion."[14] How can lecturers teach without first praying for the assistance of the Holy Spirit to be the teacher and guide, and thanking him at the end for that help? Whole-life disciple-making involves the heart, soul and mind of both lecturer and student.

> An astonishingly high 60 percent did not feel that they had grown spiritually as a result of several years of theological study.

---

13. Banks, *Re-envisioning Theological Education*, 200.
14. Shaw, "John Stott," 319.

Conclusions

A good curriculum design process is essential to the development of a curriculum which reflects the goals and values of the institution. We need input from educators, from students and from those whom they will work with – churches and Christian organizations, the external stakeholders. We need to recognize that the curriculum has different layers and facets. Building knowledge, developing and testing skills, changing behaviour, instilling proper attributes and equipping for the next stage of ministry are all essential outcomes of curriculum. To be successful, the creation of whole-life disciple-makers needs to be woven into the DNA of the curriculum. Its evidence should be present at each level and facet.

> If we are living out the commandment to "love the Lord your God with all your heart and soul and mind," then we will also be worshipping as we study.

We need to regularly reflect on how successful we are being at meeting our curriculum goals. This can be done by looking at our graduates and alumni. But it is also worth trying to look at your seminary with the eyes of an outsider to see what underlying attitudes and assumptions might strike the visitor. What is the hidden curriculum, and what influence does it have? Does the culture of making whole-life disciples stand out?

As well as what is written, and formally committed to, there is a crucial need to fully embody strategies to overcome the SSD. As Ferris and Enlow observe,

> To a profound degree, the primary curricula of our schools are not those we publish: the faculty is the curriculum. It is the way we handle God's Word. It is the way we relate to one another, to students, and to others on and off campus. It is the way we relate to Christ's church. It is the way we relate to the non-Christian world around us.[15]

---

15. Ferris and Enlow, *Ministry Education*, 75.

Reflective Questions

1. What are the core "goals and values" in your institution's curriculum?
2. To what degree is creating whole-life missionary disciples present in the curriculum of your institution?
3. How much does the implicit curriculum reflect the explicit curriculum?
4. In what areas of curriculum is change needed?
5. What approaches to curriculum change will you take?
6. How will you review and evaluate the effectiveness of your institution's curriculum?

9

Overcoming the SSD through Programme Design

Ian Shaw

Having considered how to address the issue of the sacred-secular divide through curriculum in its broadest sense, including the important areas of implicit (or "hidden") curriculum and the "null" curriculum, we now turn our attention to addressing the issue through the design of specific programmes.[1] The goals and values that inform the overall curriculum should be reflected in all its components – the specific programmes, the courses/modules that make up those programmes, and the lectures and teaching activities that are delivered in those modules. This section considers overcoming the sacred-secular divide at programme level and sets out a number of examples that show how this can be done, and how it has been done in different institutions. Examples of programmes might be a BA level programme in holistic child development; or a master of divinity programme in pastoral ministry; or a master of theology programme in biblical interpretation.

As has already been stated, the goal of creating whole-life missionary disciples cannot be resolved by simply making sure each programme has one

---

1. In this section the term "programme" is used. Some institutions use the term "course." The focus is on organized periods of study that lead to a specific award – bachelor of arts in theology, master of divinity, master of theology, etc. They may have a specific outcome in terms of training for a certain ministry. The individual components that make up the programme are referred to as courses. See chapter 10 in this book.

or two courses on the issue. That would in fact serve to perpetuate the SSD issue by compartmentalizing it into just one small area of the overall curriculum. Instead, it needs to be integrated into all programmes and all subject areas and courses within those programmes – biblical studies, theology, church history, missiology, pastoral theology, ethics, etc. We have identified this as a systemic problem, and the values that are necessary to overcome it need to intentionally be integrated globally throughout the institution.

This does not necessarily mean huge changes are necessary to what is already being done. Much of what seminaries do is already good and appropriate and does not need to be totally dismantled. During the international consultations that were at the heart of the Langham/LICC project on overcoming the sacred-secular divide through theological education, there was no appetite for revolution or iconoclastic activity by the participants. A number of the participants had been in institutions where there had been attempts at revolutionary change, not well planned and too sudden, which had caused a great deal of hurt and pain. Others spoke of colleagues who tried to start a revolution in their own cause and antagonized other faculty members without listening to the attitudes of others.

Instead, in the consultations held in London, Medellín, Nairobi and Singapore, comprised of participants with decades of wisdom in theological leadership around the world, much emphasis was placed on the value of "one-degree shifts" (see chapter 13 for a full discussion of this). A small change of emphasis, some careful changes in wording, might not seem much, but over a long time they can make a huge difference to what the institution, or the programme leader, or the individual module lecturer, achieves. These small changes in goals and values have a leavening affect throughout the culture of the institution, bringing small but pervasive impact.

The Nature of Programme Design

A programme is an organized set of learning experiences. It involves what both teachers and learners do. We want knowledge to grow, but skills and behaviour should also be shaped by the process. So there needs to be an aim, or goal, for each programme – a statement of what will be achieved by that specific set of learning experiences. The programme will enable the student to master a discipline, obtain a qualification, develop skills for the future and also, through this process, progress in their personal development. So, a programme in holistic child development will have the aim of developing knowledgeable, skilled and experienced practitioners of child development who understand their strengths and weaknesses in that particular ministry and also themselves at a deeper level.

> A small change of emphasis, some careful changes in wording can make a huge difference to what the institution achieves.

The aim of the programme is then reflected in a series of learning outcomes, or objectives, which help test whether learners have achieved the goals of the programme. These then need to be reflected in the learning outcomes of the individual courses that make up the programme, and a mapping exercise should be undertaken to ensure they are reflected across the courses. If new courses are added, or removed, from the programme, the mapping exercise needs to be repeated to ensure consistency. Programme leaders need to avoid the proliferation of courses that don't serve the overall programme aims or objectives. In a number of institutions, courses are taught that have little to do with the overall programme aims – some are more to do with the strong desire of a lecturer to teach something in his or her specialist field. In these cases, the wishes of the faculty override the educational needs of the student, to the detriment of the coherence of the training they receive. Instead, the decision of what is to be included in a programme should be focused on what students need in order to be equipped with personal and future ministry skills. In order to help students overcome the sacred-secular divide, the programme should have outcomes that reflect the overall goals and values of whole-life missionary disciple-making. These learning outcomes need to be achievable within the scope of the programme, and they need to be teachable.

Programme Outcomes

In a number of institutions, well-developed programme outcomes are lacking. These usually exist for the courses (or modules) that make up the overall programme, but they have sometimes not been developed for the programme itself. As a result, the programmes look like a collection of courses grouped around a theme, rather than an intentional scheme of learning that is a coherent whole.

In other locations, the programme outcomes seem to have little relevance to the ministry outcomes the graduates will go into. As one participant in our Latin America consultation warned, "If we send leaders to the churches who are not fully prepared to face the real problems of life, problems that the church tends to overlook because of its lack of direction and preparedness to deal with them, the church becomes totally irrelevant for society."[2]

The structure of the programme should be such that students can progress through its different levels to achieve the aims and learning outcomes of the programme and, by doing so, qualify for the award. A programme document will set out the level at which courses are normally required to be studied, and which courses are prerequisite, core (compulsory) and optional.

Evaluating Programme Outcomes

As a working exercise in the consultations, we took the generic wording of a set of overall programme outcomes, and then revised them in the light of the intention to train students who will challenge the SSD. The programme outlines discussed were already well-developed and had many strengths, but we worked on making some one-degree shifts within them to see how they could achieve the goal of training whole-life missionary disciple-makers. This involved changing some words and introducing others, all reflecting the values we were seeking to achieve. The focus of these discussions was particularly upon the aims of the programme and its learning outcomes – those skills and attributes students would have at the end of the programme that they did not have at the start of the programme or that had been enhanced during the course of the programme. Through the process of curriculum design, these programme learning outcomes would then need to be reflected in the courses that made up the programme, so there was internal coherence throughout. In these changes, the DNA of the programmes was being shaped by whole-life missionary disciple-making. Once the learning outcomes were established, then content could be added which enabled lecturers to teach subjects that achieved these.

What follows is a series of worked examples to show ways our global theological leaders integrated the principles. They are not set out as models simply to be repeated, but instead they exemplify the thinking necessary to

---

2. Barro, "Theological Education."

effect change and achieve the desired goals. Each programme, even with shared overall values and common core characteristics, will be different because the contextual needs in each location vary a great deal. The role of the curriculum development team in each institution is to ensure this is done appropriately.

The Aim (or Purpose Statement) of the Programme

The aim of the programme sets out how it will address something lacking in the student's knowledge, understanding or skill set. It shows that without this programme, there will be something missing in the learner's preparation for Christian ministry. So, the aim establishes the importance of the programme, and the vital equipping it will provide. The aim conveys more than information about the programme; it is its vision or mission statement. The curriculum goals and values should be reflected here. The aim establishes the context for the learning outcomes of the programme. It should be fairly short and concise.

Example of Generic Aims for a BA Theology Programme

This programme seeks to:

1. Provide students with professional, academic, spiritual and practical preparation for participation in the contemporary service and witness of the Christian community, particularly in the areas of pastoral leadership, church planting, communication, children's ministry, urban ministry, social action and holistic cross-cultural mission.

2. Equip students to think in relation to issues arising in ministry, through fostering their knowledge and acquiring understanding of the Christian Scriptures (which the college regards as foundational in their preparation for such ministry roles), and developing their critical awareness of theology and Christian history.

3. Prepare students for effective, practical engagement in Christian service in varied settings, including urban, children's and cross-cultural ministry settings, taking account of contextual features, such as intellectual, social, cultural, spiritual and global factors and the contemporary realities of post-Christian, religiously plural, secular and consumerist societies.

Critique of Aims in the Light of Whole-Life Missionary Disciples

These aims have many strengths. They set out the specific focus of the different components of the programme. They are ministry-focused, with a range of ministry outcomes outlined which the programme will help prepare students for. They also set out the contexts in which that ministry will be exercised. The foundational place of the Christian Scriptures are also emphasized, as is the need for both academic and spiritual formation.

As the consultations assessed this set of aims, they felt there was much that needed to be retained as of great value. However, in the light of the goal of training whole-life missionary disciple-makers, they felt there was need for some changes.

There was a feeling that in aim one the term "professional" emphasized the division between those in employed ministry and others – the laity. It had the value of showing that ministry should be taken seriously and needed proper training (as in the medical or legal professions), but use of the word "professional" served to promote the SSD. The pastor, or Christian leader, is depicted as doing the real "professional" ministry, and this created an unhelpful differentiation between their role and the ministries of church members. This could perpetuate the false idea of the pastor as the one on the frontline, the missionary "hero," whereas the church members were merely in a supportive role.

There was also a feeling that the focus of the aims centred the outcome of the programme in the learner's own ministry, rather than on their impact on their contexts. There was little about how to train and equip others as whole-life missionary disciples. So, the end point was the student's ministry, rather than how others would receive and be empowered by it.

There was also a feeling that the issues addressed in aim three were rather Western-focused. In other parts of the world, the contexts students were being equipped for had other priority issues, which might include the following: systemic corruption or oppression; tribal loyalty, ethnicity or caste

> So, the end point was the student's ministry, rather than how others would receive and be empowered by it.

divisions; living as a Christian minority in a context where a majority religion predominated; violence and political instability; and issues of Christians as the poor or dispossessed. So, although the aims were helpful, they needed to be adapted to reflect the varied regional or national contexts for which whole-life missionary disciple-makers were being trained. This did not necessarily mean that the subjects covered would be different, but the way they were taught, and the skills developed, would be shaped by what the students would be facing in future ministry contexts.

Programme Specific Learning Outcomes

Learning outcomes are sometimes called objectives or learning intentions. The focus is on what students can do as a result of studying the programme. Outcomes are not just about the knowledge and understanding that students have gained through studying on the programme, but they include the skills they have developed and used. To be sure that they have been achieved they need to be tested by examination or some form of assessment. However, the passing of assessments can unhelpfully become an end in itself. Instead, there should be a focus not only on what students have learned and recalled in an assessment, but the skills they have developed for a lifetime of future ministry. We don't just want students entering Christian ministry to have the skills to write an essay or get through an exam but to be equipped with different and more ministry-focused skills. We want to see enhanced knowledge but also changed attitudes, enriched behaviour and wider experience for ministry practice as a result of theological study. Students also do not just need to learn but to develop metacognitive skills – to learn how to learn, manage their learning and understand how learning is taking place. This means equipping students for lifelong learning and self-evaluation of learning. They also need to learn how to train others because much of Christian leadership has an educational dimension – whether preaching, leading Bible

> We don't just want students entering Christian ministry to have the skills to write an essay or get through an exam but to be equipped with different and more ministry-focused skills.

studies, training ministry teams or equipping and supporting Christians in their ministries.

Example of Adapting Generic Programme Learning Outcomes for a BA Theology Programme

In the consultations we did an exercise based on the same generic BA theology programme, this time focusing on the specific learning outcomes, again critiquing them and assessing what might need to change to ensure that students left equipped to train whole-life missionary disciples.

Original wording

Students should be able to:

1. Participate effectively and creatively, at a professional level, in the service and witness of the Christian community in varied settings.

2. Demonstrate an understanding of the Christian Scriptures and an ability to explain and apply them with discernment, relevantly and appropriately to the needs of those to whom they minister, and in the light of an informed grasp of theology and Christian history.

3. Respond creatively and imaginatively to issues arising in Christian ministry in varied settings, in ways which reflect an informed and sensitive awareness of the context and which remain faithful to the Christian message.

• • •

Pause for Reflection

Please pause for a moment before reading on, and reflect on what you might want to change in the above programme learning outcomes in order to ensure that those graduating from the programme were equipped as whole-life missionary disciple-makers.

• • •

Revised programme learning outcomes

In the discussion of these learning outcomes, it was felt that many strengths were seen in what was already there, and the learning outcomes would certainly work positively to help students prepare for ministry. However, there were areas that needed to be developed. After our group of Majority World leaders reworked this in the light of our intention to help students overcome the SSD, this is what the outcomes looked like.

The first programme learning outcome originally read:

> As a result of taking this programme, students will be able to participate effectively and creatively, at a professional level, in the service and witness of the Christian community in varied settings

This became:

> Participate effectively and creatively in the *service, disciple-making* and *witness* of the Christian community in *varied settings*, including family, community, place of study, work and locality.

You can see, especially from the words in italics, that these were not big changes, but adding a few significant words to the outcomes of the programme made notable differences. As with the aim, it was felt that the word "professional," as noted above, could be seen to perpetuate an aspect of the SSD, distancing those in paid ministry from whole-life missionary disciples who they were to support in their everyday ministry in different contexts. So it was decided to remove it.

"Service and witness" were retained. Witness was understood in the sense of speaking Christian truths but also of being a Christian presence. It was felt important to amplify this by adding "disciple-making." This brought a focus not just on what the students would in themselves achieve in terms of faithful ministry as disciples but also the work of preparing and equipping others to be disciples. The programme would therefore graduate not just faithful disciples but faithful disciple-makers.

The wording "varied settings" was considered important because it was a recognition that there would be more than one ministry/job outcome for students, and this needed to be exemplified. A series of ministry frontlines were identified and added to the learning outcome – family, community, place of study, work and locality. As a result of this, theological education would be directed towards wider intentions than just producing good graduates. It would be designed to help graduates in the variety of settings they may work in (whether pastoral ministry, the workplace, the home or the community), as well as the people they will work with. The missional intention of training whole-life missionary disciple-makers is written into the DNA code of the programme.

The second programme learning was also developed from the original wording:

> Demonstrate an understanding of the Christian Scriptures and an ability to explain and apply them with discernment, relevantly and appropriately, to the needs of those to whom they minister, and in the light of an informed grasp of theology and Christian history.

It was adapted by the global leaders in theological education to read:

> Demonstrate a mature understanding of Christian Scripture, theology and history and the *ability to use them effectively, creatively and with discernment, in mission and the enabling of others in mission.*

Again, the classic theological aim of producing mature biblical, theological and historical understanding in students is retained. So is the need to deploy this in future ministry contexts "with discernment." But to these were added the word "effectively," which has a stronger connotation of *using* the skills learned transformatively to effect change than does "relevantly and appropriately," which could suggest it was important just to know about this. The word "creatively" adds another dynamic, moving students away from unthinkingly delivering a set of pre-set responses, or formulas, to specific issues. Instead, the possibility of opening up new approaches, where appropriate, in different contexts, is thereby brought out.

The final section of the learning outcome was enhanced with a missional focus, directing purpose of the study away from just exams or assessments, or even a narrowly focused ministry context, to "mission and the enabling of others in mission."

The third programme learning outcome was originally:

> Respond creatively and imaginatively to issues arising in Christian ministry in varied settings, in ways which reflect an informed and sensitive awareness of the context and which remain faithful to the Christian message.

This already has many strengths. It recognizes the variety and complexity of Christian ministry, and the need to proclaim an unchanging gospel in changing contexts. However, the focus could be seen as being the rather closed one of "Christian ministry" – of the professional Christian worker. So, the following enhanced wording was developed:

> Respond creatively and imaginatively *to issues arising in discipleship and whole-life missionary disciple-making in various settings*, in ways which reflect an informed and sensitive awareness of the local context and which remain faithful to the Christian message.

Again, the ability of the student to function as both a disciple and a disciple-maker is emphasized by the addition of the words in italics. Students are to respond not just to current scholarship, which is essential for students to grasp, but also to the theological challenges and implications of living as a disciple, and in whole-life missionary disciple-making. This emphasizes preparing students for their ministry frontlines and also the ministry frontlines on which the Christians they minister to will be working. The outcomes remain both theological reflection *in* practice and theological reflection *on* practice, rather than just pragmatic solutions.

These revised outcomes ensure that the making of whole-life missionary disciples filters into all subjects. Because all the learning outcomes in different subject areas and courses should reflect the programme learning outcomes, making these changes at programme level ensures that these principles have been woven into the DNA of the rest of the curriculum. All course (module) learning outcomes are derived from, and must reflect, those at programme level. This means that all who are involved in teaching this programme will need to embrace whole-life missionary disciple-making. It pushes them to address the issue in individual course design and also in their individual lectures. At all levels the curriculum is integrating ways for students to develop the necessary skills to be whole-life missionary disciple-makers. Faculty will also need to discuss with other faculty how each aspect of teaching interrelates with the others.

An Example from Southeast Asia

One of the examples of programmes from the Majority World that was presented as an example for discussion was called Foundations for Organisational Transformation, taught in Southeast Asia. The programme was developed to enable participants to create strategic plans for transformation programmes that would address the problems of apathy, inefficiency and corruption that plague many organisations in the context. The aims and learning outcomes of the programme deliberately relate learning to ministry outcomes. They show the potential for well-constructed learning outcomes to be related to whole-life disciple-making.

The aim of the course was to "equip Christian leaders with the theory, tools and practice to launch gospel-driven transformation in their respective organizations."[3]

The learning outcomes related to *character* included the ability to:

> Exhibit commitment to spiritual integrity (wholeness) by seeking expressions of the gospel not only at home and in "Christian" activities, but also at work and in the community.

This outcome intentionally required teachers, and their students, to work in such a way that there was integration of academic and spiritual formation, and also in a range of contexts – from working in a Christian organization to home and community life. This demonstrated the "whole-life" learning expected from students.

The learning outcomes for *knowledge* included the ability to:

1. Explain the biblical basis for organizational transformation in the light of the biblical metanarrative (creation, fall, redemption, restoration).

---

3. Course developed by Dr Steve Hobson at International Graduate School of Leadership, Manila, Philippines.

2. Discuss the salient features of key human behaviour principles and change frameworks as they relate to organizational transformation.

These outcomes required developing a biblical rationale for organizational transformation, and an understanding of key human behaviour principles and change frameworks as they relate to organizational transformation. These outcomes require significant engagement with the traditional disciplines of theological study, especially biblical and doctrinal areas, and the relation of these to organizational transformation. There is also an interdisciplinary element, drawing on social science fields in terms of the study of human behaviour and the science of change management. Again, the outcome is an integration that creates a wide-ranging understanding of the issues.

The learning outcomes for *skill* in this example from Southeast Asia included:

1. Plan, implement, and evaluate initiatives that seek to advance transformation in a strategic sector of society.
2. Coach leaders who are trying to advance transformation in their respective areas of influence.

This wording demonstrates that in this programme there is an expectation that learners will be able to deploy their learning in contexts with a view to transformation – moving from planning to implementation and evaluation – but also that they will be able to train others in these skills for their own frontlines. In this way the outcome is measured as more than success in the classroom, and includes future transformation in society. The objective to "coach leaders" who will advance transformation requires investment not just in transferring knowledge to them but also in equipping them with skills for practice in their "respective areas of influence." In this way, the programme serves to train people for whole-life mission – to serve "in their respective areas of difference."

These intended outcomes show great potential for this programme to overcome the SSD. When they were discussed by the Asian consultation, one potential weakness identified was in the area of not specifying the goal of making "whole-life missionary disciple-makers." So, the graduates of this programme would be strong as missionary disciples, but they would have less equipment for whole-life missionary disciple-making. This emphasis on training others for their ministries could easily be added into the objectives. So, one learning outcome could become to "coach leaders to coach leaders."

Conclusions

This section has focused on how the goals and values of training whole-life missionary disciples need to flow from the institutional level, down to the curriculum, and then to the specific programme level. The stated learning intentions at each of these levels should reflect the goals and values of the institution and curriculum and should eventually be evidenced in the outcomes and impact of graduates. This needs to be clearly stated. But the changes in programme outcomes do not need to be vast; instead, alternative words and emphases, small one-degree shifts, can produce significantly different outcomes that help students achieve the goals and values of training whole-life missionary disciple-makers.

Reflective Questions

1. In what ways are the core "goals and values" of your institution reflected in the stated learning intentions of its programmes?
2. To what degree is the intention to create whole-life missionary disciples reflected in the programmes on which you teach?
3. In what ways can your institution's programmes be changed to reflect the intention of training students who can train others to be whole-life missionary disciples?
4. What steps will you need to take to bring this change about?

10

Overcoming the SSD through Individual Courses (Modules)

Ian Shaw

We have been exploring ways in which theological education can help overcome the SSD in and through theological education itself. The aim is encouraging seminaries to have the overall intention of training whole-life missionary disciples, who will become whole-life missionary disciple-makers. The overarching curriculum for the institution has been considered, including the importance of the hidden curriculum. We then looked at the programmes (such as Theology BA, MDiv, MTh) which make up the overall curriculum, and which need to reflect the goals and values of the curriculum in their learning outcomes (objectives). We now move on to the individual courses (modules)[1] which build together to create the programme. This is where the individual lecturer can have considerable impact. Even if it is not possible, for a range of reasons, to begin to tackle the SSD through major curriculum revision all at once, even one-degree shifts in individual courses can make significant impact.

In this section we will have opportunity to look at how the global consultations in the Langham/LICC project worked to integrate principles

---

1. In this section, the term individual courses is used, although others will be familiar with the terms modules or units. They are the constituent parts that make up the overall programme.

of overcoming the sacred-secular divide into some generic course outlines. We will then share some specific examples that the leaders from the Majority World seminaries who attended the consultations were using in their work.

Designing Individual Courses

Each course will have its own specification document, which sets out the aims, learning outcomes and content of the course, as well as the bibliography and assessments. Usually there is a schedule of the lectures and other learning activities to be undertaken by the students.

The Aim (or Purpose Statement) of the Course

The aim of the course is to address something lacking, to achieve something missing in the student's knowledge, understanding or skill set. It will be related to the aim of the programme but will fulfil an aspect of the overall programme aims that the other individual courses within it do not.

The aim sets out why the course is important – the vital equipping it provides. It acts as a vision/mission statement for the course. It may refer to some of the issues to be addressed, and how the course will do this. By reading it the students understand how important the course is, and why they should take it as part of their training for ministry. If the overall aim of the programme is to create whole-life missionary disciples, then the aims of the individual courses that make up the programme must reflect this.

The Learning Outcomes

The aims of the course will then flow into the learning outcomes. They, too, will reflect the overall learning outcomes of the programme but will be specific to what the students will learn to do in this specific course. Learning outcomes are sometimes known as learning objectives or intentions. A learning outcome is a statement of what a student is expected to know, understand and be able to do at the end of a module or qualification. It establishes what students can do which they could not do before taking the course, or which they can now do in an enhanced or a more advanced way. The learning outcomes of the course are achieved through a set of learning activities. These need to be tested in some form of assessment – essay, exam, project, presentation or other assessed activity.

If the aim is to develop skills for ministry, the learning outcomes should not focus narrowly on mastery of issues within the scholarly field. Bob Ferris and Ralph Enlow comment on how often students enter theological training with a passion for ministry but leave it with a passion for scholarship.[2] For those moving into academic ministry this is valuable, but that will not be the primary outcome for most. Curriculum produced by scholars often produces scholars, rather than students equipped for ministry practice. There is certainly a place for the scholar-pastor and the scholar-practitioner, but it is important to ensure the learning outcomes do not simply test whether information has been successfully imparted and grasped. They should also help measure the growth and maturing of the student, and their equipping for future mission. So, the teaching of skills for future ministry to be gained through this course should be embedded in the outcomes. We don't just want students to get a good grade or get through an exam but to be equipped in new and better ways.

> Curriculum produced by scholars often produces scholars, rather than students equipped for ministry practice.

Once these intended outcomes are established, they feed into the content and they drive the teaching content and the way the lecturer teaches. The primary goal of the teacher is not simply to transfer information successfully but to enable students to employ that information in ways that will transform their lives and the lives of others. Through studying a specific course, we want to see enhanced knowledge but also changed attitudes and enhanced practice as a result. Theology BA and MDiv level work is often done by learners preparing for ministry activities, and the learning outcomes should reflect this and be at the appropriate level. Masters-level work is often done by people reflecting on, or extending, the ministry practice in which

> We don't just want students to get a good grade or get through an exam but to be equipped in new and better ways.

---

2. Ferris and Enlow, *Ministry Education*, 77.

they are already engaged, and again, the learning outcomes need to be set at an appropriate level.

It is important to remember the role of the student in all this. Teaching is not an activity done by the lecturer in isolation: learning is a collaborative effort. Students do not just need to learn, but to learn how to learn, and manage their learning, and understand how learning is taking place. This means equipping students for lifelong learning and self-evaluation of their own learning, and each individual course contributes to this.

As Christian teachers, we must also remember the role of the Holy Spirit, who is our teacher and guide (John 16:13). In teaching his people his will and his ways, God works through means, primarily through Scripture. The text of the Bible, and the way it has been interpreted, is explained to students by their theological teachers, so that they can integrate it within their own thinking and experience and open themselves to God's transforming power in this process.[3] It is exciting, a privilege and a great responsibility, for the theological lecturer to be involved in this process as students are transformed and equipped with life-skills through study of the word of God and related theological disciplines. In creating whole-life missionary disciples, it is important that they also learn how to work towards the transformation of others.

> It is exciting, a privilege and a great responsibility, for the theological lecturer to be involved in this process as students are transformed and equipped with life-skills through study of the word of God.

Important aspects of course learning outcomes

- Learning involves knowledge and understanding, but also the development of key cognitive skills (i.e. analysis, synthesis, evaluation) and transferrable skills which can be used in other contexts. These include being able to communicate subject knowledge effectively and appropriately.

---

3. Ferris and Enlow, 146–147.

- Learning outcomes should be kept in view during all teaching and learning activities in each course so that students have opportunities to demonstrate their skills and knowledge. Study is therefore a progressive developmental process, working towards achieving these outcomes.
- Students need feedback to help them improve, so the testing of learning outcomes is a key element of learning. This can be done by means of formative assessments, which help build skills, and summative assessments, when the skills are tested at the end. Providing feedback on assessments is also an often-overlooked part of the learning process for students. It is more than simply giving a grade, but also enables students to grow through the comments and advice given.

The importance of learning outcomes in training whole-life missionary disciples

- An outcomes-based approach helps to shift the emphasis from the lecturer to the student, from teaching to learning.
- Students are able to understand where they are going in their studies, so they can identify things they will be able to do at the end of the course and what they will do during their studies in order to achieve this.
- Learning outcomes should emphasize the equipping of students with skills to be lifelong learners, able to adapt and learn for themselves. This is essential if they are to be able to go on in future ministry and train others as whole-life missionary disciple-makers.
- They enable teachers to connect teaching and learning with the assessment, which should test the learning outcomes.
- Learning outcomes also create a framework for quality assurance, so that markers and any external assessors, such as external examiners, can assess whether students have gained the skills intended in the course.

Skills that should be tested in course learning outcomes

There are a range of skills to test in learning outcomes, which go far beyond simply recalling the content of lectures.

- *Knowledge and understanding* – these focus on testing mastery of subject matter and depth of coverage.
- *Cognitive skills* – such as analysis, synthesis and critical reasoning. Students are asked to show not only that they know about certain issues but also how to think about them. They can deploy the learning they have gained using the methods and approaches appropriate to the field. In terms of training/creating whole-life missionary disciples, students will need to be able to integrate their theological reflection into the approaches they take and be able to articulate a biblical and theological basis for doing so.
- *Key academic skills* – such as communication, IT skills, the ability to find and retrieve information. Students are asked to show whether they have learned how to learn, and whether they have the skills for lifelong learning.
- *Practical and ministry skills* – those are skills specific to a particular subject area and future employment. Again, it is important that these are integrated at all levels, rather than only being tested in some. This missional outcome should inform all other skills being developed.

The size and shape of learning outcomes

- A smaller number is easier to manage than a larger number. It is hard to test a large number of learning outcomes in one or two assessments, so they should be kept focused.
- The number is dictated by the number of skills that are going to be developed and tested.
- Learning outcomes must be testable (i.e. students can show in set exercises that they have demonstrated them) and must be tested.

A taxonomy of key words for learning outcomes

- *Learning outcomes testing knowledge and understanding*: Describe, identify, demonstrate, organize, employ, (critically) understand, define, give examples of, summarize, discuss, explain, clarify.
- *Learning outcomes testing cognitive skills*: Account for, (critically) analyze, appraise, (critically) assess, assimilate, challenge, compare, consider, construct, contrast, critique, debate, defend, define, demonstrate, design, develop, differentiate, distinguish between, engage with, evaluate, (critically) evaluate, explore, interpret, (critically) reflect, review, synthesize.
- *Learning outcomes testing key transferable skills and professional/practical skills*: apply, communicate, compare, compile, enhance your work practice, improve, make informed decisions, manage, negotiate, participate, perform, plan, practise, present, process, programme, record, report, summarize, test, weigh arguments, work independently, work with a group, write.

The assessment of learning outcomes is important and will be addressed in chapter 12.

Evaluating Generic Course Learning Outcomes

One of the exercises in the four consultations in the Langham/LICC project was to take a series of learning outcomes from a generic course and assess how they might be adapted to reflect the need to train whole-life missionary disciples. We were again working on the DNA of the curriculum, but this time more at a micro-level than with curriculum or programme development.

The example used was from a generic introduction to New Testament module, NT 101. It may be a familiar example from when you began your own theological study, or you may teach something similar.

Generic introduction to New Testament course description
Aims

To introduce students to the academic study of the New Testament narrative texts (Matthew–Acts), and to equip them to begin to interpret these texts in an informed way

Learning Outcomes

As a result of studying this module, students will be able to:

1. Demonstrate knowledge of the New Testament narrative texts in such matters as their historical origins, general contents and literary relationships to each other.
2. Explain the significance and relevance of historical context for interpreting the New Testament narrative texts.
3. Exegete selected passages from the set texts in the light of critical discussion relating to them.

• • •

Pause for Reflection

It is worth reflecting for a few moments on how you might change this generic course description to support our stated aim of training students who train whole-life missionary disciples.

• • •

Our group of global seminary leaders reworked these in the light of the intention to teach in such a way that students would be helped, and help their congregations, to overcome the SSD. This was the result.

The aim was developed from:

• To introduce students to the academic study of the New Testament narrative texts (Matthew–Acts), and to equip them to begin to interpret these texts in an informed way.

It became:

- To introduce students to the collaborative study and interpretation of New Testament narrative texts (Matthew–Acts), and to equip students to relate them to everyday mission and discipleship in different local contexts.

In this way the aim of the course changes from simply understanding the materials and using them within the defined subject area of the course, to developing the skills to be able to deploy them in "mission and discipleship." Although this is a foundational, entry-level module, it is important that it is informed by the goals and values of training whole-life missionary disciples. This direction of travel is introduced into the programme from the outset, and students are being shaped in their skills with this in mind. Learners are also being prepared to relate the New Testament to "different local contexts," so they are immediately developing an awareness that they will need to do this in different ways on different ministry frontlines – whether speaking about the Bible in church, or hospital, or old peoples' home, or with children, or in a workplace, or with their neighbours.

Learning outcomes

The first generic outcome for this NT 101 module the group worked with was:

Demonstrate knowledge of the New Testament narrative texts in such matters as their historical origins, general contents and literary relationships to each other.

This became:

Demonstrate knowledge of the historical context and culture in which the New Testament narratives were written and their intended audience.

You will see there was no great change here. The importance of the core elements of the discipline of the study of the New Testament are retained as integral to the course. In the consultations there was a strong commitment that there be no "dumbing down" of academic level or content in what was being attempted. A reference to the "context and culture of the New Testament" was added, which was perhaps implicit in the original, but which needed to be made clear. Similarly, the addition of a reference to the "intended audience" of the texts enabled students to explore some of the purposes for which the Scriptures were written, helping them understand the literary relationships between the texts. The task of the interpreter of Scripture is highlighted as building a bridge between the world of the text (which needs to be accurately understood), and the world of the contemporary reader.

The second generic learning outcome was:

> Explain the significance and relevance of historical context for interpreting the New Testament narrative texts.

This was revised to become:

> Develop exegetical skills and make use of a range of commentaries in order to interpret the New Testament narrative for their own culture.

Again, the group sought to extend the intention of the course from simply meeting the demands of the discipline, giving a specific focus to the interpretation of the New Testament narrative texts with the addition of the words "for their own culture." Again, this is building a bridge between the world of the text and the world of the reader and interpreter. It was also thought important to bring in a focus on "exegetical skills" which would be essential for future ministry, ensuring students had skills to use the tools they would need after leaving the seminary – including a "range of commentaries." Students are made to understand that the skills they are developing have a clear ministry purpose and are not an end in themselves.

The consultation in Nairobi developed a slightly different version of this learning outcome which they felt was particularly appropriate for their context. It became:

> Explain the significance and relevance of historical context for interpreting the New Testament narrative texts *for practical daily living in Africa*.

This African version retains the original wording, but it shifts the skill being developed from one of simply interpreting the New Testament narrative accurately, to the use of that important skill in the African context. And it is not just the African context in general, but "for practical daily living in Africa" (i.e. on the ministry frontlines where students, and those they minister to, will work). So that might mean interpreting the text with a view to working with people in business in Nairobi, or employed as matatu drivers, or living in the slums, or working on a farm. Students are being equipped to handle the text faithfully with a view to their ministry outcomes.

The third generic learning outcome in this NT 101 module was:

> Exegete selected passages from the set texts in the light of critical discussion relating to them.

The groups felt that the dominant objective here was using current critical scholarship, which is undoubtedly important. But they wanted to emphasize the reasons why students would use this skill. So, the third outcome in fact became two learning outcomes:

> Identify the theological and relational implications of selected passages for contemporary contexts such as family, work and community (local or national).

> Read and interpret the New Testament text as Christian Scripture with the eyes of a disciple and a disciple-maker.

So, the texts were being exegeted in order to explore the theological implications for different contexts. These contexts, or ministry frontlines, were identified by means of examples. The third learning outcome is now driven by what the students will use the skills for, and the emphasis is on understanding the implications for their ministries after they have graduated.

The fourth learning outcome ensures the interpreter understands how the New Testament text functions as Christian Scripture, thereby instilling faithfulness and respect for the core text for Christian theology and living. Students are asked not just to read and interpret Scripture in a cold, critical fashion, but with the eyes of a disciple (i.e. as a reader who wants to be a follower as a result of that reading; who wants to be changed by engagement with it).

The words "and a disciple-maker" were also added – i.e. the skills to study, read and interpret from the perspective of those who want to share and inculcate those values in others, thus making disciples.

These are small changes, one-degree shifts, a few words changed here and there, but they can fundamentally re-orientate teaching approaches – what students do in class, and what they are equipped to do on their ministry frontlines.

An Example from Colombia

During the consultations, a number of examples were presented of how different seminaries and their lecturers have been developing their courses to assist with the training of whole-life missionary disciples. These show how those goals and values can be stitched into the DNA of our institutions from the level of the curriculum down to individual course level.

> Small changes can fundamentally re-orientate teaching approaches – what students do in class, and what they are equipped to do on their ministry frontlines.

In the following example, Dr Milton Acosta, one of the theological educators who participated in our consultations, shares how he addresses the SSD issue through his Old Testament teaching in his seminary in Colombia. He shows how teaching has been adapted to prepare students for the context in which they will be teaching.

Overcoming the Sacred-Secular Divide Through Teaching Old Testament Courses in Latin America

Milton Acosta

By its very vocation, the Seminario Bíblico de Colombia, located in Medellín, Colombia, pays attention to its cultural context in order to determine what is taught and how. This grows out of its mission statement which seeks to train individuals committed to God, the church and society at large. As an accredited institution, the seminary is also required by the Colombian Ministry of Education to demonstrate that the curriculum of its theology degree programme is relevant to the city, and indeed the whole country. Therefore, the seminary has to familiarize itself with its context in order to understand how to respond to its most pressing needs and determine how theological education fits into all that.

This does not mean that the seminary intends to solve the problems of the world, but the school makes a conscious effort to be relevant in its mission, vision, values, curriculum and in every syllabus. Since 2000, the year when the seminary was first accredited, everything done in that regard has to be official, documented, recorded and reported to the government.

In order to illustrate the relevance of theological education for society, here are two personal examples of how I address the SSD issue through my Old Testament courses.

Being an academic and theological institution, we value classical theological knowledge, including the study of biblical languages, history, Christian theology and so on. At the same time, we acknowledge that all theology is contextual just as the Bible is a thoroughly contextual text. It's written by people in real-life circumstances for people in the real world and about issues such as personal piety, family life, politics, economics and international trade. The cause of the SSD is not the sacred text but what we do with it. This includes how we teach it in the church and in theological institutions. I will illustrate this with a few examples.

The Psalms are filled with prayers where penitents protest against injustice, denounce bribes, condemn oppression and reject empty religion (Pss 26, 37, 71, 73).[4] We need to ask how texts such as these can help Christian teachers trying to do their ministry in gang-infested high schools or Christian business people and professionals trying to work in a society thoroughly permeated by corruption and inequality. In a theology faculty, our job is to work with our students in order to help them speak of God in a context of poverty, oppression, corruption and forced migration.

> The cause of the SSD is not the sacred text but what we do with it.

Statistics show that some of the most corrupt countries are also the most religious ones. Why does religion have little or no effect in society, be it Christian, Buddhist or Muslim? Because religious people focus mainly on their

---

4. Brueggemann and Bellinger, *New Cambridge Bible Commentary*, 136–137.

object of worship and very little on the social and ethical implications of their faith.[5] And when they do, their ethics is limited to a few select issues that excite and mobilize religious crowds in Latin America, such as abortion, same-sex marriage and bioethics. If theology students are able to understand the social and ethical implications of the biblical message for society, they will also see more clearly the presence of the church throughout society. This will happen as all church members are equipped to serve as whole-life missionary disciples, carrying out the mission of God while doing their daily work within their professions.

> Religious people focus mainly on their object of worship and very little on the social and ethical implications of their faith.

A Colombian referendum in 2016 made it evident that the most prominent evangelical Christian leaders had a very narrow view of justice. A rich biblical concept has been reduced to a political slogan: "el que la hace la paga" (You do the crime, you do the time). As we know, politicians will do and say whatever it takes to win an election. Christians should not fall prey to those political games, but it happens.

In the light of this, I suggested that a bright student should write her thesis on the contrast between the idea of justice in the Old Testament and that of Colombian Christian political discourse. The result was an outstanding piece of work that demonstrates how the Old Testament prophets challenge the SSD, speaking to believers involved in politics, economics, social work, teaching and so on. Theological and biblical studies do play a significant role at bridging this divide. It starts in the classroom.

Integration of Overcoming the Sacred-Secular Divide into a Latter Prophets Course Description – A Colombian Example

Colombia is a country that has experienced significant social and political challenges in past years, and it is important for all Christians (not just pastors) to be able to relate their faith, derived from the Bible, to their contemporary

---

5. Wijaya, "Constructing," 221–236.

context to avoid the SSD. In a country of widespread Christian profession this is a major issue. Therefore, the justification for the course on the Latter Prophets sets out the significance of the Old Testament materials for the students' context.

Course justification (aim)

The Latter Prophets represent a decisive contribution to the interpretation of the history of the people of Israel, of the people of God in the New Testament and for the theological construction of the student of theology. The course shows they are also of permanent relevance for their message against injustice, oppression and corruption in all areas of society.

Learning outcomes (what students will be able to do as a result of studying the course)

1. Identify the historical circumstances and essential literary characteristics of each of the books of later prophets.
2. Point out at least three salient aspects in the message of each prophet.
3. Articulate the exegetical and hermeneutical principles in the study of the later prophets to create a theological reflection about one current reality.

By use of these learning outcomes, the classical elements of Old Testament study are retained, allowing students to understand the nature of biblical prophecy, especially in the Old Testament. The context in which the prophecies were written is established, and the distinctives of each prophet are established. But these skills are then used by the students in reflecting on the ministry context into which students are going, thus equipping them to use their biblical and theological training in challenging the SSD.

The assessments that are used to assess this course will be discussed in chapter 12, p. 186.

Reflective Questions

1. To what degree is the intention to create whole-life missionary disciples reflected in the courses you teach?

2. In what ways can the courses you teach be changed to reflect the intention of training students who can train others to be whole-life missionary disciples?

3. What "one-degree shift" can you attempt in the next month to begin the process of change?

4. What further steps will need to be taken to fully integrate the training of whole-life missionary disciple-makers into your courses?

5. In what ways will you review the effectiveness of the courses you teach in meeting their intended outcomes of training whole-life missionary disciple-makers?

11

Overcoming the SSD through Lectures

Ian Shaw

Having discussed ways in which we can work to overcome the sacred-secular divide through curriculum, programmes and individual courses, we now turn to the individual lecture. A variety of learning strategies should be encouraged, but the lecture remains a key means of teaching. What is included in this section about lecture preparation can also be applied to seminars, workshops, tutorials, small group discussions, etc. Indeed, the principles outlined here should be used to shape the teaching capacities of students when they move into ministry situations, where they may be preaching, teaching, leading small group studies, etc.

Many lecturers begin their work with a postgraduate qualification, such as a PhD, but have received no systematic preparation for their teaching role, so develop their pedagogy through trial and error. They are left to learn as they go along, drawing on feedback from students if there is a process for it to be taken. Sometimes there is help from other colleagues through peer review and observation. Often, lecturers model their teaching on those that have taught them, or, if it was a negative experience, consciously avoiding what they disliked. All this is often unplanned and non-systematic, leaving lecturers with significant doubts about what they are trying to do, or whether they are proceeding on the basis of ill-founded understandings of what makes teaching effective. Yet, lectures are very much the interface between students and the institution. They are where the goals, values and standards of the seminary are exemplified in the most tangible way, and thus contribute significantly to whether the student learning experience is excellent or not. Our students learn not just from what we teach them but also from how we teach them. Our communication practice will shape theirs. If our students are to teach others in their future ministries on how to overcome the sacred-secular divide, lecturers need to be modelling and imparting ways in which they can do this – adapting their approach to that particular goal. Sadly, if we slip into poor teaching and communication practice, it is likely that our students will repeat that, and important opportunities will be lost.

> Our students learn not just from what we teach them but also from how we teach them.

Current thinking about pedagogy encourages a variety of learning activities to meet a variety of learning styles. This section sets out some of the key approaches to preparing and delivering lectures, and it discusses ways they can be adapted to develop teaching and learning approaches that help students to tackle SSD.

The Importance of Well-Planned Lectures

Once, when preparing a seminar on lecture preparation, I typed into the library catalogue search page of a major university the words "lecture preparation." The book title that instantly appeared in response was this: *Preparation for Death: The Best Preservative Against the Plague*, Benjamin Grosvenor, 1721! I'm not sure what algorithm within the library search engine led to that result, but it might be a good summary of how many students view the pain of enduring lectures! One famous nineteenth-century Scottish missionary described some of his lectures at Glasgow University as like "descending into the depths of the caves of Orpheus" – the dwelling place of Hades in Greek mythology. The overcoming of SSD through lectures will not be accomplished by dull and unimaginative teaching.

Studies of teachers who achieve high student ratings generally find they have an extensive, complex and flexible understanding of what it means to be an effective teacher. They challenge their students intellectually and draw on a range of strategies for enhancing student learning, and they are convinced that they play a significant role in their students' learning. They are also confident that they have the teaching skills needed for their work.[1] Studies show that good teachers are well organized, with well-planned lectures, use a variety of teaching strategies which have clear goals and have high expectations of their students. They give students regular feedback about their courses and provide remedial activities for those who are facing difficulties in their learning. They use many examples to make course content relevant to their students and connect learning outcomes to the experiences of their students.[2] All these principles of excellence need to be drawn on when helping students to challenge the SSD.

An important attribute in exemplary teachers is their enthusiasm and respect for their subject. Students find this infectious. This results in a commitment to prepare clear, well-organized and interesting lectures, and ensures a good relationship with their students.[3] A passion for creating whole-life missionary disciples must inform our teaching strategies, and students will quickly identify this and relate positively to it.

The studies of Nira Hativa have identified other positive attributes of successful teachers.[4] One is to make sure students don't lose sight of the whole picture (the goals and values of the curriculum). In earlier sections we have discussed how overcoming the sacred-secular divide should be woven into the DNA of the institution, and this important dimension should not be lost sight of at the individual lecture level. Good teachers should present a clear lesson outline at the start of the class, so that students are aware of the topics and subtopics, with clear transitions to the next point indicated. Many practical examples should be included, with regular checks on whether students are understanding the material. The provision of such examples, and check points,

---

1. See Hativa, "Exemplary University Teachers," 699–729; Hilgemann and Blodget, "Profile"; Dunkin, "Concepts of Teaching," 21–33.

2. Horan, "Attributes."

3. Kelly and Kelly, *Backgrounds*; Lowman, "Characteristics of Exemplary Teachers," 33–40.

4. Hativa, "Exemplary University Teachers," 699–729.

are important when teaching students to train whole-life missionary disciples. The ability to see the relevance of teaching material is enhanced by positively encouraging students to ask questions by providing affirmations during the class: "Excellent question!" or "You have raised a very important point."[5] When questions have been answered, good teachers check whether additional explanation is needed. There should be regular challenges to students' thinking, and good teachers relate material to situations and contexts that students are familiar with.

These portraits of excellence in lecturing help us avoid the scenario in some lectures where the lecturer does most of the talking, most of the thinking and, sadly, most of the learning. Training whole-life missionary disciples means using the best skills and practice in our teaching to achieve this high ambition, engaging the interest and capacities of learners so they feel confident in taking on the role of trainers of others in the future.

Lecturing Requires Hard Work

Some time ago I saw a sign which described the nature of gardening, something which I enjoy. It said, "The secret of a successful garden is plenty of water, and 80 percent of that is in the form of perspiration!" Well, the secret of successful teaching is hard work. Many hours and often late nights of preparatory work are needed. The great theologian Karl Barth's first academic post as professor at Göttingen came in 1921. He spoke of working long into the nights, often to three or five o'clock, with the lecture due at 7 a.m., learning to mount, as he put it, "the academic donkey (I could hardly call it a horse), and rid[e] it to the university" – sighing regularly "over the mountains of material which I haven't mastered." Barth concluded, "So, 'teaching' is groaning, there is nothing 'splendid' about it."[6]

If we are to think through ways of training students to help others to overcome the SSD, we need to invest time in this, and go on investing time in this. The Langham/LICC project has shown it is a widespread and deep-seated problem. We can't overcome it by simply repeating materials and approaches we have used for many years. The seminary teacher must be a lifelong learner,

---

5. Hativa, "Exemplary University Teachers," 704–721.
6. Quoted in Busch, *Karl Barth*, 127, 128, 129.

taking every opportunity for further research and writing, and thinking through ways to use teaching materials to challenge the "great divide."

Freshness and Creativity

The great twentieth-century philosopher Ludwig Wittgenstein did not have a particularly happy time as lecturer at Cambridge in the1930s. He was appalled at the staleness of many lectures delivered by his colleagues. Wittgenstein argued that a lecture should be seen as advancing an investigation – it was said that in a lecture he *thought* before the class. Wittgenstein's lectures were certainly challenging for students as he drew on his vast store of knowledge and intellectual reflection, but they proved highly effective.. This literally thought-full exposition would lead up to a question, to which the class were supposed to propose answers, and then he would respond to their answers – so the success of the lecture depended on the class as much as the lecturer. His biographer, Norman Malcolm, reports that, despite the difficulty of the subject matter, "he succeeded because he had done a vast amount of thinking and writing about all the problems under discussion."[7] Malcolm notes how this was inspirational to others, and Wittgenstein attracted some of the most gifted and able people from various fields in the university to study with him, a number of whom went on to become leading philosophers in England, America and Australia.[8] His approach was to constantly think, and re-think, then apply, responding to questions and problems raised. This sort of approach is essential to training whole-life missionary disciples. Responding to the questions and problems that are raised by our students, and the complex realities in which they live, will make our teaching fresh and creative. Our thinking and teaching should inspire our students to realize the complexities of whole-life disciple-making and also inspire them to teach and train others to overcome the SSD.

Establishing the Lecture's Learning Outcomes

As with each course, so every lecture should have a purpose. The lecturer should enter the room with a clear reason for delivering that lecture, and what

---

7. Malcolm, *Ludwig Wittgenstein*, 15, 24.
8. Malcolm, 16.

it will achieve within a course which no other lecture is able to achieve. The lecture should build on what has gone before and lay the foundation for what is to follow. The learning outcomes of that lecture should be connected to the learning outcomes of the course as a whole.

In preparing an individual lecture, it is important to set out the most important things students need to know about this subject. These form learning outcomes associated with knowledge and understanding. Then the lecturer should consider learning outcomes that identify what students will be able to do at the end of the lecture that they could not at the beginning – the skills and capacities they will develop – and how these will serve them in future ministry.[9]

The lecture's learning outcomes should be related to those for the overall course, which will be connected to the learning needs and future ministry of individual students. If a key value in the curriculum is that of training students who will overcome the SSD in their future ministries, this should be apparent not just in the learning outcomes of the programme, and the course, but also of the lecture. So, the question should be asked, How will this lecture material support students in their own training as whole-life missionary disciples, and also in the training of others?

The Size and Shape of Lecture Learning Outcomes

In planning the learning outcomes for a lecture, a number of factors need to be kept in consideration.

They should be:

- *Manageable* – usually between two and four is achievable.
- *Measurable* – you should be able to find out what students have learned.
- *Achievable* – they should be at the right level.
- *Realistic* – within the format of the lecture and resources you have.
- *Time-limited* – within the time available that students have.

---

9. Further thoughts on lecture preparation for seminaries are given in Shaw, *Transforming Theological Education*, 165–179.

• • •

Pause for Reflection

At this point, please pause and think of some lecture-specific learning outcomes for something you are currently teaching. Consider how they will ensure that students are developing skills to create whole-life missionary disciples.

• • •

Students Knowing What They Are Doing, and Why

During a lecture, students should have a clear idea of what they are learning and why. So, this needs to be clearly established in the lecture schedule (tied to preparatory reading if possible) and also stated overtly at the outset of each learning unit. If someone came into the room and asked what the students were doing, they should be able to give a coherent explanation of the learning activity and its purpose.

There are two useful acronyms that express this.

WALT: We are learning to . . .

WALTBAT: We are learning to be able to . . .

These should be informed by the goals of the course. So, students should be able to explain (without prompting) how what they are doing is of relevance to the training of whole-life missionary disciples. Even if they are discussing some of the finer points of theology, they should be able to understand and explain its relevance to this greater value and goal. Students should be able to say, "If I understand this, and learn how to do this, then I will be equipped to do the following in my future ministry. . . ."

Structuring the Lecture

A restaurant critic was once served a plate of food in an establishment he was reviewing and was asked what he thought of it. His answer was "it lacks a theme!" It was an undifferentiated substance of some sort, without the chef presenting a clear idea of what it was. Similarly, a lecture should not be delivering an undifferentiated mass of information.

In planning a lecture, work out what is the theme and what are the central points.

The lecture should be designed so that it amplifies, illustrates and applies these main points, which are connected to the learning outcomes. At the end, the students should have a clear idea of what these are, rather than having a mass of material dumped on them. So, what was the theme of the lecture you just delivered? How does that theme serve the creation of people who can serve on ministry frontlines?

Then, build a structure around the theme that is related to creating whole-life missionary disciples.

- Start with something that attracts attention to the theme, arouses curiosity or draws the student in.
- Demonstrate the theme's importance and relevance.
- Present key content in accessible ways.
- Provide opportunities for questioning, analyzing and challenging.
- Create exercises that help students to understand more deeply.

Pivotal Moments

There should be an element of creativity, even drama, in a lecture, all of which help reinforce the learning intentions.

- Look for strategic opportunities to take the material in a new direction.
- Look for suitable places where you can take the material to a new level.

The old joke used to be that a lecture was "transferring a body of information and ideas from the notes of the lecturer to the notes of the student without passing through the minds of either!" If that is all that is going on, then just give out a handout. Students should have strong engagement with the material, and that requires more than just writing down notes.

- Include application to the key goal of whole-life disciple-making.
- Look for transformation of students into whole-life disciple-makers, not just the delivery of information.
- Explain what difference this teaching, idea, theme or event is going to make in future ministry on the frontlines.

- Explore how thinking in the class has changed – you can ask students this at the end of the lecture.
- Identify what actions should follow that will further the creation of whole-life missionary disciples as a result of the lecture.

There is a need to shift the focus in lecturing from "teaching tasks" to "learning tasks," from what the lecturer does to what the students do. The emphasis is not on providing simple answers to students' questions, but equipping learners to be able to answer those questions now and in the future. Students need to not just know about the SSD, but they need to have the skills to teach others how to overcome it. They may not go on to be lecturers themselves but, in ministry contexts, will be involved in teaching, preaching and church-based learning situations, and they need teaching and communication skills to do that well.

Delivery

Once the lecture has been planned, it then needs to be delivered. Students learn not just from what they are taught, but also how they are taught.

- Pause and reflect on the way the teaching is delivered. Is your style lively, engaged, inspirational or boring? I once heard a senior lecturer at a university describe a lecture setting in which, as she put it, "it was clear neither the students nor the lecturer wanted to be there." Instead of that, passion and enthusiasm should be evident, not just for that material that is taught, but also for what it can accomplish in enabling students to change the thinking and living of others. Training whole-life missionary disciples is important and exciting – so demonstrate this!
- Be prepared to illustrate and apply. As we noted earlier, the lecturer's asides reveal their true heart. When they go off the formal lecture script, you can see what interests and motivates them. You can also see how they relate the subject to the goals of making whole-life missionary disciples.

> The lecturer's asides reveal their true heart.

- How you handle visual materials is also important. Avoid "death by PowerPoint." My son studied at one of Scotland's leading universities, and got a very good degree there, but whenever he hears I am going to do a seminar on lecturing always says to me: "tell them not just to read it all off the PowerPoint!" Some lecturers have clearly adapted to modern technology by dumping their entire lecture content onto PowerPoint slides. These are carefully filled with densely packed script in small font, and there can be dozens of them! This is neither a good model for lecturing nor is it a good model for training whole-life missionary disciple-makers, because your students may repeat it in ministry contexts!
- Think about how the classroom is set out and how the interpersonal dynamics created can feed into the process of overcoming the SSD through theological education. A very distant, authoritarian model of teaching will serve to accentuate the SSD by encouraging it to be repeated in future ministry by creating a huge division between those employed in ministry and the rest of the congregation.

Creating Koinonia

There is a tendency to think of lecturing as a one-way process, with the only major contributor being the lecturer. However, in lecturing, creating a context of collaboration – or *koinonia* – between students and faculty is needed. This should be a community of learning, not just of the teachers and the taught. In this, there is an unseen dynamic in learning as described by E. D. Hirsch:

> In language use, there is always a great deal that is left unsaid and must be inferred. This means that communication depends on both sides, writer and reader, sharing a great deal of *unspoken* knowledge.
> This large body of tacit knowledge is precisely what our students are *not* being adequately taught in our schools.[10]

> This should be a community of learning, not just of the teachers and the taught.

---

10. Hirsch, "Creating a Curriculum," 7–8.

It is important to release the experience of students within the classroom about the topics being discussed; they will already have much experience of the realities of the SSD.

Setting Further Reading

The learning in the lecture does not end with the lecturer's closing sentence. Look to give students reading and questions for reflection for next time, or in a seminar or tutorial. Then develop activities to consolidate the learning – these can be formative or summative assessments, or other practical or reflective activities. This can include opportunities for students to apply what they have learned to an aspect of whole-life disciple-making before the class meets again.

Assessments

The role of assessments as a further teaching tool, and in evaluating whether learning intentions have been fulfilled, is very important. This will be discussed in chapter 12.

Are We Achieving What We Intend?

With the overall goals and values of the curriculum in mind, through each stage of lecture preparation and delivery, reflect on how the themes of overcoming the SSD can be integrated. This focus on outcome and impact helps to avoid the "banking" form of theological learning, where the lecturer is the expert, the fount of knowledge at which the students sit. The tendency of this model is to create trained pastors who arrive in the church as the "experts" who seek to deploy that expertise and assert status and distance. The role of the congregation becomes one of supporting that person in their "professional" role. We instead want to reverse this and turn out servant-hearted leaders who are trained to equip others for their frontline ministries in their places of study, workplaces, families, neighbourhoods, etc.

A significant emphasis on reading and handling text (biblical, theological, historical, missiological, etc.) is still needed, but students need to be taught not only how to understand that text, but also how to apply that understanding to helping people in everyday Christian living. Students need to learn how to think biblically and theologically about key issues. We need students to use critical reflection to consider theological matters and how they play out in life and ministry, and in equipping others for ministry service. The goal of the educator is not just to inform but to provoke change – to achieve transformation.[11]

A Summary of the Learning Process and Its Ultimate Outcome and Impact[12]

ACTIVITY	→	OUTPUT	→	OUTCOME	→	IMPACT
Teaching the curriculum	→	Change in students	→	Change as a result of what students do	→	The impact achieved by the people your graduates will work with
Lecturers committed to overcoming the sacred-secular divide	→	Graduates who are whole-life missionary disciple-makers	→	Churches filled with whole-life missionary disciples	→	Lives transformed, the kingdom of God extended and society transformed

This chart, which is adapted from the one given by Perry Shaw in *Transforming Theological Education*, indicates the desired process whereby learning is able to impact different contexts in which students go on to work.

Activity

Students are busy in class.

They are taught, they read, they do their assignments, sit tests and exams, write papers, do placements.

Output

Students learn, they develop – then they graduate and leave.

Is that the job done? Is that where they stop asking questions? Is it enough to say we taught them well, that they passed with good grades? Clearly not.

Outcomes

Output is not the end of the process. Output should lead to change.

---

11. See Ferris and Enlow, *Ministry Education that Transforms*, 39–55. Note Elmer's helpful cycle of learning on pp. 54–55.
12. See Shaw, *Transforming Theological Education*, 53, where this is outlined more fully.

Students go back to do what they have been trained for – to their churches or ministries. Through the process of theological education, they should be better equipped for that. As a result of their ministries, churches should change, develop and grow.

Impact

But does the story of training for Christian work stop there – with graduates now settled in ministry positions? No. The role of the equipped Christian leader should be to impact the church or Christian organization where they work. Those they work with should also be trained and developed, and they, too, should impact society. One trained leader, training dozens of leaders, who in turn impact hundreds of people. In reality, the way to measure the effectiveness of our teaching is not to simply look at our graduates as they leave, but also to assess the impact of their subsequent ministry in the lives of those they work with and their congregations.

Some Examples
Example 1: Building Whole-Life Missionary Disciple-Making into a Lecture in a First Year BA Church History Course

Title of the lecture

Lecture on the Ascetic Movement

Aim of the lecture

To develop in students an understanding of Christian asceticism in the third and fourth centuries and its ongoing influence on spirituality, mission and learning.

Learning outcomes of the lecture

At the end of this two-hour learning session, students will be able to:

1. Understand the reasons for the rise of ascetic practice in the early centuries of Christianity.
2. Evaluate the different forms of asceticism promoted by key individuals like Antony, Pachomius and Basil of Caesarea.

3. Analyze dimensions of asceticism necessary for contemporary Christian discipleship and mission, such as in family, workplace or local community.

Outline of the lecture

This teaching session will enable students to develop their historical knowledge, understanding and skills in order to understand a key movement in Christian history and be able to consider reasons for its popularity in its context. They would then use these insights to explore the sorts of ascetic living needed for contemporary Christian discipleship – such as commitment to a simpler lifestyle, sexual purity for singles, fidelity in marriage or the practice of prayer and fasting. Through understanding the choices made by some in the early church, and assessing whether they were right or wrong, students can reflect on the sacrifices they, and other Christians they will train, may need to make for contemporary whole-life missionary discipleship. The final section of the lecture would evaluate the strengths and weaknesses of the monastic movement's work in extending Christianity through mission, and the implications of this for Christian witness in different contexts today.

Example 2: Building Whole-Life Missionary Disciple-Making into a Second Year BA Lecture in a Course on the Atonement

Title of the lecture

Lecture on the Teachings of the Reformers on the Atonement

Aim of the lecture

To develop in students an understanding of what the Reformers taught about the atonement, and its significance for Christian belief, practice and whole-life missionary disciple-making.

Learning outcomes of the lecture

At the end of this two-hour seminar, students will be enabled to:

1. Understand the key teachings of the Reformers on the death of Christ and their significance for the Christian's personal experience of salvation.
2. Apply key elements of the teachings of the Reformers, such as Luther's "Theology of the Cross," to contemporary Christian discipleship.
3. Evaluate the practical implications of the assertion that "the shape of all mission is cruciform."

Outline of the lecture

The lecture will explore the key teachings of the Reformers and demonstrate how much contemporary evangelical soteriology draws on their work. Students need to be able to understand the biblical basis for the Reformers' teachings, and their significance for the Christian experience of, and understanding of, salvation. They need to be able to explain this to others in their Christian disciple-making, teaching them about salvation founded on the work of Christ on the cross and the application of this to the believer by the grace of God. The implications of Reformation teaching on the cross are very important for how Christians live. Luther's "Theology of the Cross," and his rejection of a "Theology of Glory," is significant for training servant-hearted disciples of Christ, modelled on the pattern of the Saviour himself, who laid down his life for his sheep. This feeds into contemporary discipleship and also mission. The "cruciform" dimensions of whole-life discipleship in workplace, family life, place of study and wider society can then be evaluated and applied. The Christian's primary calling in the workplace is thus not to make as much money as possible, or to get as many promotions as possible, but to honour God in how work is done and show a Christ-like attitude in working with, witnessing to and serving others. This involves sacrificial living. Whole-life missionary discipleship is thus a loving, obedient, response to God's grace in salvation and is the fruit of that salvation, rather than an attempt to win or maintain the favour of God.

> Whole-life missionary discipleship is thus a loving, obedient, response to God's grace in salvation and is the fruit of that salvation, rather than an attempt to win or maintain the favour of God.

Reflective Questions

1. In what ways are the core "goals and values" of your institution reflected in the stated learning intentions of the lectures you teach?
2. In what ways is the intention to create whole-life missionary disciples reflected in the lectures you give?
3. Think of a very successful lecture you delivered. Why was it successful? What did you do that was different to your less successful lectures?
4. How can you build on the successful parts of your lecturing to equip students to challenge the SSD?
5. What specific activities can you introduce into your teaching to equip students to become those who can train others to be whole-life missionary disciples?
6. What feedback processes can you develop to ensure that lectures meet their final intended outcomes?

12

Overcoming the SSD through Assessments

Antony Billington

In discussions relating to theological education, the term "assessment" is increasingly used to refer to the quality assessment of an institution's effectiveness.[1] Specifically, the assessment of a school's "impact" has become a significant factor.[2] While those areas are vital to consider – not least with respect to the topic at hand in this collection – the type of assessment under discussion in this section is student learning assessment.[3] In particular, how might a concern for liberating God's people for whole-life discipleship impact the nature and scope of our assessments?

Revisiting Assessment: Some Reflections
Reintegrating Assessment in the Teaching/Learning Process

Assessment is a key part of curriculum design and teaching. Changes in curricula, programmes, modules and individual lectures (as discussed in earlier sections) lead inevitably to changes in assessment.

---

1. See Jaison, *Towards Vital Wholeness*.

2. See Brooking, *Is It Working?*, which gathers together reflections from the triennial ICETE international consultation of 2015.

3. Shaw, *Transforming Theological Education*, 241–251. For a helpful overview from a broader educational perspective, see Suskie, *Assessing Student Learning*.

There is a helpful feedback loop here. As Linda Suskie notes, while traditional approaches to assessment were "used only to evaluate and grade individual students, with decisions about changes to curricula and pedagogies often based on hunches and anecdotes rather than solid evidence," contemporary approaches enable faculty "to improve teaching, learning, and student success as well as to assign grades and otherwise assess individual students." In addition, assessment can be "used to tell our story: What makes our college or program distinctive and how successful we are in meeting societal and student needs."[4] Further, assessment is more effective when integrated across multiple settings: "Student learning is deeper and more lasting when students can see connections among their learning experiences. . . . The need for coherence, integration, and collaboration affects each part of the teaching-learning-assessment process."[5]

Given the integrated nature of the teaching-learning process, programmes and modules which seek to tackle various sacred-secular divided perspectives will reflect that same concern in their student assessments.

Reviewing the Nature of Assessment

Just as assessment in the wider sense of the evaluation of the institution as a whole has moved from "a purely quantitative orientation to a more comprehensive and qualitative nature,"[6] so has assessment of student learning. The biggest shifts are from a focus on teaching to learning, recognizing that "learning has an impact not only on knowledge (which is mostly assessed in terms of information) but also on understanding, reflective capacities, skills, attitudes and application."[7]

A multidimensional strategy is inevitably complex, with several areas to assess: (1) cognitive acquisition of appropriate knowledge – what we know; (2) competence in required ministerial skills – what we do; (3) character development and spiritual formation – who we are.[8] As Perry Shaw

---

4. Suskie, *Assessing Student Learning*, 9.

5. Suskie, 19.

6. Jaison, *Towards Vital Wholeness*, 119.

7. Jaison, 129.

8. Cf. Harkness, "De-schooling the Theological Seminary," 142.

acknowledges, such a holistic approach "is not always straightforward," but it "somehow needs to impact our assessment and evaluation processes," for "to ignore the affective and behavioural dimensions is to deny something of our missional-ecclesial purpose."[9]

Reflecting Theologically on Assessment

In a suggestive article, Allan Harkness identifies six theological values which he sees as significant for assessment in theological education: (1) we value God's creative variety; (2) we value the worth of individuals; (3) we value the interplay between judgement and love; (4) we value education for transformation; (5) we value collaboration in community; (6) we value education with a missional focus.[10] Harkness encourages theological educators to reflect on how assessment flows out of such convictions. In this case, a set of theological commitments around the significance of whole-life discipleship and mission will carry entailments for assessments.

For instance, with respect to valuing education with a missional focus, Harkness draws on the work of Robert Banks on reconceiving the task of theological education through a missional lens.[11] In part, Banks takes his cue from the strategies adopted by Jesus, and then Paul and his fellow apostles – where the training of Jesus's disciples and the leaders of the early Christian communities was shaped primarily by the realities of missional concerns. Such leaders need knowledge, but they also require the ongoing transformation of attitudes and dispositions, with an outflow in acts of service and ministry. The outworking of this value may lead to a curriculum with appropriate assessment shaped by the issues arising in and from the ministry involvement of learner and teacher alike,

> A set of theological commitments around the significance of whole-life discipleship and mission will carry entailments for assessments.

9. Shaw, *Transforming Theological Education*, 249.
10. Harkness, "Assessment in Theological Education," 183–201.
11. Banks, *Re-envisioning Theological Education*.

where biblical studies, hermeneutics, theology and church history are driven by pastoral and missiological concerns.

Reframing Assessment: Some Examples

Perry Shaw notes that "the purpose of assessment is learning," and that "in this as in all that we do, our focus should be

> Such leaders need knowledge, but they also require the ongoing transformation of attitudes and dispositions, with an outflow in acts of service and ministry.

on the developing of whole people who are effective in helping the church fulfil its missional task."[12] This being the case, what sort of assessments best fulfil the vision to develop men and women to be agents of God's mission in different spheres of everyday life?

To take one example which emerged from the consultations, an assignment for a module on the Latter Prophets at the Seminario Biblico de Colombia requires students to write "a documented description (one thousand words) of one current national issue that is in some way analogous to the issues presented in the biblical text." Students need not only to identify the characteristics of the messages of each of the prophets studied but also to explore the implications of their messages for injustice, oppression and corruption in areas of contemporary society. The module thus seeks to encourage students not to reduce biblical texts to matters of personal piety alone, but to relate them to some aspect of Colombian reality to which the text under study is applicable. In this case, given a general lack of knowledge of history and current national issues, as well as a lack of theological reflection on those matters, students are expected to devote as much attention to understanding the contemporary context as they are to the biblical text. An added advantage is that, as an accredited institution, the seminary is required by the Ministry of Education to demonstrate that the curriculum for the theology program is relevant to the immediate location around the seminary, to the city and to the country as a whole.

Another example: a master's Introduction to the Old Testament module from the South Asia Institute of Advanced Christian Studies, carries four

---

12. Shaw, *Transforming Theological Education*, 250.

different types of assessments – seminars on critical issues, tests on Old Testament history, a reflection assignment and a miniature research paper.

The latter two are particularly instructive. The reflection assignment is designed to assess the affective and behavioural take-away from the learning, with students required to choose from several options, including keeping a journal with entries reflecting on their learning, writing up a series of short devotions for a designated group, composing a mini-portfolio of sketches or photographs, making a five-minute film or composing an anthology of poems or short stories or songs, with accompanying notes.

The mini research paper takes the form of a seven-hundred-word response (drawing on commentaries, books, and articles) to possible issues raised by friends when reading the Old Testament. Space limits us to a few representative examples:

> Ankita is your friend and a recent convert from Hinduism. She has written you a mail: "Hey! I am going through the book of Kings these days. For the Israelites, obedience to God led to blessing and disobedience to punishment. Reward and punishment are directly related to their actions, good or bad. With my Hindu background, I'm reminded of Karma. Am I right in thinking that the Bible supports Karma?" Mail Ankita back explaining the concept of reward-retribution in the OT and if it is same as the concept of Karma.

> Because of all the recent events of violence in the world, a friend of yours is increasingly losing her faith in the goodness of God. Recently, in a discussion, she cited the death of Bathsheba's child (2 Sam 12) and argued that it shows that God is cruel, as he wants an innocent party to pay for a sin committed by their parents. How would you explain the character of God to her with respect to this incident from 2 Samuel 12?

> You were chatting on WhatsApp with your long-time friend Karim. He is a Muslim but has been asking you about Christianity and the Bible. He has sent you this message: "David is suppsd to follo Gods ways completely (1 Kgs 11:6), yet he marrid mny wivs. Does

ths mean tht God of Bible is ok with polygamy?" You have messaged back saying that you will discuss this when you meet next. Now work out an explanation of "God and polygamy in the OT" for Karim for when you discuss with him. (Remember Karim's religion allows him four wives. Maybe he's hoping Christianity allows more?)

In this case, the variety of assessment allows greater scope for students to explore the whole-life implications of Old Testament texts and themes in a way that is contextually located and missionally sensitive. Nor is it difficult to see how some of these modes of assessment could be transferred to modules in other subjects.

Helpful insights have emerged from work undertaken by Alistair Mackenzie and Will Messenger as part of a joint curricular development initiative of the Oikonomia Network, the Theology of Work Project and three seminaries.[13] While the focus of the initiative is on the workplace, the insights gleaned are more widely applicable. They report, in line with their prior perception, "that most theological coursework doesn't train students to equip congregants for their work outside the church," and that it is "rare to find specific ways in which course content is designed to ensure that pastors are trained to equip people to live as Christians in their workplaces." They also note what many faculty will be familiar with, that "course curricula are so full that in order to be considered, new elements must be small and directly relevant bite-sized modules or short videos that can be creatively integrated within present topics and assignments."[14]

Across several blog posts, Mackenzie reports on conversations with faculty in various subject areas – including Old Testament, New Testament, systematics, ethics, church history, hermeneutics and homiletics – reflecting on their experience and offering specific advice.[15] The initiative also provides

---

13. Mackenzie, "Curricular Integration Workshops."

14. Mackenzie.

15. Much of the resulting material is available via the Theology of Work Project website. See https://www.theologyofwork.org/scholars.

"sample assignments to help inspire fresh thinking about how to incorporate a concern for vocation, flourishing and economic justice across the curriculum."[16]

To take some examples, in biblical studies, students could be asked to take one of the twelve elements or four central themes of the Economic Wisdom Project and trace the element or theme through the Bible or a part of the Bible.[17] In theology, students could be asked to write a paper explaining the theological development of a concept such as stewardship, vocation or poverty in a specific era or tradition, possibly even turning their findings into a lesson plan for teaching a congregation.[18] In church history, students could be asked to write a lesson plan along with application questions for use in a church educational setting about some aspect of church history dealing with work, vocation or discipleship.[19]

In the area of formation, Mackenzie recognizes that "most of our models for prayer, contemplation and conversing with God are based upon the idea of retreat . . . withdrawing from the distractions and busyness of everyday life," even though "the lives of Daniel, Nehemiah, the woman in Proverbs 31, Jesus and Paul demonstrate creative combinations of contemplation and action, prayerful reflection and purposeful work."[20] In the light of these biblical examples, he suggests the following assignment:

> Most of our models for prayer and conversing with God are retreating models. Where in the Bible and in Christian tradition do we find distinctively active everyday models and instructions for prayer and conversing with God? What are some practices that can help us to connect prayer and worship with work? Describe some of these examples and explain ways in which they differ from retreating models. What have you personally found most helpful in this exploration?[21]

---

16. Tait, "Sample Assignments," 14 March 2017.

17. Tait, 14 March 2017, drawing on the Economic Wisdom Project (see https://oikonomia network.org/economic-wisdom-project/).

18. Tait, 14 March 2017.

19. Tait, "Sample Assignments," 9 May 2017.

20. Mackenzie, "Teaching Formation."

21. Mackenzie.

Interpreting and preaching Ecclesiastes 2 and 3 provide two different ways of assigning a topic in hermeneutics and homiletics modules, allowing opportunity for class debate and the writing of a sermon. The aim of the first exercise would be "to get students thinking carefully about how to deal hermeneutically with a portion of Scripture that seems to communicate different, perhaps even contradictory, messages about the meaning of work." The aim of the second exercise would be "to get students to explore how the different messages about the meaning of work in Ecclesiastes 2 might help people with very different experiences of work make sense of their working lives."[22]

While these last few examples focus on work, it would not take too much imagination to reapply them to other spheres of life, such as family or personal relationships or politics, or to other topics, such as money, shopping, eating, health and technology.

As can be seen, in spite of the hurdles – and recognizing that the sacred-secular divide must be addressed in core, non-elective subjects – small but significant shifts are possible. Ongoing reflection on the form as well as the content of appropriate assessment has much to contribute to a vision of theological education which is committed to the significance of the everyday lives of Christian disciples and the wider public dimension of God's mission in the world.

---

22. Mackenzie, "Teaching Hermeneutics and Homiletics."

Section 3

Effecting Change

13

Effecting Change of Culture

Mark Greene

Effecting Change – One Nudge at a Time

Changing the culture of any organization is a challenge. The larger the organization, the harder it can seem and the less it can feel that it has anything to do with me. It is easy to think, "I'm 'just' an Old Testament lecturer or an administrator, that's not really part of my responsibility. That's for the principal, the president or the chair of the board." But the reality is different. We all play a role in shaping or maintaining the culture of our college precisely because of the nature of culture and how it works. You may or may not be able to change the culture of the whole seminary by teaching Old Testament with a concern to see every student live out every aspect of their lives in God's ways and teach others to do the same. However, if you teach Old Testament that way, you will almost certainly not only have an impact on the students but shift the overall culture too, even if only in a small way.

After all, we know that small things can make a big difference over time. We know that a mustard seed can grow into a tree, that a dash of salt can flavour a whole dish, that an ounce of yeast can leaven five pounds of bread, that a life can be changed by a sentence or one act of kindness. We know too that in thinking about changing theological education, we must remember that we are not just operating with flesh and blood, with systems and structures, but that we are operating in the spiritual realm. Satan is not at all interested in seeing theological education create cadres of disciple-making pastors. There is a spiritual battle. Similarly, for ourselves, there are not just actions to be taken but perhaps actions and attitudes to repent of. And there are not just actions to be taken but wisdom to be sought from above – we are walking a path largely untrodden. We need the Lord's guidance.

In chapter 14 we'll explore examples of how theological educators have made changes to curriculum, to modules, to individual lectures, to the whole way an organization is run. However, in LICC's work with churches and organizations, we've learned that before educators start the process of doing this, it's helpful for the people to have a framework for how culture works and how it can be changed. So, in this section we're going to look at what culture is, the simple framework for culture change that we've been using, and explore the potential of one-degree shifts – small changes that carry the new DNA and which, like one-degree changes in the course of a ship, take the organization to a different place over time.

"Culture is the way we do things round here," said Archbishop Derek Worlock. And the way we do things round here often seems obvious to us, entirely rational, completely benign, optimal even. Now, the story goes that a group of Vatican prelates went to visit Derek Worlock when he was archbishop of Liverpool. When they returned, the pope asked them, "So what is culture?" "Culture," he was told, "is the way they do things in Liverpool." A statement that no one from Manchester or Medellín or Manila or Mombasa would agree with. Different countries do things in different ways – some of those differences hardly matter, some of those differences can make a big difference. What is clear is that behind the things that people do lies a set of beliefs – conscious or unconscious. And those beliefs direct behaviour and tend to shape every aspect of that culture: the stories we tell, the people we celebrate, the structures we put in place, the priorities for our use of time, of money, of resources and so on. Take food, for example. There's not much pork eaten in Saudi Arabia, not much beef eaten in Delhi, and not much horse eaten in the UK. Religious beliefs shape the first two choices and national sensibility the third.

> Behind the things that people do lies a set of beliefs. And those beliefs direct behaviour.

Or take another example. Who are the heroes in your stream of the church? Who are the heroes in your seminary?

Whose pictures are on the wall? Former principals? Outstanding scholars? Significant donors?

In my former seminary, one of the "heroes" was Sir John Laing (1879–1978). There was a building named after him and an annual lecture endowed in his name. He didn't ask for either of those honours. The seminary made that decision. Every year, at the annual lecture in his name, we would be reminded that he was a Carlisle builder who had created one of the largest construction companies in the UK and that he had been critical to the founding of the college and to its capacity to move to its new location. The focus was on his generosity. And our gratitude for it. The impression, inadvertently given, was that what mattered about him was the money he gave.

However, Sir John Laing was not only a gifted, successful and generous business person, he was an extraordinary disciple of Christ and a man who changed the industry he was a part of. He pioneered higher standards of health and safety for his employees and offered sick pay, bad weather pay and holiday pay long before these became statutory requirements. He created employee savings schemes for school fees and holidays at a time when most workers didn't even have a bank account. He demanded commitment but gave loyalty. Discovering through a manager that a former employee was destitute and seriously ill, he sent a telegram: "Relieve immediate distress and report – further instructions will follow."[1] Examples abound. He directly impacted the wellbeing of hundreds of thousands of people in mainstream society, as well as indirectly through his support of a host of Christian initiatives.

Furthermore, he conducted his business in conscious partnership with Christ. Early in his career, he was faced by a financial crisis in the construction of a reservoir near Barrow caused by an inaccurate survey done by a third party. So John Laing walked out into a nearby field and sought God and vowed that "if He would show him the way through his troubles, he would make Him a participating partner in his business." Despite the precarious state of the business, the Lord agreed. Around fifty years later, John Laing was taking Fred Robinson, a friend, for a drive out that way. At one point he stopped the car and walked into a field. When he came back, he told Fred the story, and added,

---

1. Coad, *Laing*, 94.

"The Lord has kept His part of the contract and I wanted to assure myself that I had kept mine."[2]

Everyone at my former college knew that Sir John Laing was a generous donor; very few knew how remarkable a disciple he was.

The stories we tell reflect what's most important to us.

So do the emphases we choose in curriculum and lecture.

> The stories we tell reflect what's most important to us. So do the emphases we choose in curriculum and lecture.

An Overall Framework for Change

In LICC's work, we've found a simple model that helps clarify the key requirements for initiating significant change: the Beckhard-Harris Model. It is based on a simple formula:

$$D \times V \times F > R$$

Dissatisfaction x **V**ision x **F**irst Steps
must be greater than the **R**esistance to change

To generate change, to overcome resistance to change you need three things.

1. You need some level of dissatisfaction. Otherwise why bother? Your seminary may be recruiting enough students, your students performing well academically, the feedback on your own teaching very positive and the reports from receiving churches may also be positive. In such a situation, there is not much incentive to change. But if you are dissatisfied with the impact your students are having in the churches they serve, if you are frustrated by the thinness of Christian

---

2. Coad, 50, 51.

impact in your nation, well, then you might be open to doing the hard work of getting a radical change to your module on doctrine approved.

2.   The "V" for vision has to be compelling. If there's no compelling alternative to the current situation, there's no incentive to change. Do we want to see the church make whole-life disciples or not? Do we want to see Christians in our nation making more of an impact or not?

3.   Third, there need to be some doable "F" for first steps. If I can't see how to begin, I won't begin.

One of my very favourite doable first steps came from Dr Edwin Tay, the vice principal of Trinity Theological College in Singapore. When a new administrator joined his office, as part of her induction, he asked her to read three one-page articles from Robert Banks and R. Paul Stevens's *Complete Book of Everyday Christianity*. One on vocation. One on the theology of work. One on ministry at work. And each week they discussed one of those articles together for half an hour. And, as it happened, it transformed his administrator's vision for her role, enabling her to go beyond brilliantly efficient task-fulfilment to creating a warm, relational, service-oriented culture and atmosphere.

I love that example because it reflects the reality that if a seminary is to change, it has to change in my bit of the seminary. It reflects the reality that the administrative and support staff need a biblical view of work and vocation which shapes the way they do their work. It reflects a determination that if we are sending people out in the world to disciple people who work in organizations, it would be helpful if we could model to them what a good organization might look like. And in Dr Tay's case, it reflected his conviction that if he was going to create a whole-life disciple-making culture in the seminary it needed to begin in his office.

Now, in this formula it's important to note the "multiply" sign. In mathematics any number multiplied by zero creates a total of zero. So it is in this model: if any of the elements are missing, the result will be zero. You need all three to be operational. As such, it's not enough to

> If we are sending people out in the world to disciple people who work in organizations, it would be helpful if we could model to them what a good organization might look like.

communicate dissatisfaction and offer a compelling vision, you have to show someone how they can begin.

So, for example, our research in UK churches has collected scores of one-degree shifts that have contributed to change in local churches, and we've also identified seven that have had significant impact in lots of different types and sizes of churches. Here's one:

> • This Time Tomorrow – A short three-minute interview in a church worship service where someone in the congregation who is not in church-paid work is asked four questions:
>   1. Where will you be this time tomorrow?
>   2. What do you like?
>   3. What are the challenges?
>   4. How can we pray for you?

Now the questions can vary. As a church grows in appreciation of the scope of their ministry in God's world, the fourth question might be What do you see God doing on your frontline? Or it might be What difference does following Jesus make to you in that context?

But this simple practice can contribute to considerable change:

- It shows the congregation that our Monday to Saturday lives matter to the clergy and to us as a community.
- It expands people's imagination for what ministry looks like.
- It triggers conversations about Monday to Saturday mission after the service and thereby enriches the scope of relationships within the congregations.
- It facilitates congregational prayer for Monday to Saturday mission.

You can find the other six key initiatives on the LICC website.[3]

---

3. See www.licc.org.uk/resources/getting-started-now/.

First Steps on the Road to Change

One way to begin is to look at the short questionnaire (see pp. 99–100) which sets out twenty possible marks of a seminary with a whole-life orientation. They aren't intended to be definitive, or exhaustive, and there are obviously lots of other ways to express a commitment to the whole-life *missio Dei*. You may be doing none of them, you may be doing them all, but they are all potential one-degree shifts that could be taken. But even if none of those are within your power, even if you can't make any changes to the overall curriculum, you can begin. Because beginning does not require any money, or any permission from anyone, or indeed any change to the curriculum. Take, for example, a standard lecture. What's in your power?

How can you shape a whole-life consciousness? A whole-life imagination?

- *Classroom Visuals*: Put a notice on the door to the lecture room that reflects some aspect of your whole-life concerns.
  - A "No SSD" poster.
  - A whole-life missional quote.
  - A question like Where are your future congregants right now?
  - A question like Who are you bringing to this lecture today? Perhaps with pictures of different people.
- *Projection*: If you use it, put a slide up with a visual of a ministry context beyond the church. For instance, 1 Corinthians 13 over a picture of the business district or industrial area of your town.
- *Handouts*: What quotes or data can you use that opens students' minds to possible applications in Monday to Saturday life?
- *The Opening Prayer*: How might your prayers shape the students' expectations of God's longer-term purposes for the material you're teaching and the skills you're seeking to develop?
- *Course Introduction*: How does your course introduction help students see potential for the material even beyond the limitations of the course itself?
- *Asides, Illustrations and Applications*: How do these shape the students' consciousness? Are they all about domestic and church contexts? Or do they reflect a wider concern for mission and discipleship in all of life?

- *Student Bios*: What do you seek to discover about the people in the class that might inform how you teach them and might inform the kind of conversations they have in class? Ask for short mini-bios that help you and your students know what they each have done before college and thereby give the class avenues for discussion and application.

Opportunities abound. None of those ideas cost anything and none of those ideas require any change to a module descriptor or assignments.

The good news here is that because culture is expressed through everything an organization does, you can begin to shift that culture through almost any mechanism.

> Because culture is expressed through everything an organization does, you can begin to shift that culture through almost any mechanism.

The bad news is that because culture is expressed through everything an organization does, you need to initiate a number of changes to begin to create a new culture. Otherwise things will simply default back to the way they were. Of course, every institution is different and therefore every institution will need to work out what their first steps are, what their one-degree shifts are. Even so, it is very likely that over time we will discover that there are some actions that almost any seminary can do and that prove to be really helpful in almost every instance.

However, the point here is to think about what small things can begin to change the consciousness and dynamics and scope of conversations in your college. And to consider where you might have an opportunity to do so. Are you part of the chapel team? Do you interview prospective students?

Imagine what one-degree shift might be introduced into a chapel service that could begin to create a different kind of consciousness? At LICC, our team prays for specific individuals in daily mission twice a week and for a sector of workers once a week, following a Diocese of London prayer cycle created for that purpose.[4] Last week it was people working in airports. This week it's people

---

4. See www.london.anglican.org/articles/diocese-weekly-prayer-cycle/.

working in retail. As we do so, we find ourselves thinking about particular people we know in those areas and praying for them. It's a small thing, but it ensures our praying embraces a wide range of areas in society.

Similarly, suppose you interview prospective students, what one-degree shift question might you ask, even before they come, that begins to shape them for a future of whole-life disciple-making?

Your Ministry at Work

Now, the reality is that if you are seeking to pursue this vision, you, as scholars, as seminary educators, have a ministry in your workplace in ways quite similar to the ministries that people in "secular work" are called to.

Like most Christians in work, you operate in a broadly successful organization with much to affirm but some things that you believe before God need to be done differently for the shalom of the organization, the customers you serve and the nation you're in.

Like most Christians in work, you operate in the context of a set of convictions and values that have served the organization well but that are not, in your view, optimal for the organization or the people they serve.

Like most Christians in work, if you are to see the fruit you'd like to see, you are going to have to gain the support of others in the organization. Right now many of them might agree with your ideas but still think that "we're doing just fine, that really what you're talking about is a side-issue, that the robust whole-life gospel won't make any material difference to the seminary's health. Besides we have bigger issues to deal with." All of which is not dissimilar to a Christian in a workplace seeking to bring biblical principles, overtly or covertly, to bear on organizational development and appraisal systems where the organizational leadership believes there's really no need, we're doing fine.

Your challenge is, like theirs, a formidable one, a long-term one and a vital one. You are not "just" a lecturer in systematics, or an office manager, you are an agent of kingdom change. And to do that over the long-term requires prayerful support and an understanding that is continually deepening regarding the challenges God's people face in their Monday to Saturday worlds.

This is a challenge we address a lot when we work with pastors who assent to the vision and want to pursue it but don't yet know what it might look like for their people out in the world. They haven't seen too many people living it out themselves and they haven't seen many pastors helping them do it. Now, I believe pastors can disciple people for contexts they haven't been in, but they can't disciple people for contexts they don't understand. Similarly, if the end goal of theological education is the fruitfulness of Jesus's disciples in context – if work, for example, is not so much a topic to be addressed but a context to disciple people for – then it's important that we understand the texture of those contexts. This involves not only developing our understanding of the macro-cultural forces at play in our society, in our state, in our city, but also deepening our understanding at the micro-level: what does it feel like to follow Jesus in that frontline context?

> Pastors can disciple people for contexts they haven't been in, but they can't disciple people for contexts they don't understand.

We cannot give students a fresh imagination for mission in the world if we don't have one ourselves. And we can't train seminary graduates to disciple people for frontline contexts they don't understand unless we have a feel for those contexts and give them tools to understand them. Of course, this has implications for the kinds of conversations we ourselves choose to have with the people we know in our churches and outside.

> We cannot give students a fresh imagination for mission in the world if we don't have one ourselves.

The challenge for theological educators is that historically our two primary dialogue partners are our colleagues in the academy and church and denominational leaders. We have an ear to the scholars in our guild and an ear to the church leaders who ask us to train their leaders. But we need a third ear, an ear for the disciple in context.

Maybe you try to have an intentional conversation about someone's Monday to Saturday context once a week in the coffee lounge after church.

Maybe you tell people that you made a new year's, or mid-year's, resolution to find out about one new person's frontline context every month.

Maybe you choose a prayer partner whose calling is to an ordinary job.

Maybe you visit someone in your small group in their workplace. If you do, that will permanently broaden the scope of your relationship and the kinds of conversations you have and the kinds of ways you can minister to one another. And as it happens, pastors tell us that it is visiting people on their frontline that has had more impact on their ministry than any other thing.

Again, it's obvious. You go into someone's gym or their workplace, and you pick up so much, the atmosphere, the clothes, the signs on the wall, what the rest rooms are like. And because you are there, stories come out.

You go, for example, to the London Fan Company, and you notice the shards of metal on the floor, and you ask one of the workers, "What do you do with those?" And they tell you that they pick them up and take them to the scrap metal merchant who weighs them and gives them a cheque. And then they give the cheque to a local charity. And perhaps it reminds you of gleaning, picking up the leftovers for the poor. Or perhaps of how Boaz changes the way his workers harvest the barley (Ruth 2:15–16) to benefit Ruth, the Moabite widow, who is so impoverished that she has to glean to eat. And that leads to a broader discussion of how businesses might be better structured to maximise the prevention of poverty.

When you step into the CEO's office at Bridon in Doncaster, and you see the cartoon on the wall of a rubber dinghy crammed with people going down some foaming rapids, and you ask about it, you get the story of the company and the challenges ahead. And you begin to understand. And then you read your Bible differently: you see the connections perhaps with the life and psalms of David, and the range of decisions he had to make under a huge range of pressures, not least mortal threat. You gain an imagination for how God's word comes to life through his people out there. Maybe God has something to say to you as you go into these places, as he did to Jeremiah (18:1–3): "This is the word that came to Jeremiah from the LORD: 'Go down to the potter's house, and there I will give you my message.' So I went down to the potter's house, and I saw him working at the wheel."

The more deeply we grasp God's interest in the world he has created and his purposes for it, and for his people in it, and the more deeply we appreciate the texture of people's lives in that world and the opportunities and challenges they have, the more likely it is that we will be able to teach and train the church leaders of the future to empower all God's people for their ministry in his world.

Cultural change begins with us and begins in us.

And it can begin today, simply with a question to a student about what they did before they came to seminary and what it was like.

> Cultural change begins with us and begins in us.

14

Effecting Change

Ian Shaw

This book has set out some of the key thinking about the problem of the SSD, and discussed the ways overcoming it can be integrated into educational practice: from establishing the goals and values of the institution, to reflecting those in the curriculum and on down into all other levels. We want to promote change, even if it is only small and incremental (see chapter 13). This section sets out some examples of ways seminary leaders and teachers are effecting change in order to overcome the SSD. All the examples and quotes in this section come from those who attended the Langham/LICC consultations. Some of these examples were already being implemented when we met, but others reflect developments introduced as a result of attending the consultations.

The changes and enhancements to approaches come from across a variety of subject areas, and some are more far-reaching than others. These range from a new programme, to the creation of different assignments. As in earlier sections, because of the nature of some of the material, the names of contributors will not be given.

Changes Being Made
New Programmes

One new programme has been introduced in this area through the work of a participant in the Overcoming the Sacred-Secular Divide through Theological Education project. This is a new MA degree programme, called Faith and Life, which will be delivered in a Romanian secular university. It is specifically designed to enable students to explore ways in which the SSD can and should be addressed.

New Courses/Modules

Others from the consultations have introduced new individual courses to bring a focus on this issue. Awareness of a significant divide between the sacred and the secular in East Africa (as described earlier) has led one institution to develop a course on the Biblical Foundations of Christian Service, which helps students understand how Christianity should impact all aspects of life, and how all of life is an aspect of Christian service. The course seeks to bridge the gap and to break down the unhelpful divide that characterizes the Christian mindset in this context. This course has not been introduced in isolation because, alongside this, all the institution's staff are taken through theology of work training, which helps them relate what the institution teaches to their own work, opening their eyes to the reality of the undue divide.

Other changes are being introduced in some seminaries, which although not as widespread in scope, operate on the principle that smaller developments can have a valuable impact, as the one-degree shift principle outlined in this book demonstrates.

Focus on Relevance

In chapter 11, the importance of two acronyms was set out.

WALT: We are learning to . . .

WALTBAT: We are learning to be able to . . .

It is important that, at any given point in a programme, a course, or a lecture, students know what they are learning. Alongside this they need to know *why* they are learning this. So, we could also speak of WWALT: Why we are learning to . . .

WALTBAT, with its emphasis on "to be able to," also stresses the relevance of the skills that are being taught. If we are to overcome the sacred-secular divide, students need to know the "why," the relevance of what they are being taught to the task of creating and training whole-life missionary disciples.

One of the participants in the consultations spoke of their teaching in the subject area of the sociology of religion. By its nature, the content focuses on sociological processes in society, including secularization. However, through attending the consultations, they came to the conclusion that their previous focus had been on the secular, without drawing connections to the sacred. This prompted a change of focus, as they reported: "I have deliberately changed in my delivery of lectures by showing students the direct relevance to our Christian ministry of some of the insights of the Sociology of Religion." They had added an emphasis on "why we are learning to," and the usefulness of the skills taught, opening up the implications for whole-life missionary disciple-making in what might otherwise be a closed and narrowly defined academic subject area. This understanding of sociological processes also, they believed, had "the potential to avoid unnecessary conflicts in the church or any community of believers."

Another of the participants emphasized the importance of stressing relevance in winning the attention of students, observing "very real interest and excitement for the students who now feel that the learning makes greater sense and that the underlying principles are relevant to life-situations."

Changing Methodology

Another participant stressed the importance of ensuring that the first changes she would make would be in the area of methodology. If overcoming the sacred-secular divide was made integral in the method used in the subject, then these new approaches would filter into the way the course was taught. Once this new method was embedded in teaching, the changes to content would follow more easily.

Including Examples from Church and Society

One significant comment made during the consultations stressed how a lecturer's asides reveal their heart. So too do the examples they use. Sadly, much teaching involves delivery without application, and for application to come to life students need to see examples. When teaching students about an issue so closely applied to everyday life as making whole-life missionary disciples, students need clear ideas of what this will look like in practice. Some of the participants emphasized the new focus they were bringing to their teaching. As one explained, "I intentionally give more attention to Christian living and challenges in the workplace and secular realm." Another was planning on giving a range of examples from the contexts where most students would work, especially "helping students to identify the problem in their churches."

In addressing the need to provide examples of the cause and effect of the SSD, one seminary leader had decided to go even further in their teaching, and require the students themselves to supply the examples: "This semester I taught Christian history as every year, but this year I requested students discuss the topics by looking at an issue from their social context or from their church's life which exemplified the theme."

Through such student-led learning, the students are able to make the connections for themselves between the material taught and examples of social and pastoral realities. Such skills, when acquired, make it more likely that, when the students move on into ministries after they graduate, they will find it natural to use theological understandings and skills to enable their congregations to overcome the SSD.

Assessments and Practical Activities

Although students will be engaged in learning activities during lectures, seminars and workshops, it is during the writing of their assessments that their learning becomes especially active.

One of the participants described how they had subsequently become "more intentional in setting assignments that relate what students are learning with life issues affecting society." For example, one teacher had now started asking students to prepare sermons that directly deal with the SSD, again building skills for future ministry in training whole-life missionary disciples. There were also examples of lecturers making conscious efforts to ensure students were aware of the relevance of key issues in theology to life. One Old Testament teacher now requires a one-to-two page paper on "How the study of Genesis impacted my life as a whole-life missionary disciple."

Teaching Locations

The location in which much teaching takes place was raised by a number of the leaders at the consultations. Was it possible that, by centring most of the teaching on a seminary campus, often in a very different location to that in which most would be working after graduation, this contributed to the SSD? A possible consequence of this was that theology might be seen as distant from, if not irrelevant to, life, especially if there were no tangible connections between the study and the working contexts. This brought to my mind visiting a large seminary in Africa some years ago, where many students were interested in working in inner city areas and the slums and shanty towns where many of Africa's population were living. However, after three years of study on their campus, which was in a leafy suburban location, few went to work in the slums, and those who did often did not stay long. As a result, the seminary started an urban mission training course and taught it in the centre of one of Africa's largest slums. Suddenly the theology they taught students became relevant to their context, as they spent time living in the urban mission training centre or walked to it each day. Through this, many students experienced a strong call to urban ministry and took up posts in the slums and stayed there. It seems evident that some use of a future ministry workplace as a location for study does help break down the contribution that theological education can make to the SSD.

Another approach is to take classes on exposure trips to working and living contexts and discuss theological issues and their relevance in situ. One seminary was running a models of leadership class, which visited people in different leadership roles in society in the locations where they work: a businessman who runs a successful fish-distribution operation and is also the pastor of a four-hundred-member church that he has developed in a hostile context; a famous neurosurgeon in his hospital and theatre; and a member of parliament in his parliament offices.

The Faculty Is the Curriculum

At the end of the section on curriculum development, the pivotal role of the faculty in implementing and modelling the curriculum was emphasized. As Ferris and Enlow concluded, "The faculty is the curriculum."[1] Those who attended the consultations spoke of a deeper appreciation of this and also spoke of seeking to change thinking in some of their colleagues. One delegate subsequently wrote, "I have experienced a renewed passion to dispel this false dichotomy." If all can demonstrate this same passion, surely significant

---

1. Ferris and Enlow, *Ministry Education*, 75.

> One faculty member making one-degree shifts can start ripples that fan out to influence and inspire many others to adopt new approaches.

change will follow. Another leader wrote: "One of the clear changes that I have seen personally is that I have become more vocal in advocating to get rid of the unnecessary divide. As a result of the project, I am striving my best to address whole-life discipleship in my teaching."

One faculty member making one-degree shifts can start ripples that fan out to influence and inspire many others to adopt new approaches.

Evidence of Change

While making changes to teaching approaches and content is important, the aim through this is to "effect change." So, a question posed to those who had attended the consultations was Has it made any difference? Have your students, and your fellow faculty members, changed?

The Response of Students

For some participants, it was still early days as new approaches were being implemented. One wrote, "I think, it is well received and many of my students have been challenged." This note of "challenge" is important because, from it, new ways of thinking and practice are likely to follow. Almost all consultation participants spoke of the enthusiasm of their students. One noted that students had responded to the changes being introduced "Very enthusiastically! The programme is a success." Others noted "much more enthusiasm and interest in the subject, and students participated eagerly in this method." There was evident excitement at the new approaches to teaching that promoted whole-life missionary disciple-making, but also more "participation" – engagement with the material and seeking outcomes in practice. A number spoke of students now having an "open mind" to considering how to address the SSD. A leader wrote of how students had "expressed their great joy and desire to change their mindset at work." There was evidence of a changed worldview, a new mindset, with a desire to create solutions to this problem. All this bears out the words of the educationalist, Susan Ambrose: "Learning is not something done *to* students, but rather something students themselves do."[2] The crucial importance of motivation in learning is stressed by Peter Lindsay, "Being excited to learn is learning."[3]

Such change was not without its difficulties. As one wrote, "The students are struggling but they are becoming increasingly appreciative of the assignments they do." Others were actively applying this holistic understanding of the gospel, both in their "everyday living and the relevance of the mission in their world apart from the church." What particularly drove the desire to create a new mindset, and a new approach that focused on whole-life disciple-making, was the awareness that this made their theological learning particularly relevant. One leader spoke of the "excitement for the students who sense that the learning makes greater sense and that the underlying principles are relevant to life situations." Another described the influence of the varied backgrounds his students came from – "but most of them are committed Christians and some pastors of evangelical and charismatic churches. Consequently, they always appreciate when I go out of the way to explain the relevance of some of the things I teach them to our Christian lives, thereby minimizing the sacred-secular divide." All this emphasizes the key role played by the teacher in promoting change. If learning such things was easy, we would not need teachers!

> Being excited to learn is learning.

> If learning such things was easy, we would not need teachers!

Responses to Change from Faculty Members

Change is never easy, especially for those who have had a set pattern of thinking and practice for many years. In the consultations a number spoke of their expectation that some faculty members would resist new approaches, being wedded to their traditions and previous practice. Most commented that it was "too soon to see," and that the impact of the changes was "not felt yet."

---

2. Ambrose, *How Learning Works*, 3.

3. Lindsay, *Craft of University Teaching*, 36.

That resistance being faced was clear: "Some are enthusiastic about it but most are quite suspicious, not understanding why all the 'classical' approaches one would find in an MA in theology do not appear in our programme." Another person was of the view that the mixed faculty of their institution was likely to increase resistance: "Due to the various backgrounds of the teaching staff, not all appreciate such an approach, but those that are committed Christians are very much appreciative of such changes." Some faculty treat teaching and their classroom as their private space, and resist input from other faculty, even when this is constructive, so patience is needed.

In other institutions, there has been a very positive response. One participant who taught at a Christian university was clear that the issue had been embraced at the highest level: "The university is emphatic about faith, life and learning integration. All faculty are expected to ensure they overcome the sacred-secular divide." One institution had issued a "special call that courses like Christian Worldview, Christian Ethics and Science and Faith be interdisciplinary courses for the entire university. The process is well underway to incorporate this proposal. Christian Worldview is already taught in some non-theological programme domains."

Two Key Lessons

Based on the responses received by those who were seeking to bring change in their institutions, two key lessons can be learned.

1. **The importance of finding and working with like-minded faculty.** One leader rejoiced to find that several faculty had similar approaches – "so we encourage one another!"

2. **Students are the best advocates for change.** Where change had been made, and the new approaches were being successful, this owed much to the advocacy of students, who shared their excitement with the faculty. One delegate commented, "The course has also been highly regarded by the other faculty who have said that it is one of the subjects that the students have appreciated." The infectious and enthusiastic response of students was rippling through institutions: "students have been the natural communicators of the method among other students and professors." One of the secrets in successfully introducing new

approaches focused on whole-life missionary disciple-making was to win the students.

One Seminary Lecturer's Testimony of Effecting Change

One of the participants at the project's consultation in Colombia was Rafael Zaracho, who teaches in a seminary in Paraguay. What follows is his testimony of the change he is seeking to introduce in helping students overcome the sacred-secular divide.

My Working Context

Rafael Zaracho

Even though religion "is central to the lives of many Latin Americans,"[4] the level of corruption, injustice, bribes and poverty is huge. It is possible to find people claiming to be a profound religious person but at the same time cheating without much consciousness of the religious dimension. At least in Latin America, it does not, at first appearance, seem that it is caused by the sacred and secular separation. It is common to see people doing things in the name of God or calling on the name of God to initiate or to finish a soccer game, to initiate or finish the day, to initiate or to finish a project, to apply for a job. It is common for children to be given very religious names such as María or José, or the combination of them such as José María, and religious holidays and stores using religious names, etc., is common. Yet such people are not averse to also praying to win the lottery or to be successful in deceiving the authorities. On the one hand, it is possible to perceive a deep-rooted religiosity that has shaped and still shapes the many aspects of our everyday life, work and thinking in Latin America. In most circles, the sacred and secular dimensions are presented as opposed worldviews. The reality for most people in Latin America is that they live with a confused worldview. The legacy of deep-rooted religiosity from traditional Catholicism can be seen in many aspects of life, work and thinking

---

4. Pew Research Center, "Religion in Latin America," 40.

in Latin America. Even though the number of Catholics is declining, the region of Latin America remains overwhelmingly Catholic.[5]

For evangelical theological seminaries in this context, a burning question is how to prepare the current and future leaders of our congregations, bearing in mind the reality of this context? Even more, most of the current leaders of the church and church-related organizations are still first-generation evangelicals, and the question is how much of the DNA of this confused worldview, perpetuating the sacred-secular division, is present in the life and work of these leaders? What are the implications of this reality?

Initial Steps

Bearing in mind these realities, here are some of the initial steps that I have introduced in my teaching, preaching and interactions, as I have become more aware about the "sacred-secular separation" as a result of the Langham/LICC consultations:

At the seminary

I am more intentional to include readings, tasks and final papers in my courses (systematic theology, Anabaptist theology, etc.), where students can reflect and attempt to integrate their theological knowledge with arts, politics and culture. For instance, I have invited my systematic theology students to propose a "solution" for church cases that they know happened in one of the churches (involving moral, ethical, theological and leadership-centred conflicts) by applying their knowledge and tools gained during the semester. As final work for my Old Testament theology class, for instance, I have allowed an original painting together with an explanation of how it conveys main themes or doctrines of OT theology. Another student for the same class wrote a poem dealing with the images of God in the OT. At the same time, I have invited my students to be intentional in the process of seeking out students from different backgrounds and ages to work on the tasks with. In addition, I have invited the students to explore different approaches and find their own styles of learning. The main idea with these options is to promote the notion of a community of learners. This notion invites us to give full voice and create spaces for those in

---

5. Pew Research Center, 32–39.

these communities to play active parts in the process of learning and taking responsibility for their present and future.

Preaching

When I have the opportunity to preach, both in my local congregation and in other congregations, I am more intentional to include everyday experiences and relate them to the text under study. In addition, I am more intentional in inviting the congregation to find "points of contact" between the biblical text and their everyday work, business, school, and housekeeping experiences. Furthermore, I am very careful with some expressions and their local meanings, especially those that have a tendency to promote a sacred-secular division, such as *trabajo para el Señor* (work for the Lord), *casa del Señor* (Lord's house), *servicio al Señor* (service for the Lord), *estamos en la presencia del Señor* (we are in the presence of the Lord), etc. All of these affirmations have rich and profound implications, and are very important to promote and help the congregation to understand and practice, but the reality is that all of them are limited and relate only to the activities (attendance of prayer, worship and service time) done in the context of the local congregations.

> The reality is that all of them are limited and relate only to the activities (attendance of prayer, worship and service time) done in the context of the local congregations.

Spirituality and discipleship

A common understanding of spirituality, as part of the Protestant tradition that came with the missionaries, is that it is something internal and is described using abstract concepts (as internal strength and energy that sustains us). In addition, spirituality is seen as something individual and private. Even some aspects of congregational spirituality such as prayer, Bible study and worship are for the personal edification of the members as individuals and not the corporate expression of the community of believers and their mission practices. In other words, it is possible to sense in many congregational contexts an overvaluation of the spiritual dimension over other dimensions. It is the spiritual practices – or those that contribute to spirituality, such as prayer, fasting, devotional reading, etc. – that are promoted, rather than *relational* elements (being good neighbours, co-workers, etc.), or *bodily* aspects (balanced diet, regular exercises, appropriate rest, etc.), or *attitudinal* dimensions (dealing with resentment, uncontrolled anger, lack of disposition to forgive, etc.), or *ethical and moral* choices (such as rejecting cheating, offering or receiving bribes,

> The challenge is to intentionally model a life that can communicate that following Jesus is not a purely spiritual issue in the sense of an invisible reality in the life of the disciple.

etc.). For the vast majority of believers, these dimensions are disconnected from their spiritual life. The challenge is to intentionally model a life that can communicate that following Jesus is not a purely spiritual issue in the sense of an invisible reality in the life of the disciple. Being a disciple means that each dimension of our life can be directed and guided by the spirit of Jesus. Discipleship is a visible and concrete reality that is expressed through the attitudes and actions described in the Beatitudes (Matthew 5–7).

From this, some other questions that need further evaluation and thinking are:

- How is this confused reality of these worldviews represented in our everyday life and ministry?
- To what degree has this confused religiosity shaped and still shapes everyday life, even among evangelicals?
- How can theological schools help create self-awareness of the Sacred-Secular Divide among our students?

Some Examples of Class Exercises: Systematic Theology Class
Theological forum: Deepening in a doctrine.

In pairs, class members choose one of the great theological themes and present the central elements in relation to this doctrine. For each theme there will be a forum, guided by the teacher, where each member must choose and personify the life, thought and theology of one of the great thinkers in the history of Christian theology (e.g. Ecclesiology: Augustine and Boff; Anthropology: Barth and Luther).

Each of the two class members should play the part of "famous visiting theologian." Each will have about fifteen to twenty minutes to present the context in which they lived and why this doctrine was important, and to give a brief outline of the visiting theologian's emphasis in relation to this doctrine. For each forum the "visiting theologian" must prepare an integrated didactic summary (two to three pages) that includes the life and the main emphasis on the chosen doctrine, and its influence on Christians of the time. A good presentation of the life and theology of the chosen Christian thinker is expected, and one can dress and act according to the context and time of the chosen person. After each "visiting theologian" has presented, there will be a time for exchange of ideas, questions and answers among the "visiting theologians," the class and the teacher.

Note: The forum will require about ten hours of preparation.

The purpose of this task is to evaluate to what extent the students have been able to understand the great theological issues discussed in the history of the church within its historical, political and religious contexts. In addition, to gain awareness about the impact of our particular contexts in shaping our beliefs and practices, and how our beliefs and practices can impact our current contexts.

Final exam

The first part of the final exam will require students to prepare and present one of the great doctrines studied in a way that is relevant to the context of a local church and its implications for daily life as a Christian.

You should decide with the leaders of the local church the doctrinal theme to be presented based on importance or need. These are some of the options:

1. *Theological forum in the church.* Following the model of the theological forum of the class, present one of the doctrines studied and help the congregation to understand the doctrine and the practical implications for daily life.

2. *Sermon*. Give a sermon on one of the doctrines studied and help the congregation to understand the practical implications for daily living and challenge them to take actions in response.

3. *Lesson for teenagers*. Prepare a lesson for teenagers helping them to understand the importance and practical implications of the doctrine for daily living.

4. *Case study*. Taking a real case of a local church or society (of the "world"), present and describe in detail an application of the doctrine to a case or situation observed without mentioning precise names or places. From this observation provide:
   - A theological reflection of the situation.
   - Specific steps necessary to resolve the situation in the light of theological reflection.

5. *Article*. Write an article for a popular or digital magazine (blog) presenting one of the great doctrines and helping readers to understand the importance and practical implications of the doctrine for daily life. The style and language must be adjusted to the audience, avoiding technical terms.

Note: If one of the first three options is chosen, a written report (three to five pages) will be required. This report should contain some evaluations of the activity carried out in the local church, and how successful it was in enabling church members to overcome the sacred-secular divide. For the last two options, the length of the report may vary.

This assignment seeks to evaluate the capacity for theological integration and connection with the social reality of the students and the training of whole-life missionary disciples. In each of these activities the purpose is to demonstrate the ability to connect one of the great doctrines with the daily situations of life and ministry, and so enable them to overcome the SSD.

A total of ten hours of preparation work is expected.

15

Helping the Sacred-Secular Divided Student

Ian Shaw

If the church is plagued by the sacred-secular division, then it is likely that those sent by churches for training will arrive at seminary with a deeply divided sacred-secular worldview.

The focus of curriculum design should be a vision for the ideal kind of graduate we aim to produce as a result of our teaching and learning processes. That principle, not what we can deliver or what we want to teach, should drive the design process. As chapter 8 explained, we need to design the curriculum backwards. We should work back from the outcome, and impact, that we want our graduates to make. Based on the ideas in this book, drawn out of a series of consultations spread over two years, our ideal graduate will leave seminary as a whole-life missionary disciple, with a commitment to replicate this whole-life discipleship in all Christians. In some sense this section should be the first, not the last!

Deconstructing Wrong Perceptions

In chapter 1, Mark Greene outlined how most Christians across the world perceive the mission strategy of the local church: "To recruit the people of God to give up some of their leisure time to support the mission initiatives of church-paid workers."

The pastors are the "heroes," out there on the "mission field" doing "real ministry," and the congregation are there to support them in that work. At best, the secular work of the congregation is undertaken to help pay them to accomplish that ministry – but the congregation's own work, home, family or neighbourhood context is not seen as the mission field.

As a consequence, our training strategy has often become "to train church-paid workers to recruit *some* of the people of God to use *some* of their leisure time to support the missionary activities of church-paid workers."

This book looked at how to deconstruct a number of ideas in seminaries that have unhelpfully hindered training whole-life missionary disciple-making students. But this mistaken understanding is also engrained in students as well. They have accepted a call to go and be trained to be those "church-paid workers," with an expectation that they will spend a significant part of their ministries desperately hoping that some of the people of God will spend a bit of their time in supporting them in their mission initiatives. Perhaps they have come with the expectation that they will be the missionary "hero," bravely doing most of the mission work. Now, this needs to be deconstructed. Re-thinking those perceptions will not be easy.

Replacing Wrong Perceptions with Biblical Ones

Students trained in our seminaries should have a passion to fulfil the Ephesians 4:12 mandate of preparing "God's people for works of service, so that the body of Christ may be built up." This involves a change in focus for many. There are numerous examples of sports stars who have found it difficult to make the transition to coaching. The move from ensuring your own performance is the best, to ensuring others can perform to their best. But the task of the pastor-teacher, and others with gifts in Christian leadership, is just such a coaching and training role, to equip and empower all of God's people in their everyday ministry

> Students trained in our seminaries should have a passion to fulfil the Ephesians 4:12 mandate of preparing "God's people for works of service, so that the body of Christ may be built up."

and mission – to support the congregation in their whole-life missionary discipleship.

So, with our students, we need to change the mental map of what a good leader looks like. We need our students to challenge the cultural norm even within the churches and Christian ministries they join.

Two key approaches:

- When a student says, "I'm going into 'the ministry,'" what do you say? Why not ask them, "Which particular ministry"? Pastoral ministry or workplace?
- And how will that ministry help equip other Christians to serve on their frontlines – in school, at home, in the factory, with family or neighbours, as parents or grandparents?

I know two well-known Christians who approached John Stott about going into the "ministry," and his response was that first question, which ministry? One was training to be a medical doctor, the other to be a lawyer. He showed them that they were already in ministry, and that, while it was possible that God wanted them to change the ministry in which they were serving, it was never a question of being "in the ministry" or not "in the ministry." One of those young men went on to become one of Britain's leading consultant paediatricians, and the other is a high court judge. Both continue to preach, and are fully engaged in the church, but their "ministry" is on the frontline of contexts other than the pulpit.

> When a student says, "I'm going into 'the ministry,'" Why not ask them, "Which particular ministry"?

Being Sure Students Are in Seminary for the Right Reason

In chapter 3, Edwin Tay very helpfully called for a return to the true definition and understanding of vocation – indeed, to a return to the Reformation concept of the priesthood of all believers. He quoted Luther: "A cobbler, a smith, a peasant – each has the work and office of his trade, and yet they are all alike consecrated priests and bishops."[1] So, too, William Perkins: "The action of a shepherd in keeping sheep . . . is as good a work before God, as is the action of a judge in giving sentence, or of a magistrate in ruling, or a minister in preaching."[2] Our students need to understand this, that they do not need to be in full-time church-paid ministry to serve God and others.

The ideal, non-sacred-secular divided student needs to understand this wider concept of "ministry" or "calling." Maybe some go to theological seminary for the wrong reason, thinking that it is the only route into Christian ministry. Instead, they need to realize that if they are a faithful Christian, they are already in ministry. So theological training is not for those who want training to go into ministry; it is for those who are already doing ministry and need some further training for that and for those who have a desire to study theology more deeply so that they can also teach, train and support others in their everyday Christian ministry. We also need to value those who undertake theological training not because they are intent on entering full-time church-paid service, and ensure we equip them for their calling and ministry in other areas, whether that is serving as teachers, or medical doctors, or office workers, or mechanics, or homemakers, or as retired people. This breadth of students in the seminary class can only strengthen theological education and break down the SSD, with those training for full-time paid Christian service studying alongside those intending to live out their Christian vocation in a range of other contexts. The gulf in thinking between these two groups was highlighted in the observation of one Asian seminary leader, "My students on the full-time pastoral ministry track are quite lost in the lectures on marketplace theology." Yet, how are the pastoral ministry track students to equip others for mission in the marketplace if they do not have an understanding of their working context and the issues they face there? To have

> We need to value those who undertake theological training not because they are intent on entering full-time church-paid service, and ensure we equip them for their calling and ministry in other areas.

---

1. Luther, *Christian in Society*, 130.
2. Perkins, *Treatise*, 39.

studied alongside some who are already working in the marketplace enhances that understanding. The measure of effective theological education is not just graduates with knowledge, but also those who have effective ministries in churches and Christian organizations and who inspire and empower others for service. Medical training that produces highly knowledgeable doctors, but who lack the skills to treat or care for patients, is not a success. Indeed, it may be dangerous.

> Medical training that produces highly knowledgeable doctors, but who lack the skills to treat or care for patients, is not a success. Indeed, it may be dangerous.

Portrait of the Ideal Graduate

So what does the "ideal graduate," the non-sacred-secular divided student, look like?

During the Langham/LICC consultation in Colombia, Latin America, we spent one afternoon identifying the key characteristics of the ideal graduate. Different terms were suggested – "intentional learner," "practitioner," "servant" – but none fully captured what each one means. After a great deal of friendly and animated discussion in Spanish, the following list of six key abilities emerged.

Our graduates should be faithful disciples who have the characteristics described in the following sections.

The Ability to Study, Understand and Apply the Bible to Their Context

The non-sacred-secular divided student will love the word of God and will love to study it. They will humbly submit to what it teaches. As one contributor to the Colombia consultation put it, "The ultimate source of authority rests in the Bible, not in the pronouncements of some 'big name.'" They will see such study as a dimension of the command to "love the Lord your God with all your heart, all your soul, all your mind, all your strength" (Mark 12:30). They will study the word of God not just to gain information and understanding but as a way of truly getting to know the Lord, recognizing that "the beginning of wisdom is the fear of God" (Prov 9:10). They will faithfully and lovingly hold on to the word of God because it is the truth and will be equipped to "encourage others by sound doctrine, and refute those who oppose it" (Titus 1:9). Such students will be confident users of their theological learning, prepared to stand up and defend the truth and also to challenge false and erroneous interpretations. They will be lifelong theological learners, and they will excite others to be the same. In a sense, the teaching heard in class will still be going on fifteen years later. They will know how to critique, analyze and then apply the knowledge they acquire. They will use knowledge to develop themselves in Christian ministry situations. The Bible will not be the only book the non-sacred-secular divided student studies, but, as the core discipline of Christian theology, it will permeate all other fields of their theological study. This study should work itself deeply into the life and character of the student. A student whose heart and mind are saturated in the word of God, rightly understood as the word for all of life, should not be sacred-secular divided – no aspect of their thoughts, actions or being will be untouched by the sacred.

The non-sacred-secular divided student will also be able to apply the Scriptures to their context. They will be able to build bridges between the world of the text, and that in which they currently exercise ministry. This needs a strong ability to understand and interpret both text and context, and a high capacity to train others to do the same. Theological studies should, as stated in *The Cape Town Commitment*, equip all God's people "for the missional task of understanding and relevantly communicating God's truth in every cultural context."[3]

The Ability to Serve as Part of a Community

The model of ministry that sees most mission work as done by the church-paid workers immediately creates a dichotomy in the Christian church between those in "the ministry" and the rest. Sacred-secular divided pastors often end up living a life apart from the Christian community they lead; they are encouraged not to develop friendships with members of their congregation and are viewed as professional specialists who are only called on in times of great need. All this creates isolation, loneliness and individualism. There is also a high rate of burn-out in those who adopt such a model of ministry.

---

3. Third Lausanne Congress, *Cape Town Commitment*, sec. 2F.4.

The leaders in the Latin American consultation were crying out for leaders and their church communities to develop a sense of mutual service, to break down the individualism and loneliness that characterizes much full-time paid ministry. Theological institutions need to develop such models, so that students are well-versed in community learning and support, where the contributions of all are welcomed and encouraged. Students need to know how to demonstrate the faithful practice of everyday spiritual disciplines in community, not just in their own personal quiet times.

The Ability to Identify and Enable Christians to Use Their Gifts in Whole-Life Ministry

The sacred-secular divided student will see "the ministry" as their personal fiefdom. They will see their theological learning as a matter of pride and something to be guarded rather than shared. They will feel threatened by the gifts and abilities of others and will be reluctant to give them opportunities for ministry because they are "unqualified." Their congregations will view them with respect, even awe, but will not feel empowered or enabled by them.

The non-sacred-secular divided student will be a disciple-maker. Ideally, they will make disciples because they have been trained to do this. At one consultation, the practice of one seminary that runs a course on discipleship was outlined. The key learning activity is to take on the discipling of a Christian believer over a year and write a reflective journal on that process. Through this sort of exercise, whole-life disciple-making will be stitched not only into the DNA of the institution but also into the DNA of the students that attend it.

The ideal graduate will rejoice in identifying and enabling the gifts of others. Seeing Ephesians 4:12–13 worked out will be their priority. It will be their delight to prepare others for "works of service," knowing that a hundred trained church members will have far more impact than one well-trained minister on their own. In this way, they will delight in seeing the body of Christ "built up," for it is not Pastor X's church, but Christ's body. Their longing will be for the maturing of the

> It will be their delight to prepare others for "works of service," knowing that a hundred trained church members will have far more impact than one well-trained minister on their own.

body until they attain to "the whole measure of the fullness of Christ." Their focus will be on identifying the gifts each Christian has and finding the ministry frontline on which that Christian can serve – whether that vocation is in the workplace, the home, the place of education, the family or the community. In this way, they will demonstrate the vision and imagination to equip other Christians for their mission in the world, the training that consultation participants from Latin America saw as so lacking in their context.

Some years ago, I was speaking with a man in a church who was an engineer with a major company making aeroplane engines. He said to me, "I have often though it would be good to do something useful in service for the Lord – like you are doing." I was at the time working for Langham Partnership, travelling extensively around the world to visit theological seminaries and their leaders. So I asked him about his work, which involved precision manufacturing of jet engine parts, and after listening to him describing his job, I said, "Can't you see that what you are doing is a vital part of mission, ensuring that planes carrying Christian missionaries and pastors are safe and reliable? You are also doing vital humanitarian work, showing God's love and compassion for humanity by ensuring planes don't fall from the sky. Your work saves lives." And he rubbed his chin, with a bit of a smile on his face. "Oh, I've never thought of that." I pressed on, thinking of the huge factory in which he worked, "Remember, your work brings you into contact with far more non-Christians every day than if you were in a full-time church ministry position." And there was now a clear smile on his face. "I've never thought of that either." So, I stressed to him, "you are doing useful service for the Lord on the mission field already. It may be one day God puts you in another field of Christian mission, but for now you are already on the frontline."

The Ability to Work as Part of a Team

The leaders of seminaries in the consultations were distressed by how often students were not team players. On graduation they found it difficult to work with others and could not handle disagreements or those with different approaches or emphases. Again, this suggests students who are sacred-secular divided. Their faith is lived out with a strong emphasis on the vertical axis – how they personally relate to God in their own devotions, which may be very strong – but with little emphasis on the horizontal dimension of relating to others. They have divided the command to "love the Lord your God," from the command to "love your neighbour as yourself" (Mark 12:30–31). The result is often divided teams and divided churches. Whole-life missionary discipleship involves the ability to work with others, some of whom may not agree with the graduate about everything and who may have different tastes. So, their seemingly strong devotional life is not impacting their relational life. In this the church is greatly weakened. Strong teams are stronger than lone ministries or divided ministries. As a friend of mine used to say, "One person cannot shift half a piano, but two people can shift a whole one."

This means that in preparing students for whole-life missionary disciple-making, there should be opportunities in theological education for collaborative learning and teamwork, so that these key skills and attributes can be developed and employed.

The Ability to Demonstrate Integrity and Christ-Like Witness

The opposite of integration is dis-integration. The sacred-secular divided student demonstrates such a dis-integration in their studies, and future ministry, when they are unable to connect their academic formation with their spiritual formation and Christian living. They are unable to see how theological training is designed to integrate these two elements, with a view to the transformation of the people of God according to the image of Christ, and in preparation for mission in the world. Students need to be faithful to the word of God and theological orthodoxy, and they need to connect this to right Christian living. It remains a cause of dismay that cases of academic misconduct, such as plagiarism, are common in theological seminaries. It is a problem that demonstrates this lack of integration and a failure to "love your neighbour," respecting her or his work by acknowledging it as a source. It is also a failure to use the mind as part of "worshipping the Lord your God," and instead sees studies and assignments as a means in themselves, rather than seeing them as a faithful offering to God as well as merely a requirement for the examiner.

The non-sacred-secular divided student will have a spirituality that impacts heart, hands and mind. Students should find it impossible to separate their theological studies from right Christian living. Paul called the Philippian church to have the same mind as that of Christ, "not looking to your own interests but each of you to the interests of the others" (Phil 2:4). A separation between right living and theological study demonstrated in seminary is likely to be repeated in a ministry context. Our global leaders in the consultations sadly spoke of churches and ministries ruined by corruption, immorality, infighting and division.

The Ability to Inspire, Equip and Accompany People on Their Christian Journey in a Sacred-Secular Divided World

The sacred-secular divided student will become the sacred-secular divided leader or minister, alone and separate in the pulpit, struggling to relate the gospel to the everyday realities of the congregation. They may be highly qualified, highly intellectual, widely read and theologically well-versed, but much of their ministry will be irrelevant and incomprehensible to their congregation. Excelling at parsing theological minutiae, they will be unable to relate it to a person bored and unfulfilled in their job or facing a life crisis. Their congregation will view them as remote and uninterested in their situation in life.

The non-sacred-secular divided student will be convinced of the importance of "being there" in ministry, whether rejoicing beside a cradle with the parents of a newborn or comforting the weeping at a graveside. They will be welcomed in such contexts because of their love for those they serve, and also because they have inspired and equipped their congregations for just such situations in the Christian journey. They will be there to minister, but they will also find they are being ministered to, because there is integration between what they believe and how they live.

The theological training of such students will have widely exposed them to a rich range of examples of others who are whole-life missionary disciples and are "able to inspire and equip and accompany people on their Christian journey."

Such were the aspirations and ambitions expressed by our global leaders for the ideal graduate – the non-sacred-secular divided student. They were aptly summarized by one of the contributors to the Langham/LICC consultations:

> In theology –
> The first task is to listen
> The second task is to teach others
> And the greatest task is to walk together humbly with our God.

Appendix

Project Participants

Those who attended the consultations in London (January 2017), Colombia (May 2017), Kenya (December 2017) and Singapore (February 2018) and others who contributed significantly to the project:

- Dr Milton Acosta – Old Testament Professor, Fundación Universitaria Seminario Biblico de Colombia, Colombia
- Dr George Atido – President, Université Shalom de Bunia, Democratic Republic of Congo
- Dr Collium Banda – Vice Principal, Theological College of Zimbabwe, Zimbabwe
- Dr Juan José Barreda Toscano – President and Teacher, Biblica Virtual, Argentina
- Dr Antonio Carlos Barro – General Director, Faculdade Teológica Sul America, Brazil
- Dr Mona Bias – Academic Dean, International Graduate School of Leadership, Philippines
- Mr Antony Billington – Senior Pastor, Beacon Church, Ashton-in-Makerfield and Theology Adviser, London Institute for Contemporary Christianity (LICC), UK
- Prof Sunday Bobai Agang – Director of PhD Programme, ECWA Theological Seminary, Kagoro, Nigeria
- Prof Bernard Boyo – Professor of Bible and Theology, Daystar University, Nairobi, Kenya
- Dr Oscar A. Campos – Professor of Theology and President of Seminario Teológico Centroamericano, Guatemala
- Rev Dr Clement Mook-Soo Chia – Principal, Singapore Bible College, Singapore

- Dr Havilah Dharamraj – Academic Dean and Head of the Department of Old Testament, South Asia Institute of Advanced Christian Studies, Bangalore, India
- Rev Dr Alexander Fajardo Sánchez – Online Programs Director and Board Member, Facultad Teológica Latinoamericana (FATELA), Colombia
- Dr Greg Forster – Director, Oikonomia Network, and Visiting Assistant Professor of Faith and Culture, Trinity International University, USA
- Dr Timoteo Gener – President and Professor of Theology, Asia Theological Seminary, Philippines
- Mr Mark Greene – Executive Director, London Institute for Contemporary Christianity (LICC), UK
- Miss Elizabeth Hitchcock – Executive Assistant, Langham Partnership, UK
- Rev Dr Neil Hudson – Director of Church Relationships, LICC, UK
- Miss Pippa James – Executive Assistant, LICC, UK
- Dr Theresa Lua – General Secretary, Asia Theological Association, Philippines
- Prof Marcel Măcelaru – Professor of Theology (Prof Dr Habil), Faculty of Humanities and Social Sciences, "Aurel Vlaicu" University, Arad, Romania
- Dr Dinorah B. Méndez – Professor of Theology and Church History, Mexican Baptist Theological Seminary, Lomas Verdes, Mexico
- Dr Rhodian Munyenyembe – Senior Lecturer and Head of Theology and Religious Studies Department, Mzuzu University, Malawi
- Prof David Ngaruiya – Ag. Deputy Vice Chancellor, Academic Affairs, International Leadership University, Kenya
- Prof James Nkansah-Obrempong – Academic Dean, Africa International University, Kenya
- Dr Javier Ortega – Lecturer, Christian and Missionary Alliance Seminary, Chile
- Dr Ruth Padilla DeBorst – President, Comunidad de Estudios Teológicos Interdisciplinarios (CETI), Costa Rica
- Rev Dr Finny Philip – Principal, Filadelfia Bible College, India

- Dr Ivor Poobalan – Principal, Colombo Theological Seminary, Sri Lanka
- Rev Canon Dr Alfred Uwimana Sebahene – Lecturer in Systematic Theology and Ethics, St John's University of Tanzania, School of Theology and Religious Studies, Tanzania
- Dr Ian J. Shaw – CEO of the Opal Trust, and he oversees Postdoctoral projects for Langham Partnership. He is also an Honorary Fellow of the School of Divinity, New College, Edinburgh, UK, and was formerly Provost of Union School of Theology, UK
- Mr Grant Smith – CEO, Hand in Hand Group, UK
- Dr Sylvia Soeherman – Academic Dean, Sekolah Tinggi Teologi SAAT, Indonesia
- Dr Frew Tamrat – Principal, Evangelical Theological College, Addis Ababa, Ethiopia
- Rev Dr Edwin Tay – Vice Principal, Trinity Theological College, Singapore
- Miss Anna Watkin – Personal Assistant to the Executive Director, LICC, UK
- Dr Bernard K. Wong – Associate Dean, China Graduate School of Theology, Hong Kong
- Dr Rafael Zaracho – Academic Dean, Instituto Biblico Asunción, Paraguay

Bibliography

Althaus, P. *The Theology of Martin Luther*. Philadelphia: Fortress Press, 1966.

Ambrose, S. A. *How Learning Works: Seven Research-Based Principles for Smart Teaching*. San Francisco: Jossey-Bass, 2010.

Ames, W. *The Marrow of Theology*. Edited by John Dykstra Eusden. Grand Rapids, MI: Baker, 1968.

Armstrong, Chris. "About God's Business." *Christian History* 110 (2014): 32–36.

Ashford, Bruce Riley, and Heath A. Thomas. *The Gospel of Our King: Bible, Worldview, and the Mission of Every Christian*. Grand Rapids: Baker Academic, 2019.

Athyal, Saphir. "Toward an Asian Christian Theology." In *What Asian Christians Are Thinking*, edited by Douglas Elwood, 68–84. Quezon City, Philippines: New Day, 1976.

Augustine. "Sermon LIV" in *Sermons on Selected Lessons of the New Testament*. In *Augustine: Sermon on the Mount; Harmony of the Gospels; Homilies on the Gospels*, edited by Philip Schaff. Vol. 6 of *Nicene and Post-Nicene Fathers: First Series*. Grand Rapids: Eerdmans, 1980.

Báez-Camargo, Gonzálo. "Tiempo de Saltar de las Trincheras." *Misión* (Octubre–Diciembre, 1982): 15.

Banks, Robert. *Redeeming the Routines: Bringing Theology to Life*. Wheaton: BridgePoint, 1993.

———. *Re-envisioning Theological Education: Exploring a Missional Alternative to Current Methods*. Grand Rapids: Eerdmans, 1999.

Barro, Antonio. "Theological Education for the Third Millennium." Paper presented at Langham/LICC Consultation on Overcoming the Sacred-Secular Divide through Theological Education, Medellín, Colombia, May 2017.

Bartholomew, Craig G. *Contours of the Kuyperian Tradition: A Systematic Introduction*. Downers Grove: IVP, 2017.

Bartholomew, Craig G., and Michael W. Goheen. *The Drama of Scripture: Finding Our Place in the Biblical Story*. 2nd ed. Grand Rapids: Baker Academic, 2014.

Bartholomew, Craig G., and Ryan P. O'Dowd. *Old Testament Wisdom Literature: A Theological Introduction*. Nottingham: Apollos, 2011.

Bastian, Jean Pierre. *Historia del Protestantismo en América Latina*. México: CUPSA, 1990.

———. *Protestantismo y Sociedad en México*. México: CUPSA, 1983.

Bates, Matthew W. *Gospel Allegiance: What Faith in Jesus Misses for Salvation in Christ.* Grand Rapids: Brazos Press, 2019.

Bauersfeld, H. "Research Related to the Mathematical Learning Process." In Vol. 4 of *New Trends in Mathematics Teaching*, 199–213. Prepared by International Commission on Mathematical Instruction. Paris: UNESCO, 1979.

Bebbington, David W. *The Dominance of Evangelicalism: The Age of Spurgeon and Moody.* A History of Evangelicalism. Leicester: IVP, 2005.

———. *Evangelicalism in Modern Britain: A History from the 1730s to the 1980s.* London: Unwin Hyman, 1989.

Bede the Venerable. *Homilies on the Gospels.* 2 vols. Translated by Lawrence T. Martin and David Hurst. Michigan: Cistercian Publications, 1991.

Beeley, C. A. *Gregory of Nazianzus on the Trinity and the Knowledge of God: In Your Light Shall We See Light.* Oxford: Oxford University Press, 2008.

Boersma, H. *Embodiment and Virtue in Gregory of Nyssa: An Anagogical Approach.* Oxford: Oxford University Press, 2013.

Boot, Joseph. *Gospel Culture: Living in God's Kingdom.* Cornerstones 1. London: Wilberforce Publications, 2016.

Bosch, D. *Transforming Mission, Paradigm Shifts in Theology of Mission.* Maryknoll: Orbis, 1993.

Bratt, James D., trans. and ed. *Abraham Kuyper: A Centennial Reader.* Grand Rapids: Eerdmans, 1998.

Brooking, Stuart, ed. *Is It Working? Researching Context to Improve Curriculum: A Resource Book for Theological Schools.* ICETE. Carlisle: Langham Global Library, 2018.

Brueggemann, Walter, and William Bellinger Jr. *New Cambridge Bible Commentary: Psalms.* Cambridge: Cambridge University Press, 2014.

Bruner, Jerome S. *The Process of Education.* Cambridge, MA: Harvard University Press, 1960.

Bulley, C. *The Priesthood of Some Believers: Developments from the General to the Special Priesthood in the Christian Literature in the First Three Centuries.* Carlisle: Paternoster Press, 2000.

Bullón, H. Fernando. *Protestant Social Thought in Latin America.* Oxford: Regnum, 2015.

Burke, D. "Time to Leave the Wilderness? The Teaching of Pastoral Theology in South-East Asia." In *Tending the Seedbeds: Educational Perspectives on Theological Education in Asia*, edited by A. Harkness, 263–284. Quezon City: Asia Theological Association, 2010.

Busch, Eberhard. *Karl Barth: His Life from Letters and Autobiographical Texts*. Philadelphia: Fortress, 1976.

Buxton, Graham. *Celebrating Life: Beyond the Sacred-Secular Divide*. Milton Keynes: Paternoster, 2007.

Calvin, J. *Institutes of the Christian Religion*. 2 vols. Edited by J. T. McNeill. Translated by F. L. Battles. Philadelphia: Westminster Press, 1960.

Cameron, J. E. M., ed. *The Lausanne Legacy: Landmarks in Global Mission*. Peabody: Hendrickson, 2016.

Cannell, L. *Theological Education Matters: Leadership Education for the Church*. Newburg, Indiana: EDCOT Press, 2006.

Chang, Philip. "Business as Mission in Asia." In *Emerging Missions Movements: Voices of Asia*, edited by Bambang Budijanto, 11–22. Canada: Compassion International and Asia Evangelical Alliance, 2010.

Chester, Tim. *The Everyday Gospel: A Theology of Washing the Dishes*. Leyland: 10 Publishing, 2013.

Church of England Commission on Evangelism. *Towards the Conversion of England: The Report of a Commission on Evangelism Appointed by the Archbishops of Canterbury and York Pursuant to a Resolution of the Church Assembly Passed at the Summer Session, 1943*. London: Press and Publications Board of the Church Assembly, 1945.

Coad, Roy. *Laing*. Sevenoaks: Hodder & Stoughton, 1979.

Colson, Charles, and Nancy R. Pearcey. *How Now Shall We Live?* London: Marshall Pickering, 1999.

Constable, G. *Three Studies in Medieval Religious and Social Thought*. Cambridge: Cambridge University Press, 1995.

Dahle, Margunn Serigstad, Lars Dahle, and Knud Jørgensen, eds. *The Lausanne Movement: A Range of Perspectives*. Regnum Edinburgh Centenary Series 22. Oxford: Regnum Books International, 2014.

Daley, B. E. "The Cappadocian Fathers and the Rhetoric of Philanthropy." *Journal of Early Christian Studies* 7, no. 3 (1991): 431–461.

Davis, Ellen F. *Scripture, Culture, and Agriculture: An Agrarian Reading of the Bible*. Cambridge: Cambridge University Press, 2009.

Daystar University. *Catalogue 2017–2021*. Corporate Affairs Department, 2017. https://www.daystar.ac.ke/downloads.htm.

DeGregorio, S. "The Venerable Bede on Prayer and Contemplation." *Traditio* 54 (1999): 1–39.

DeYoung, Kevin, and Greg Gilbert. *What is the Mission of the Church? Making Sense of Social Justice, Shalom, and the Great Commission.* Wheaton: Crossway, 2011.

Diehl, William E. *Thank God, It's Monday.* Laity Exchange Books. Philadelphia: Fortress, 1982.

Duara, Prasenjit. "An East Asian Perspective on Religion and Secularism." In *State and Secularism: Perspectives from Asia*, edited by Michael Heng-Siam-Heng and Ten Chin Liew, 1–6. Singapore: World Scientific, 2010.

Dunkin, M. J. "Concepts of Teaching and Teaching Excellence in Higher Education." *Higher Education Research and Development* 14, no. 1 (1995): 21–33.

Elliott, Mark. "East European Missions, Perestroika and Orthodoxevangelical Tensions." *Journal of Ecumenical Studies* 33, no. 1 (1996): 9–19.

Escobar, Samuel. "It's Your Turn, Young Ones – Make Me Proud!: Evangelical Mission in Latin America and Beyond." In *The Reshaping of Mission in Latin America*, edited by Miguel Alvarez, 9–23. Oxford: Regnum, 2015.

Ferguson, E., ed. *Encyclopedia of Early Christianity.* New York: Garland Publishing, 1998.

Ferngren, G. B. *Medicine and Health Care in Early Christianity.* Baltimore: The John Hopkins University Press, 2009.

Ferris, R. W., and R. E. Enlow Jr. *Ministry Education that Transforms.* Carlisle: Langham Global Library, 2018.

"Findings Report: Second Consultation on Theological Education and Leadership Development in Post-communist Europe in the Context of the Kingdom of God and the Kingdoms of the World." *Transformation* 16, no. 1 (1999): 1–4.

First Lausanne Congress. *The Lausanne Covenant.* Lausanne Movement, 1974. https://www.lausanne.org/content/covenant/lausanne-covenant.

Flett, John. "A Theology of Missio Dei." *Theology in Scotland* 21 (2014): 69–78.

Fox, Judith. "Secularization." In *The Routledge Companion to the Study of Religion*, edited by John R. Hinnells, 306–322. London/New York: Routledge, 2010.

Frucht, Richard, ed. *Encyclopedia of Eastern Europe: From the Congress of Vienna to the Fall of Communism.* Garland Reference Library of Social Sciences. New York: Garland Publishing, 2000.

Fyock, James A. "The Effect of the Teacher's Worldviews on the Worldviews of High School Seniors." EdD diss., Liberty University, 2008. https://core.ac.uk/download/pdf/58821457.pdf.

Gálvez, Rigoberto M. "A Guatemalan Perspective on Pentecostal and Neo-Pentecostal Theology in the Twenty-First Century." In *The Reshaping of Mission in Latin America*, edited by Miguel Alvarez, 144–160. Oxford: Regnum, 2015.

Gibbs, Mark. *Christians with Secular Power*. Laity Exchange Books. Philadelphia: Fortress, 1981.

———. "Editor's Introduction." In *Thank God, It's Monday*, by William E. Diehl. Laity Exchange Books, vii. Philadelphia: Fortress, 1982.

Gibbs, Mark, and T. Ralph Morton. *God's Frozen People*. Philadelphia: Westminster, 1965.

———. *God's Lively People*. Philadelphia: Westminster, 1971.

Gnanakan, Ken. *The Whole Gospel of God*. Bangalore: Theological Book Trust, 2014.

Goheen, Michael W. *The Church and Its Vocation: Lesslie Newbigin's Missionary Ecclesiology*. Grand Rapids: Baker Academic, 2018.

———. *Introducing Christian Mission Today: Scripture, History and Issues*. Downers Grove: IVP, 2014.

———. "A Missional Reading of Scripture for Theological Education and Curriculum." In *Reading the Bible Missionally*, edited by Michael W. Goheen. Grand Rapids: Eerdmans, 2017.

Goheen, Michael, and Craig Bartholomew. *Living at the Crossroads: An Introduction to Christian Worldview*. London: SPCK, 2008.

Goudzwaard, Bob, and Craig G. Bartholomew. *Beyond the Modern Age: An Archaeology of Contemporary Culture*. Downers Grove: IVP, 2017.

Greene, Mark. "Is Anybody Listening?" *Anvil* 14, no. 4 (1997): 283–294.

Gregory of Nazianzus. "Oration 14: On Love for the Poor." In *St. Gregory of Nazianzus: Select Orations*, translated by Martha Vinson, 39–71. The Fathers of the Church 107. Washington, DC: Catholic University of America Press, 2003.

Gregory of Nyssa. *On Virginity*. In *Saint Gregory of Nyssa: Ascetical Works*, translated by Virginia Woods Callahan, 3–75. The Fathers of the Church 58. Washington, DC: The Catholic University of America Press, 1967.

Haidar, Hasna. "What Is Liberal Arts Education?" *TopUniversities Student Blog*. 28 January 2014. https://www.topuniversities.com/blog/what-liberal-arts-education.

Harkness, Allan G. "Assessment in Theological Education: Do Our Theological Values Matter?" *Journal of Adult Theological Education* 5, no. 2 (2008): 183–201.

———. "De-schooling the Theological Seminary: An Appropriate Paradigm for Effective Ministerial Formation." *Teaching Theology and Religion* 4, no. 3 (2001): 141–154.

Hart, M. D. "Reconciliation of Body and Soul: Gregory of Nyssa's Deeper Theology of Marriage." *Theological Studies* 51 (1990): 450–478.

Hativa, Nira. "Exemplary University Teachers: Knowledge and Beliefs Regarding Effective Teaching Dimensions and Strategies." *Journal of Higher Education* 72, no. 6 (2001): 699–729.

Helm, Paul. *The Callings: The Gospel in the World*. Edinburgh: Banner of Truth Trust, 1987.

Heslam, Peter S. *Creating a Christian Worldview: Abraham Kuyper's Lectures on Calvinism*. Grand Rapids: Eerdmans, 1998.

Hilgemann, V., and J. Blodget. "Profile of an Excellent Teacher: Summary of Research." 1991. ERIC Document Reproduction Service No. ED 353017. https://eric.ed.gov.

Hinnells, J. R., ed. *The Routledge Companion to the Study of Religion*. London: Routledge, 2010.

Hirsch, E. D. "Creating a Curriculum for the American People." *American Educator* (Winter 2009–2010): 5–10.

Holmes, S. R. *Listening to the Past: The Place of Tradition in Theology*. Carlisle: Paternoster, 2002.

Horan, M. "Attributes of Exemplary Community College Teachers: A Review of the Literature." 1991. ERIC Document Reproduction Service No. ED346900. https://eric.ed.gov.

Horton, Michael. *The Gospel-Driven Life: Being Good News People in a Bad News World*. Grand Rapids: Baker Books, 2009.

Jaison, Jessy. *Towards Vital Wholeness in Theological Education: Framing Areas for Assessment*. ICETE. Carlisle: Langham Global Library, 2017.

Jayasooria, Datuk Denison. "Human Rights and Market Capitalism: A Call for Asian Social Action by the Christian Community." In *The Church in a Changing World: An Asian Response*, edited by Bruce Nicholls, Theresa Roco-Lua, and Julie Belding. Quezon City, Philippines: Asia Theological Association, 2010.

Jethani, Skye. *Futureville: Discover Your Purpose for Today by Reimagining Tomorrow*. Nashville: Nelson Books, 2013.

Jeyaraj, Jesudason Baskar. "Revitalizing the Churches to Challenge Corruption in Society." In *Light for Our Path: The Authority, Inspiration, Meaning, and Mission of Scripture*, edited by Bruce Nicholls, Julie Belding, and Joseph Shao, 286–303. Quezon City, Philippines: Asia Theological Association, 2013.

Keller, Timothy. *Shaped by the Gospel: Doing Balanced, Gospel-Centered Ministry in Your City*. Grand Rapids: Zondervan, 2016.

Kelly, N., and B. Kelly. "Backgrounds, Teaching Styles of Award-Winning Professors." Paper presented at the annual meeting of the Rocky Mountain Educational Research Association, Albuquerque, NM, November, 1982.

Kierkegaard, Søren. "Journal: 167 (1843)." In *Works of Søren Kierkegaard, Vol. 18*. Copenhagen: Søren Kierkegaard Research Center, 1997.

Kim, David, David McCalman, and Dan Fisher. "The Sacred/Secular Divide and the Christian Worldview." *Journal of Business Ethics* 109, no. 2 (2012): 203–208. https://doi.org/10.1007/s10551-011-1119-z.

Kraemer, Hendrik. *A Theology of the Laity*. London: Lutterworth, 1958.

Kuyper, Abraham. *Lectures on Calvinism*. New York: Cosimo, 2007.

———. "Souvereiniteit in Eigen Kring." In *Abraham Kuyper: A Centennial Reader*, translated and edited by James D. Bratt, 461–490. Grand Rapids: Eerdmans, 1998.

Kuzmič, Peter. "Christianity in Eastern Europe: A Story of Pain, Glory, Persecution, and Freedom." In *Introducing World Christianity*, edited by Charles E. Farhadian, 77–90. Oxford: Blackwell, 2012.

Lapiz, Ed. *Pagpapahiyang: Redeeming Culture and Indigenizing Christianity*. Manila, Philippines: (self-published), 2018.

Lay Leadership Task Group. *"Setting God's People Free": A Report from the Archbishops' Council*. Church of England, 2017. Accessed 17 November 2019. https://www.churchofengland.org/sites/default/files/2017-11/gs-2056-setting-gods-people-free.pdf.

Leckey, Dolores R. *Laity Stirring the Church: Prophetic Questions*. Laity Exchange Books. Philadelphia: Fortress, 1987.

Lind, R. E. "Origins of the Modern Mind/Body Split." *The Journal of Mind and Behavior* 22, no. 1 (2001): 23–40.

Lindsay, P. *The Craft of University Teaching*. Toronto: University of Toronto Press, 2018.

Livingstone, R. *The Future in Education*. Cambridge: CUP, 1941.

Lowman, J. "Characteristics of Exemplary Teachers." *New Directions for Teaching and Learning*, no. 65 (1996): 33–34.

Luther, Martin. *The Christian in Society 1*. Edited by J. Atkinson. Vol. 44 of *Luther's Works*. Philadelphia: Fortress Press, 1966.

Lynch, J. H. *The Medieval Church: A Brief History*. London: Longman, 1992.

Măcelaru, Marcel V. "Holistic Mission in Post-Communist Romania: A Case Study on the Growth of the 'Elim' Pentecostal Church of Timişoara (1990–1997)." In *Pentecostal Mission and Global Christianity: An Edinburgh Centenary Reader*, edited by Younghoon Lee and Wonsuk Ma, 305–322. Regnum Studies in Mission. Oxford: Regnum Books International, 2018.

Mackenzie, Alistair. "Curricular Integration Workshops at ON Schools." Oikonomia Network, 2 May 2018. https://oikonomianetwork.org/2018/05/curricular-integration-workshops-at-on-schools/.

———. "Teaching Formation: Prayer in the Fast Lane." Oikonomia Network, 9 February 2017. https://oikonomianetwork.org/2017/02/teaching-formation-prayer-in-the-fast-lane/.

———. "Teaching Hermeneutics & Homiletics: Is Work Meaningful or Futile?" Oikonomia Network, 11 April 2017. https://oikonomianetwork.org/2017/04/teaching-hermeneutics-homiletics-is-work-meaningful-or-futile/.

Maddix, M. "A Biblical Model of the People of God: Overcoming the Clergy/Laity Dichotomy." *Christian Education Journal* 6, no. 2 (2009): 214–228.

Malcolm, Norman. *Ludwig Wittgenstein: A Memoir*. Oxford: Clarendon Press, 1984.

Mangalwadi, Vishal, and Mangalwadi, Ruth. *The Legacy of William Carey: A Model for the Transformation of Culture*. Wheaton: Crossway, 1999.

Matz, B. *Gregory of Nazianzus*. Grand Rapids: Baker, 2016.

Mbiti, John. *African Religions and Philosophy*. New York: Frederick A. Praeger, 1969.

McKnight, Scot. *The King Jesus Gospel: The Original Good News Revisited*. Grand Rapids: Zondervan, 2011.

Méndez, Dinorah B. "Evangelical Mission in Mexico Today: The Challenge to Remember and Celebrate Our Heritage." In *The Reshaping of Mission in Latin America*, edited by Miguel Alvarez, 133–143. Oxford: Regnum, 2015.

Méndez, Dinorah B. "La Esfera Socio-Religiosa de la Cultura Mexicana y su Influencia en las Iglesias Bautistas de México." BTh thesis. Mexican Baptist Theological Seminary (Seminario Teológico Bautista Mexicano) (STBM), 1989.

Middleton, J. Richard. *A New Heaven and a New Earth: Reclaiming Biblical Eschatology*. Grand Rapids: Baker Academic, 2014.

Miller, Darrow L. *LifeWork: A Biblical Theology for What You Do Every Day*. Seattle: YWAM Publishing, 2009.

Miller, David W. *God at Work*. Oxford: Oxford University Press, 2006.

Morales, Michael L. *Who Shall Ascend the Mountain of the Lord? A Biblical Theology of the Book of Leviticus*. New Studies in Biblical Theology 37. Nottingham: Apollos, 2015.

More, Hannah. *The Works of Hannah More: With a Sketch of Her Life*. Vol. 1. Boston: S. G . Goodrich, 1827.

Mouw, Richard J. *Abraham Kuyper: A Short and Personal Introduction*. Grand Rapids: Eerdmans, 2011.

———. *Called to Worldly Holiness*. Laity Exchange Books. Philadelphia: Fortress, 1980.

Naugle, David K. *Worldview: The History of a Concept*. Grand Rapids: Eerdmans, 2002.

Noll, Mark. *The Rise of Evangelicalism: The Age of Edwards, Whitefield and the Wesleys*. A History of Evangelicalism. Leicester: Apollos, 2004.

Okesson, Gregg A. "Sacred and Secular Currents for Theological Education." *Africa Journal of Evangelical Theology* 26, no. 1 (2007): 39–63.

Orr, James. *The Christian View of God and the World*. Grand Rapids: Eerdmans, 1954.

Ortiz, Israel. "Beyond Numerical Growth: The Challenge of Transformation in Guatemala." In *The Reshaping of Mission in Latin America*, edited by Miguel Alvarez, 161–177. Oxford: Regnum, 2015.

Padilla, C. René, ed. *The New Face of Evangelicalism: An International Symposium on the Lausanne Covenant*. Downers Grove: IVP, 1974.

Patterson, W. B., *William Perkins and the Making of a Protestant England*. Oxford: Oxford University Press, 2014.

Pearcey, Nancy R. *Total Truth: Liberating Christianity from Its Cultural Captivity*. Wheaton: Crossway, 2004.

Perkins, W. *A Golden Chain*, in *Works of William Perkins*. Vol. 1. London: Reformation Heritage Books, 1608.

———. *A Treatise of the Vocations, or Callings of Men, with the Sorts and Kinds of Them, and the Right Vse Thereof*. Cambridge: Iohn Legat, Printer to the Vniuersitie of Cambridge, 1603.

Peterlin, Davorin. "A Wrong Kind of Missionary: A Semi-Autobiographic Outcry." *Mission Studies* 12, no. 2 (1995): 164–174.

Pew Research Center. "Religion in Latin America: Widespread Change in a Historically Catholic Region," 13 Nov 2014. https://www.pewforum.org/2014/11/13/religion-in-latin-america/.

Poythress, Vern S. *The Lordship of Christ: Serving Our Savior All of the Time, In All of Life, With All of Our Heart*. Wheaton: Crossway, 2016.

Rakoczy, S. *Great Mystics and Social Justice: Walking on the Two Feet of Love*. New York: Paulist Press, 2006.

Rogers, M. "A Dangerous Idea? Martin Luther, E. Y. Mullins, and the Priesthood of All Believers." *Westminster Theological Journal* 72 (2010): 120–127.

Rowthorn, Anne. *The Liberation of the Laity*. Wilton: Morehouse-Barlow, 1986.

Ryken, L. "'Some Kind of Life to Which We Are Called of God': The Puritan Doctrine of Vocation." *Southern Baptist Journal of Theology* 22, no. 1 (2018): 45–66.

———. *Worldly Saints: The Puritans as They Really Were*. Grand Rapids: Zondervan, 1986.

Sacks, Jonathan. *Leviticus: The Book of Holiness*. Vol. 3 of *Covenant & Conversation: A Weekly Reading of the Jewish Bible*. New Milford: Maggid Books, 2015.

Salinas, J. Daniel. *Taking Up the Mantle: Latin American Evangelical Theology in the 20th Century*. Carlisle: Langham Global Library, 2017.

Schaeffer, Francis A. *The Complete Works of Francis A. Schaeffer: A Christian Worldview*. 5 vols. Wheaton: Crossway, 1985.

Scherer, M. "Landmarks in the Critical Study of Secularism." *Cultural Anthropology* 26, no. 4 (2011): 621–632.

Schuurman, Douglas J. *Vocation: Discerning Our Callings in Life*. Grand Rapids: Eerdmans, 2004.

Scott, Luis. *Los Evangélicos Mexicanos en el Siglo XX*. México: Editorial Kyrios, n.d.

Shaw, Ian J. "John Stott and the Langham Scholarship Programme." In *Reflecting On and Equipping for Mission*, edited by K. Jorgenson and N. Jennings. Oxford: Regnum Press, 2015.

Shaw, Perry. *Transforming Theological Education: A Handbook for Integrative Learning*. Carlisle: Langham Global Library, 2014.

Smith, Ian K. *Not Home Yet: How the Renewal of the Earth Fits into God's Plan for the World*. Wheaton: Crossway, 2019.

Smith, James K. A. *Awaiting the King: Reforming Public Theology*. Cultural Liturgies. Grand Rapids: Baker Academic, 2017.

———. *Desiring the Kingdom: Worship, Worldview, and Cultural Formation*. Cultural Liturgies. Grand Rapids: Baker Academic, 2009.

———. "Worldview, Sphere Sovereignty, and Desiring the Kingdom: A Guide for (Perplexed) Reformed Folk." *Pro Rege* 39, no. 4 (2011): 15–24.

Snyder, Howard. *Salvation Means Creation Healed: The Ecology of Sin and Grace*. With Joel Scandrett. Eugene: Cascade Books, 2011.

Southern, R. W. *Western Society and the Church in the Middle Ages*. Middlesex: Penguin Books, 1970.

Stackhouse, John G., Jr. *Why You're Here: Ethics for the Real World*. Oxford: Oxford University Press, 2018.

Stanley, Brian. *The Global Diffusion of Evangelicalism: The Age of Billy Graham and John Stott*. A History of Evangelicalism. Nottingham: IVP, 2013.

Stevens, R. Paul. *The Abolition of the Laity: Vocation, Work and Ministry in Biblical Perspective*. Bletchley: Paternoster, 1999.

———. *The Other Six Days: Vocation, Work, and Ministry in Biblical Perspective*. Grand Rapids: Eerdmans, 2000.

Stott, John, with Tim Chester. *The Disciple: A Calling to Be Christlike*. London: IVP, 2019.

———. *One People: Clergy and Laity in God's Church*. London: Falcon, 1969.

Suskie, Linda. *Assessing Student Learning: A Common Sense Guide*. 3rd ed. San Francisco: John Wiley & Sons, 2018.

Tait, Jennifer Woodruff. "Sample Assignments Across the Curriculum." Oikonomia Network, 14 March 2017. https://oikonomianetwork.org/2017/03/sample-assignments-across-the-curriculum/.

———. "Sample Assignments Across the Curriculum." Oikonomia Network, 9 May 2017. https://oikonomianetwork.org/2017/05/sample-assignments-across-the-curriculum-2/.

Third Lausanne Congress. *The Cape Town Commitment*. Lausanne Movement, 2011. Accessed 19 November 2019. https://www.lausanne.org/content/ctc/ctcommitment#capetown.

Treat, Jeremy. *Seek First: How the Kingdom of God Changes Everything*. Grand Rapids: Zondervan, 2019.

Trueman, C. R. *Luther on the Christian Life: Cross and Freedom*. Wheaton: Crossway, 2015.

Volf, Miroslav. "Fishing in the Neighbour's Pond: Mission and Proselytism in Eastern Europe." *International Bulletin of Missionary Research* 20, no. 1 (1996): 26–31.

Wagenman, Michael R. *Engaging the World with Abraham Kuyper*. Lived Theology. Bellingham: Lexham Press, 2019.

Walsh, Brian J., and J. Richard Middleton. *The Transforming Vision: Shaping a Christian World View*. Downers Grove: IVP, 1984.

Watkin, Christopher. *Thinking through Creation: Genesis 1 and 2 as Tools of Cultural Critique*. Phillipsburg: P&R Publishing, 2017.

Wijaya, Yahya. "Constructing an Anti-Corruption Theology." *Exchange* 43, no. 3 (2014): 221–236.

Wiles, J. *Leading Curriculum Development*. London: Sage, 2009.

Wilson, Jared C. *The Story of Everything: How You, Your Pets, and the Swiss Alps Fit into God's Plan for the World*. Wheaton: Crossway, 2015.

Wingren, G. *Luther on Vocation*. Translated by Carl C. Rasmussen. Philadelphia: Muhlenberg Press, 1957.

Wittmer, Michael. *Becoming Worldly Saints: Can You Serve Jesus and Still Enjoy Your Life?* Grand Rapids: Zondervan, 2015.

Wolffe, John. *The Expansion of Evangelicalism: The Age of Wilberforce, More, Chalmers and Finney*. A History of Evangelicalism. Nottingham: IVP, 2006.

Wolters, Albert M. *Creation Regained: Biblical Basics for a Reformational Worldview*. Grand Rapids: Eerdmans, 2005.

———. *The Song of the Valiant Woman: Studies in the Interpretation of Proverbs 31:10–31*. Carlisle: Paternoster, 2001.

Wright, Christopher J. H. *The Mission of God: Unlocking the Bible's Grand Narrative.* Nottingham: IVP, 2006.

——. *The Mission of God's People: A Biblical Theology of the Church's Mission.* Biblical Theology for Life. Grand Rapids: Zondervan, 2010.

Wright, Tom. *Simply Good News: Why the Gospel Is News and What Makes it Good.* London: SPCK, 2015.

Yeh, Allen. *Polycentric Missiology: Twenty-First Century Mission from Everyone to Everywhere.* Downers Grove: IVP, 2016.

Zitukawa, M., and M. York. "Expanding Religious Studies: The Obsolescence of the Sacred/Secular Framework for Pagan, Earthen and Indigenous Religion." *The Pomegranate* 9, no. 1 (2007): 78–97.

About the Editors

Mark Greene grew up Jewish and joyous in Northwest London. In his last month at university, God wooed him into his kingdom and he went on to work for ten years in advertising – a fact he is still prepared to admit. Gripped by a desire to dig into God's word, he took a career break to study at the London School of Theology. The career break turned into a career change and he ended up on the staff teaching Communications, Engaging with Contemporary Culture, and serving as Vice Principal.

Mark joined the London Institute for Contemporary Christianity as Executive Director in 1999, eager to focus on the call to see all God's people empowered to live their whole lives – Monday to Saturday, as well as Sunday. He has spoken and written widely on the topic and on work in the UK and internationally; his published work includes *Thank God It's Monday, (Probably) The Best Idea in the World*, and *Fruitfulness on the Frontline*. Most recently, Mark has written the second volume of *The One About . . .* , a collection of eight true stories about God at work in our everyday lives.

Mark has degrees in Hebrew from Cambridge, Theology from LST, and Communications and Media from Edinburgh. He's married to Katriina, a Finn, and they have three splendidly different young adult offspring. Mark enjoys films and fiction (a lot), and does a passable imitation of Mr Bean and a terrible one of Sean Connery. His wife wishes it were the other way round. His children wish he wouldn't do either.

Ian Shaw is CEO of the Opal Trust, a Christian ministry which serves churches in the Majority World through resourcing them with Bibles, evangelical books and literature. Its focus is especially on giving pastors and Bible College students the books they need to study and preach the word of God faithfully. Ian was born in Bradford in Yorkshire, and served as a lead pastor in a church in the Manchester area for eight years before undertaking doctoral research in the field of urban theology and ministry. He has since then spent over twenty years in leadership positions in theological education, including serving as Provost of Union School of Theology from 2017 to 2020, and Associate International Director of the Langham Scholars Programme from 2008–2017.

Ian has travelled extensively around the world, working with seminaries and theological colleges and helping to train faculty. He is the author of eight books, including *Churches, Revolutions and Empires, 1789–1914* (2012), a study of global Christianity in the modern period, and *Christianity the Biography* (2016), a global history of Christianity through twenty centuries. He has four children, and is married to Christine who is a teacher in Scotland.

Author and Subject Index

Scripture Index

OLD TESTAMENT

NEW TESTAMENT

licc.

The London Institute for
Contemporary Christianity

About 98 percent of UK Christians aren't in church-paid work – that's most of us. And we spend 95 percent of our time away from church – at work, at school, at home, at the store, gym or club – much of it with people who don't know Jesus. But, tragically, many of us don't feel equipped to make the most of this missional opportunity.

We at LICC champion the ministry of ordinary people in all areas of life and work. We want to see God's people know him more richly and grow as fruitful followers of Christ, right where they are. And we seek to empower every Christian to bring God's wisdom, grace, and truth to the things they do every day, the people they're usually with, and the places they naturally spend time.

We work with individuals, church leaders, and theological educators from across the denominations, partnering with a wide range of organisations. We delve into the Bible, think hard about the culture we're in, listen carefully to God's people, and explore the challenges and opportunities they face. From what we learn, we prayerfully develop biblical frameworks, lived examples, practical skills, and spiritual practices that encourage whole-life, everyday discipleship.

For the salvation of many and the flourishing of the nations, to the glory of God.

To find out more, including ways you can receive alerts on new resources, events, and articles, by email or post, go to licc.org.uk.

ICETE

International Council for Evangelical Theological Education
strengthening evangelical theological education through international cooperation

ICETE is a global community, sponsored by nine regional networks of theological schools, to enable international interaction and collaboration among all those engaged in strengthening and developing evangelical theological education and Christian leadership development worldwide.

The purpose of ICETE is:

1. To promote the enhancement of evangelical theological education worldwide.
2. To serve as a forum for interaction, partnership and collaboration among those involved in evangelical theological education and leadership development, for mutual assistance, stimulation and enrichment.
3. To provide networking and support services for regional associations of evangelical theological schools worldwide.
4. To facilitate among these bodies the advancement of their services to evangelical theological education within their regions.

Sponsoring associations include:

Africa: Association for Christian Theological Education in Africa (ACTEA)

Asia: Asia Theological Association (ATA)

Caribbean: Caribbean Evangelical Theological Association (CETA)

Europe: European Evangelical Accrediting Association (EEAA)

Euro-Asia: Euro-Asian Accrediting Association (E-AAA)

Latin America: Association for Evangelical Theological Education in Latin America (AETAL)

Middle East and North Africa: Middle East Association for Theological Education (MEATE)

North America: Association for Biblical Higher Education (ABHE)

South Pacific: South Pacific Association of Evangelical Colleges (SPAEC)

www.icete-edu.org

Langham
PARTNERSHIP

Langham Literature and its imprints are a ministry of Langham Partnership.

Langham Partnership is a global fellowship working in pursuit of the vision God entrusted to its founder John Stott –

> *to facilitate the growth of the church in maturity and Christ-likeness through raising the standards of biblical preaching and teaching.*

Our vision is to see churches in the Majority World equipped for mission and growing to maturity in Christ through the ministry of pastors and leaders who believe, teach and live by the word of God.

Our mission is to strengthen the ministry of the word of God through:
* nurturing national movements for biblical preaching
* fostering the creation and distribution of evangelical literature
* enhancing evangelical theological education

especially in countries where churches are under-resourced.

Our ministry

Langham Preaching partners with national leaders to nurture indigenous biblical preaching movements for pastors and lay preachers all around the world. With the support of a team of trainers from many countries, a multi-level programme of seminars provides practical training, and is followed by a programme for training local facilitators. Local preachers' groups and national and regional networks ensure continuity and ongoing development, seeking to build vigorous movements committed to Bible exposition.

Langham Literature provides Majority World preachers, scholars and seminary libraries with evangelical books and electronic resources through publishing and distribution, grants and discounts. The programme also fosters the creation of indigenous evangelical books in many languages, through writer's grants, strengthening local evangelical publishing houses, and investment in major regional literature projects, such as one volume Bible commentaries like *The Africa Bible Commentary* and *The South Asia Bible Commentary*.

Langham Scholars provides financial support for evangelical doctoral students from the Majority World so that, when they return home, they may train pastors and other Christian leaders with sound, biblical and theological teaching. This programme equips those who equip others. Langham Scholars also works in partnership with Majority World seminaries in strengthening evangelical theological education. A growing number of Langham Scholars study in high quality doctoral programmes in the Majority World itself. As well as teaching the next generation of pastors, graduated Langham Scholars exercise significant influence through their writing and leadership.

To learn more about Langham Partnership and the work we do visit **langham.org**